The Principle of Mercy

The Principle of Mercy

Taking the Crucified People from the Cross

Jon Sobrino

ORBIS BOOKS

Maryknoll, New York 10545

The Catholic Foreign Mission Society of America (Maryknoll) recruits and trains people for overseas missionary service. Through Orbis Books, Maryknoll aims to foster the international dialogue that is essential to mission. The books published, however, reflect the opinions of their authors and are not meant to represent the official position of the society.

English translation copyright © 1994 by Orbis Books

First published with the title *El Principio-Misericordia: Bajar de la cruz a los pueblos crucificados* © 1992 by Editorial Sal Terrae, Guevara, 20—39001 Santander, Spain.

The following chapters have been published in English; permission of the publishers to reprint them here is gratefully acknowledged: the Introduction, "Awakening from the Sleep of Inhumanity," copyright © 1992 Christian Century Foundation. Reprinted by permission from *How My Mind Has Changed* (April, 1992 *The Christian Century*); "Theology in a Suffering World," in *Pluralism and Oppression,* ed. Paul Knitter (The Annual Publication of the College Theology Society vol. 34, 1988. Published by University Press of America, Inc.); "The Crucified Peoples," in *1492-1992: The Voice of the Victims,* eds. Leonardo Boff and Virgil Elizondo, *Concilium* 1990/6 (London: SCM Press, 1990); "Latin America: Place of Sin and Place of Forgiveness," in *Forgiveness,* eds. Casiano Floristan and Christian Duquoc, *Concilium* 184 (Edinburgh: T & T Clark, 1986). Essays from *Concilium* used by permission of Stichting Concilium, Netherlands; "Bearing with One Another in Faith," in *Theology of Christian Solidarity* by Jon Sobrino and Juan Hernández Pico (Maryknoll, N.Y.: Orbis Books, 1985).

Queries regarding rights and permissions should be addressed to Orbis Books, P.O. Box 308, Maryknoll, NY 10545-0308.

Manufactured in the United States of America.

Library of Congress Cataloging-in-Publication Data

Sobrino, Jon.
    [Principio-misercordia. English]
    The principle of mercy : taking the crucified people from the
Cross / Jon Sobrino.
       p. cm.
    Includes bibliographical references and index.
    ISBN 0-88344-986-2 (pbk.)
    1. Liberation theology. 2. Mercy. 3. Christianity and justice—
Catholic Church. 4. Catholic Church—Developing countries.
5. Developing countries—Religion. 6. Catholic Church—Doctrines.
I. Title.
BT83.57.S69513   1994
230'.2—dc20
                                   94-18075
                                     CIP

Contents

Preface   vii

Introduction: Awakening from the Sleep of Inhumanity   1

PART ONE

1. The Samaritan Church and the Principle of Mercy   15

2. Theology in a Suffering World   27
   Theology as Intellectus Amoris

PART TWO

3. The Crucified Peoples   49
   Yahweh's Suffering Servant Today

4. Latin America   58
   Place of Sin and Place of Forgiveness

5. Five Hundred Years   69
   Structural Sin and Structural Grace

6. Personal Sin, Forgiveness, and Liberation   83

PART THREE

7. Toward a Determination of the Nature of Priesthood   105
   Servitude to God's Salvific Approach to Human Beings

8. Bearing with One Another in Faith   144
   A Theological Analysis of Christian Solidarity

9. The Legacy of the Martyrs of the Central American University   173

Epilogue: A Letter to Ignacio Ellacuría   187
Notes   191
Index   197

Preface

This book is a collection of articles that have appeared in various periodicals over the last ten years. Their topics vary, and the level of their reflection is in some cases mainly occasional, in others mostly testimonial, in still others more theoretical. Still, we have gathered these articles together in a single volume: They all bear on the most flagrant reality that exists in today's world, and on the reaction to that reality that is most urgently demanded of us. We hope to establish, in this volume, that the sign of the times *per antonomasiam*, par excellence, is "the existence of a crucified people"—in the words of Ignacio Ellacuría—and that the prime demand on us is that we "take them down from the cross."

Thus, a basic unity spans the several parts of this book. With a view to affording a better grasp of that unity, however, we may be permitted to offer a brief overview of the parts. Our Introduction is more biographical in tone, as we have been asked to make it, and is intended to point in a personal way to the fundamental problem of our world: ignorance, dissimulation, and torpor in the presence of a most cruel inhumanity. Part One focuses on the essential character of mercy and on the importance of shaping the mission of the church and the task of theology in function of that mercy. Part Two mainly analyzes the crucified reality of the Third World, a reality calling for a reaction today as yesterday (we have come to the fifth centenary now), and we add considerations of salvation, forgiveness, and the grace of being forgiven. Part Three presents two manifestations of mercy: the reality of priesthood, and solidarity. Finally, in our Epilogue, we recall the memory of certain individuals who have exercised mercy with ultimacy. Although we could have selected any number of others, the reader will understand that I have chosen to focus on the martyrs of Central American University, my Jesuit brothers.

This is the intent of this book: To demonstrate the imperative need that the crucified peoples be shown mercy. The limitations of these pages, besides any the reader may discover independently, are of two sorts. One consists in a certain repetitiveness in this collection of essays, a shortcoming that I have not had time to correct. In addition to my usual daily occupations, the martyrdom of my brothers, and now—happily—the work of the peace process, have absorbed my efforts.

The other limitation is more basic, and bears on the title of the book.

While our own composition is infinitely more modest, readers may be reminded of Ernst Bloch's monumental work, *The Principle of Hope*. Again in the matter of the title, it may seem to some readers, rightly enough, that the language of "mercy" is too soft, even too dangerous, an expression of what the crucified peoples need. But we have retained the title, in the hope that it may have the necessary strength to arouse and shake society and the church. After all, mercy bespeaks ultimacy, human and Christian, in the presence of a crucified people. Its adequate forms will have to be sought out, of course (especially structural justice). Nevertheless, it bears emphasizing that in the primary reaction of mercy, for which there is no ulterior argumentation or motivation but the sheer fact of the crucifixion of peoples, both the human and the Christian are at stake. Mercy is not sufficient, but it is absolutely necessary—in a world that does all that is possible to conceal suffering and avoid a definition of the human—in terms of a reaction to that suffering.

There are many things to do, of course; and there will be much to "think," philosophically and theologically, in order to do them well. But unless reason becomes—also—compassionate reason, and unless theology becomes—also—*intellectus misericordiae*, I greatly fear that we shall be leaving the crucified peoples to their catastrophe, by dint of much reasoning and many theologies.

This, then, is our hope in publishing this book: To help the First World halt its slide down the slippery slope of misunderstanding, dissimulation, and oppression of the crucified peoples. We should like to help the First World look these peoples straight in the eyes and decide to take them down from their cross. (And so we earnestly hope that others will overcome the limitations, in basic content as in style, of this book.) Above all else, we desire to help the North to hear and accept the cries of the South. We want to cooperate in bringing it about that the North not close itself off from these crucified peoples, but open itself to them generously.

We believe that what is at stake in the "principle of mercy" is the very notion—and real possibility—of all of us coming to form a single human family. In Christian language, what is at stake is the possibility of praying the "Our Father." We hear it said that, in speaking in this way, we are preaching a utopia. We know that very well. That is the reason it is ignored, and even scorned: It is utopia. But unless we aim for this utopia, an ill future awaits us all. And we approach this utopia, we believe, when we shape our lives and our institutions on the basis of the principle of mercy. There is no other way.

San Salvador
March, 1992

INTRODUCTION

Awakening from the Sleep of Inhumanity

I have been asked to write about "how my mind has changed," and I must say that it has changed indeed—though not just my mind, I hope, but my will and heart as well. Because the changes that I have experienced and will write about have also been experienced by many others in El Salvador and throughout Latin America, I will be using singular and plural pronouns interchangeably.

I am writing for the North American reader, who, almost by definition, has difficulty understanding the Latin American reality and the deep changes which that reality can bring about. I will therefore try to explain the essence of such fundamental change from the perspective of El Salvador, comparing it with another change which is often said to lie at the heart of so-called modern Western civilization. From the time of Kant, such change has been described as an awakening from a "dogmatic slumber"—an awakening that is like the liberation of reason from subjection to authority and which, in turn, gives rise to the dogmatic proclamation that the fundamental liberation of the human being lies in the liberation of reason.

In the Third World, the fundamental change also consists of an awakening, but from another type of sleep, or better, from a nightmare—the sleep of inhumanity. It is the awakening to the reality of an oppressed and subjugated world, a world whose liberation is the basic task of every human being, so that in this way human beings may finally come to be human.

Such is the change that has occurred in me and in many others. And what has brought about such a profound and unexpected change is encounter with the reality of the poor and the victims of this world. In order to put all this in simple terms, permit me to offer a bit of biographical background prior to more deliberate reflection.

I was born in 1938 in Spain's Basque region, where I grew up. In 1957, I came to El Salvador as a novice in the Society of Jesus, and since then I have lived in this country, with two notable interruptions: five years in St. Louis studying philosophy and engineering, and seven years in Frankfurt studying theology. So I know fairly well both the world of development and abundance and the world of poverty and death.

I must confess that until 1974, when I returned to El Salvador, the world of the poor—that is, the real world—did not exist for me. When I arrived in El Salvador in 1957, I witnessed appalling poverty, but even though I saw it with my eyes, I did not really see it; thus that poverty had nothing to say to me for my own life as a young Jesuit and as a human being. It did not even cross my mind that I might learn something from the poor. Everything which was important for my life as a Jesuit I brought with me from Europe —and if anything had to change, that would come from Europe as well. My vision of my task as a priest was a traditional one: I would help the Salvadorans replace their popular "superstitious" religiosity with a more sophisticated kind, and I would help the Latin American branches of the church (the European church) to grow. I was the typical "missionary," full of good will and Eurocentricity—and blind to reality.

Further studies in philosophy and theology induced a rude awakening from "dogmatic slumber." During those years of study, I and my fellow students went through Kant and Hegel, through Marx and Sartre, and engaged in serious questioning at every stage. To put it bluntly, we began questioning the God we had inherited from our pious Central American, Spanish, and Basque families. We delved into exegetical criticism and Bultmann's demythologizing, into the legacy of modernism and the relativism of the church—all of which took one logically to a profound questioning not only of what we had been taught by the church, but also of the Christ.

We had to awaken from the dream. Awakening was painful and wrenching in my case; it was as if layers of skin were being removed one by one. Fortunately, there was light as well as darkness in the awakening. Karl Rahner's theology—I mention him because he was for me the one who left the most lasting and beneficial impression—was my companion during those years, and his pages on the mystery of God continue to accompany me even today. Vatican II gave us new insights and new enthusiasm; it helped us realize that the church is not itself the most important thing, not even for God. In working on my doctoral thesis on Christology, I began again to discover Jesus of Nazareth. He was not the abstract Christ I had imagined before, nor was he the Christ being presented by Pierre Teilhard de Chardin as "the final point of all evolution," nor by Rahner as "the absolute bearer of all salvation." I discovered that the Christ is none other than Jesus and that he conceived a utopia on which all too few have focused: the ideal of the kingdom of God.

The churchly triumphalism of our youth was far behind us now. We considered ourselves avant-garde and "progressive," even thinking ourselves well prepared to set the Salvadoran people on the right track. Nevertheless, even with many changes for the better, we had not changed fundamentally. I, at least, continued to be a First World product, and if I were changing, it was in accordance with that First World's process, at that world's pace, and by that world's laws. Although it was a necessary change in many ways, it was insufficiently radical and, from a Third World point of view, it was superficial. For me, the world continued to be the First World, the church continued to be the European church of Vatican II, theology continued to be German theology, and utopia continued to mean that in some way the countries of the south would become like those of the north. That was what many of us wanted, consciously or not, to work for at that time. We had awakened from the dogmatic slumber, if you will, but we continued to sleep in the much deeper sleep of inhumanity—the sleep of egocentrism and selfishness. But eventually we did wake up.

Through one of those strange miracles which happen in history, I came to realize that while I had acquired much knowledge and gotten rid of much traditional baggage, deep down nothing had changed. I saw that my life and studies had not given me new eyes to see this world as it really is, and that they hadn't taken from me the heart of stone I had for the suffering of this world.

That realization is what I experienced upon returning to El Salvador in 1974. And I began, I believe, to awaken from the sleep of inhumanity. To my surprise, I found that some of my fellow Jesuits had already begun to speak of the poor and of injustice and of liberation. I also found that some Jesuits, priests, religious, farmers, and students, even some bishops, were acting on behalf of the poor and getting into serious difficulties as a consequence. Having just arrived, I didn't know what possible contribution I might make. But from the beginning it became quite clear that truth, love, faith, the gospel of Jesus, God, the very best we have as people of faith and as human beings—these were somehow to be found among the poor and in the cause of justice. I do not mean to imply that Rahner and Jürgen Moltmann, whom I studied avidly, no longer had anything to say to me. But I did come to understand that it was absurd to go about trying to Rahnerize or Moltmannize the people of El Salvador. If there was something positive I could bring from the perspective of my studies, the task would have to be the reverse: If at all possible, we needed to Salvadorize Rahner and Moltmann.

At this point, I was fortunate enough to find others who had already awakened from the sleep of inhumanity, among them Ignacio Ellacuría and Archbishop Oscar Romero, to name just two great Salvadoran Christians, martyrs, and friends. But beyond those happy encounters, little by little I came face-to-face with the truly poor, and I am convinced that they were the ones who brought about the final awakening. Once awakened, my questions—and especially my answers to questions—became radically different. The basic question came to be: Are we really human and, if we are believers, is our faith human? The reply was not the anguish which follows an awakening from dogmatic sleep, but the joy which comes when we are willing not only to change the mind from enslavement to liberation, but also to change our vision in order to see what had been there, unnoticed, all along, and to change hearts of stone into hearts of flesh—in other words, to let ourselves be moved to compassion and mercy.

The jigsaw puzzle of human life, whose pattern had broken apart as we went through a period of analysis and questioning, again broke apart when we met the poor of this world. But there was a significant difference. Following the awakening from dogmatic sleep, we had the hard task of piecing the puzzle together again, and we obtained some rather positive results. But such a first awakening was not enough to shake us from ourselves. Wakening from the sleep of inhumanity was a stronger jolt, but a more joyous one. It is possible to live an intellectually honest life in this world, but it is also possible to live sensitively and joyfully. And then I realized another long-forgotten fact: The gospel is not just truth—which must be reconciled in the light of all our questioning—but is, above all, good news which produces joy.

In reflecting on this questioning and this joyful change, I would like to zero in on what is most important: the new eyes we receive when we awaken from the sleep of inhumanity to the reality of what is fundamental.

For the past 17 years in El Salvador, I have had to witness many things: the darkness of poverty and injustice, of numerous and frightful massacres, but also the luminosity of hope and the endless generosity of the poor. What I want to stress, however, is the discovery which precedes all this: the revelation of the truth of reality and, through it, the truth of human beings and of God.

In El Salvador, a phrase of Paul's in his Letter to the Romans was driven home to me: "The wrath of God is revealed from heaven against all ungodliness and wickedness of men who by their wickedness suppress the truth" (Rom. 1:18). I began to understand that it is not enough to go beyond ignorance to truth, as we are often taught to believe. It is pointless to aspire to truth unless we are also willing to distill its consequences. From that moment, I considered myself fortunate to have reality show forth its truth to me.

The first thing we discovered in El Salvador was that this world is one gigantic cross for millions of innocent people who die at the hands of executioners. Father Ellacuría referred to them as "entire crucified peoples." And that is the salient fact of our world—quantitatively, because it encompasses two-thirds of humanity, and qualitatively, because it is the most cruel and scandalous of realities.

To use plain Christian talk, we have come to identify our world by its proper name: sin. Now this is a reality which a lot of believers and nonbelievers alike in the First World do not know how to handle. We call it by that name because, Christianly speaking, sin is "that which deals death." Sin dealt death to the Son of God, and sin continues to deal death to the sons and daughters of God. One may or may not believe in God, but because of the reality of death, no one will be able to deny the reality of sin.

From this basic reality of the cross and of death, we have learned to place in its true perspective the massive poverty which draws people to death—death which is slow at the hands of the ever-present structures of injustice, and death which is swift and violent when the poor seek to change their lot. We are currently numbering 75,000 dead in El Salvador.

We have learned that the world's poor are practically of no consequence to anyone—not to the people who live in abundance or to the people who have any kind of power. For that reason, the poor may also be defined as those who have ranged against them all the powers of this world. They certainly have against them the oligarchies, the multinational corporations, the various armed forces, and virtually every government. They are also of no great consequence to the political parties, the universities, or even the churches. (There are notable exceptions, of course, such as Archbishop Romero's church and Father Ellacuría's university.) If the poor are of no consequence as individuals within their own countries, they are also of no consequence as entire peoples amid the nations of the world. The First World is not interested in the Third World, to put it mildly. As history shows, it is only interested in ways to despoil the Third World in order to increase its own abundance.

People do not want to acknowledge or face up to the reality of a crucified world, and even less do we want to ask ourselves what is our share of responsibility for such a world. The world of poverty truly is the great unknown. It is surprising that the First World can know so much and yet ignore what is so fundamental about the world in which we live. It is also frustrating, because the problem is not a lack of means by which to learn the truth. We have enough knowledge to place a man on the moon or on Mars, but we sometimes do not even know how many human beings share this planet, much less how many of them die every year from hunger (the number must be around 30 million), or what is happening in Guatemala or in Chad, or how much destruction was caused in Iraq by the 80,000 bombing sorties of the so-called allies.

It isn't that we simply do not know; we do not want to know because, at least subconsciously, we sense that we have all had something to do with bringing about such a crucified world. And as usually happens where scandal is involved, we have organized a vast cover-up before which the scandals of Watergate, Irangate, or Iraqgate pale in comparison.

To "wake from sleep" in El Salvador goes far beyond the endless discussions on secondary topics which go on within churches and parties, even progressive churches and parties. The important thing is to remember that such an awakening is made possible by the world of the poor and the victimized. And it requires a fresh reading of some basic scriptural passages.

In El Salvador, we have rediscovered how God looks at God's crucified creation. To recall the anthropomorphic but eloquent words of Genesis: "The Lord saw that the wickedness of humankind was great in the earth.

And the Lord was sorry that he had made humankind on the earth, and it grieved him to his heart." To put this in even more anthropological terms, we do not know how it is possible to be a human being and not sometimes feel the shame of belonging to inhuman humanity. We have rediscovered many other passages from Scripture whose original power far exceeds any meaning uncovered by exegetical and critical scholarship—passages such as "the darkness hated the light" and, even more radically, "the Evil One is an assassin and a liar."

This world of poverty and crucified peoples has allowed us to overcome blindness and discover mendacity. As Scripture says, in Yahweh's suffering servant there is a light, and in the crucified Christ there is wisdom. If we are blessed enough to look closely at those peoples, we begin to see a little more of the truth of things. The discovery can be startling at first, but it is also blessed, because in this way we are true to ourselves and because the truth of the poor is more than just suffering and death.

Indeed, the poor of this world continue to demonstrate that they have hope, something which is close to disappearing elsewhere, other than the hope generated by an optimistic belief in progress or by the possibility of life beyond death. And the latter is not at all what Christian faith postulates. What Christian faith says is that God will grant definitive justice to the victims of poverty and, by extension, to those who have sided with them. This is an active hope which unloosens creativity at all levels of human existence—intellectual, organizational, ecclesial—and which is marked by notable generosity and boundless, even heroic, altruism.

Such is the deepest reality of our world, and that is the totality of its reality: It is a world of both sin and grace. The First World shows little or no interest in either aspect, but such is the reality from the perspective of the poor and the victimized.

In El Salvador, we have also learned to ask ourselves what is truly human about human beings. To put it bluntly, we have learned to place under suspicion the Western understanding of the nature of humanity. There are many partially valid philosophical, theological, and critical anthropologies. But historically and operatively these generally seem to suggest that what is human is "the way we are," or at least the way we imagine ourselves to be. Much political speech making and even much philosophical and theological discourse presuppose this notion, if in more subtle terms. The ideal consistently held up for all people is that of "modern man" or "Western man," even though here and there an occasional lament is voiced as to this ideal's failures and shortcomings.

The war in the Persian Gulf has shown, among other things, that the Western world has discovered or invented almost everything—except justice, solidarity, and peace. The sum total of the West's scientific and technological knowledge, its impressive political democratic and Judeo-Christian traditions, the power it has amassed in its governments, its armies, its enterprises, its universities, and its churches has not been sufficient to enable it to find a just and humane solution to conflict.

Yet despite this failure we continue to suppose that we know what it is to be human and that everyone else must be like us in order to become human. The same dangerous premise holds sway in religious circles: Primitively religious people must overcome any indigenous or superstitious elements in their Christianity before becoming genuinely religious in today's world.

All of this has changed for me since returning to El Salvador. The most important change is the very way of seeking the answer to the question of what it means to be human, coupled with the nagging suspicion that we have asked the question in a rather "dogmatic" and uncritical manner.

I am appalled at the triumphalist naïveté with which *human being* becomes interchangeable with *Western human being*, when the truth of the matter is that the latter has not humanized anyone or become more human. Those who lavish praise on Western individualism ignore how such an attitude has fostered insensibility toward the human community and even encouraged selfishness and aloofness. The Western capacity to achieve, to struggle and emerge victorious, has been so highly valued that it has enabled the westerner to feel like a Prometheus, unneedful of anything or anyone else, including grace—a subject few First World philosophies and theologies know what to do with. Western human beings have to a great extent produced an inhuman world for those in the Third World and a dehumanizing world in the First World. And still, no change seems imminent.

I am also appalled at the lack of a sense of history in Western efforts to understand humanity, as if there were a human essence which is replicated with slight variations throughout the planet. Of course, there is some truth to this view. But it is really an affront to continue to say to the many millions of the poor and the victimized that they are human beings "like everyone else," or to continue to exhort them to "hold out" because someday they will be like everyone else, complete with democracy and television sets.

In the face of this circumstance, we need to place the human reality in historical context. We must realize that there are fundamental differences in the way people live. There are those who take life for granted and those who take anything but life for granted. To be a human being today has much to do, for instance, with whether one has food to eat.

At the level of human worth, it might be said that things are improving, since the modern world, the U.S. Constitution, the United Nations' Declaration of Human Rights and so on have all proclaimed equal rights for all human beings. But that is not the way things are. Whether one has dignity, self-respect, and rights depends to a great degree on an accident of birth. It helps considerably to have been born in the United States or Germany rather than in El Salvador or Pakistan.

Finally, I am troubled by the lack of dialectic in discussions about humanity. People naively speak of a common destiny for all humanity, ignoring the basic fact that a sharp division exists between those who have and those who do not—a gap which is ever growing.

We have discovered in El Salvador that we really did not know very precisely what it means to be a human being. Now, at least, I suspect that the mystery of the human being is not exhausted in what I knew before; there was much inhumanity in the ideal of humanity to which I formerly adhered. Above all, I have discovered that what is truly human has been showing itself to me where I once would have least expected it—in the faces of the poor. Although the mystery of what is human goes beyond any one particular instance, I have concluded that in order to comprehend our human essence, it is necessary to do so from the point of view not of the powerful but of the poor, and on their behalf. As the gospel says, the truth of the human being manifests itself in the Beatitudes of Jesus and in the parable of the good Samaritan.

From the perspective of the poor, we have rediscovered the need for a new kind of civilization, a civilization of poverty or at least of austerity, rather than one of impossible abundance for all—a civilization of work and not of capital, as Father Ellacuría would say. That more humane civilization can be made concrete by considering first the community rather than the individual, by upholding transcendent values over crass pragmatism, by favoring celebration over mere diversion, and by emphasizing hope over calculated optimism and faith over positivism.

To come to know God, to hold and keep faith in God, is the ultimate mystery of the human being. It is not an easy thing to accomplish, and it cannot be achieved automatically from any perspective, not even a Salvadoran perspective. But I am convinced that true knowledge of God is facilitated in this milieu—at least of a God who resembles the God of Scripture—and faith in God becomes possible and sustainable here.

I believe in the God made manifest in Jesus, a God on whom one can rely, a father who continues to be God and therefore will not let us be. To put it another way, I believe in the goodness and the mystery of God, and both of these have become sharply real to me in El Salvador.

The goodness of God is made real in the fact that God tenderly loves those dispossessed by life and identifies with the victims of this world. This fact can be difficult to accept in other places, but here it becomes patently clear and is reinforced in Scripture. A long-standing tradition has led us to think of a God who is directly universal, even though in reality this God is essentially a European and North American construct.

The mystery of God emerges even more clearly in this world of victims, for this is a God who not only favors the victimized but is at the mercy of their torturers. There are those who think that in a religious Latin America, faith in God is not as serious an issue as in the more secularized world. However, given the fact of so many victims, Latin America is the quintessential place to question God—as Job did, and as Jesus did from the cross—especially since God is confessed as a God of life. That God should permit victims to suffer and die is an insurmountable scandal. In the midst of such a situation, a believer can only accept the fact that God on the cross is as impotent as the victims themselves, and then interpret such impotency as God's way of being in solidarity with those victims. The cross on which God is placed is the most eloquent proclamation that God loves the victimized of this world. On that cross, God's love is impotent yet believable. And it is from that perspective that the mystery of God must be reformulated.

Finally, from a Salvadoran perspective, it is clear that the true God is at war with other gods. These are the idols, the false divinities—though they are real enough—which Archbishop Romero has concretized for our time in speaking of the absolutization of exploitive capitalism and "national security." Idols dehumanize their worshipers, but their ultimate evil lies in the fact that they demand victims in order to exist. If there is one single deep conviction I have acquired in El Salvador, it is that such idols are real. They are not the inventions of so-called primitive peoples but are indeed active in modern societies. We dare not doubt this, in view of such idols' innumerable victims: the poor, the unemployed, the refugees, the detainees, the tortured, the disappeared, the massacred. And if idols do exist, then the issue of faith in God is very much alive.

I have also learned in El Salvador that to believe in God means to cease having faith in idols and to struggle against them. That is the reason we humans must make a choice not only between faith and atheism but between faith and idolatry. In a world of victims, little can be known about a person simply because he calls himself a believer or a nonbeliever. It is imperative to know in which God she believes and against which idols she does battle. If such a person is truly a worshiper of idols, it matters little whether he accepts or denies the existence of a transcendent being. There really is nothing new in that: Jesus affirmed it in his parable of the last judgment.

In order to speak the whole truth, one must always say two things: in which God one believes and in which idol one does not believe. Without such a dialectic formulation, faith remains too abstract, is likely to be empty and, what is worse, can be very dangerous, because it may very well allow for the coexistence of belief and idolatry.

Moreover, I have learned that to have faith in God means to do the will of God, to follow Jesus with the spirit of Jesus in the cause of God's kingdom. In El Salvador, I have seen this faith quite clearly; innumerable martyrs have witnessed to it. I have learned that faith is difficult but entirely possible, that it is very costly but deeply humanizing. In El Salvador, God's solemn proclamation in the prophet Micah becomes very real: "What does the Lord require of you but to do justice, and to love kindness, and to walk humbly with your God?" Reproducing justice and love in human history is the way we respond to God's love. Walking humbly throughout history is the way we respond to the mystery of God.

Such is the reality that has been revealing itself to us in El Salvador. In itself, it is at once a clear clarion and good news. The reality that is a curse represents a call for us to transform it, but it also becomes a blessing and good news which transforms *us*. These become one in the response of mercy toward crucified peoples.

In El Salvador, we have rediscovered that the faithful response to this world of victims is the constant exercise of mercy, as in the parable of the good Samaritan, which Jesus uses to describe the true human being. The Samaritan sees someone wounded along the way, is moved to pity, and treats his wounds. The importance of mercy in the gospels can be deduced also from the fact that Jesus himself and the Father who receives the prodigal son are described as being merciful.

We are speaking here not of "works of mercy" but rather of the basic structure of the response to this world's victims. This structure consists in making someone else's pain our very own and allowing that pain to move us to respond. We are to be moved simply by the fact that someone in need has been placed along our way. Even though Jesus presents the Samaritan as an example of one who obeys the commandment to love his neighbor, there is nothing in the parable which would lead us to conclude that the Samaritan acts in order to fulfill a commandment. He was simply moved to pity. It needs also to be emphasized that mercy is not only a fundamental attitude at the root of every human interaction but also a principle which affects subsequent interactions.

In El Salvador, we have awakened to the fact that a heartless humanity manages to praise works of mercy but refuses to be guided by the mercy principle. Guided by this principle, we have discovered some important things.

First of all, we well know that in our world there are not just wounded individuals but crucified peoples, and that we should enflesh mercy accordingly. To react with mercy, then, means to do everything we possibly can to bring them down from the cross. This means working for justice—which is the name love acquires when it comes to entire majorities of people unjustly oppressed—and employing in behalf of justice all our intellectual, religious, scientific, and technological energies.

Second, we must realize that mercy that becomes justice will automatically be persecuted by the powerful, and therefore mercy must be clung to vigorously and consistently. The Salvadoran martyrs—alternately called subversives, communists, and atheists—were consistently merciful. That is why they struggled for justice, and that is why they were assassinated.

Third, we must give mercy priority above all else. This is no easy task for any civil institution, any government, business, political movement, or army, nor for any religious or ecclesial institution. One must be willing to risk for mercy, the way Archbishop Romero did, risking not only one's personal life but even the ecclesial institution itself. That is why he had to witness the destruction of his archdiocese's radio and printing operations and why some of the priests around him were assassinated. All must be risked, because what is first of all is the ultimate.

Fourth, I have learned that the exercise of mercy is the measure of freedom—that state of being universally hailed as a human ideal in the Western world. When he healed on a Sabbath, Jesus was violating the rules and norms of his time because he was merciful, not because he was a liberal. Jesus understood freedom from the point of view of mercy, not the other way around. For him, freedom meant that nothing could stand in the way of the exercise of mercy.

This mercy is the demand which has been placed in our hearts by the Salvadoran reality. But the demand is also a blessing, is also good news. "Happy are the merciful," Jesus says. From this point, we can reinterpret the other Beatitudes. "Happy are those who hunger and thirst for justice. Happy are those who work for peace. Happy are you when you are persecuted for the cause of justice." And if we use the Beatitudes to reinterpret what we said above about acquiring new eyes, we can also say, "Happy are those with a clean heart." Finally, if mercy and new vision are placed at the service of the poor and we thus participate to some degree in their lot, we too can hear, "Happy are the poor."

The reader may be surprised that I have not mentioned several topics one might expect to be discussed in a piece coming from El Salvador. I have not spoken of liberation theology per se, of Marxism, of revolution, of problems with the Vatican. True enough, the changes in Latin America have brought about a new theology, a new way of being church as a church of the poor, new relationships with popular movements, new ways of solidarity, and so on. But we have tried to set forth what is at the root of these changes. Without the roots, one cannot understand the changes.

To sum up, then: We have awakened from a sleep of inhumanity to a reality of humanity. We have learned to see God from the point of view of the victimized, and we have tried to see this world of the victimized from the point of view of God. We have learned to exercise mercy and find joy and a purpose for life in doing so.

Remembering my dear Jesuit brother Ignacio Ellacuría, rector of Jose Simeon Canas Central American University, who was murdered with five other Jesuits and two pious women on November 16, 1989, I have learned that there is nothing as vital in order to live as a human being than to exercise mercy on behalf of a crucified people, and that nothing is more humanizing than to believe in the God of Jesus. As I have seen this way of life become very real in many Salvadorans, in many other Latin Americans, and in many who sympathize with us in various places, another new thing I have learned in El Salvador is the importance of saying "Thank you." Then life and faith still make sense.

—Translated by Dimas Planas

PART ONE

1

The Samaritan Church and the Principle of Mercy

The theme of this monographic issue of *Sal Terrae*—"The Other Marks of the Church"—has something of the shocking about it, and much of the needful. The reference to "other marks" is shocking. Are "One, Holy, Catholic, and Apostolic" no longer enough to "mark" the true church of Jesus? And yet the topic must needs be dealt with, because these "other marks" afford us an access—a different access—to that which is fundamental: Before all else, a true church is a church "like unto Jesus." We all share the intuition that, were we to bear no resemblance to Jesus, we should not be his church, nor would that church be recognized as the church of Jesus. And so we ask: What is a church that resembles Jesus?

To resemble Jesus is to reproduce the structure of his life. In gospel terms, the structure of Jesus' life is a structure of *incarnation*, of becoming real flesh in real history. And Jesus' life is structured in function of the *fulfillment of a mission*—the mission of proclaiming the good news of the Reign of God, inaugurating that Reign through all signs of every sort, and denouncing the fearsome reality of the anti-Reign. The structure of Jesus' life meant *taking on the sin of the world*, and not just standing idly by looking at it from the outside. It meant taking on a sin that, today, surely, continues to manifest its greatest power in the fact that it puts millions of human beings to death. Finally, the structure of Jesus' life meant *rising again* and *raising again*—having, and bestowing on others, life, hope, and gladness.

What endows the structure of Jesus' life with its ultimate consistency can be "thought" in various ways. It can be conceptualized in terms of his fidelity, his hope, his service, and so on. Of course, none of these realities excludes any of the others. All are mutually complementary, and any of them could well serve to point up the unity of Jesus' life. What we wish to set forth in this article is that the principle that seems to us to be the most "structuring" of all, as we examine Jesus' life, is the element of *mercy* in that

Published originally in *Sal Terrae* 927 (1990/10): 665-678

life. Therefore it ought to be the "most structuring" element of the life of the church, as well.

The Principle of Mercy

The term *mercy* must be correctly understood. The word has good and authentic connotations, but it can also have inadequate connotations, even dangerous ones. It suggests a sense of compassion. The danger is that it may seem to denote a sheer sentiment, without a praxis to accompany it. It may connote "works of mercy." Here the risk is that the practitioner of such works may feel exempt from the duty of analyzing the causes of the suffering that these works relieve. Mercy can connote the alleviation of individual needs but entail the risk of abandoning the transformation of structures. It may connote "parental" attitudes, but risk paternalism. In order to avoid the limitations of the concept of mercy and the misunderstandings to which it is open, we shall speak not simply of mercy, but of the principle of mercy—just as Ernst Bloch spoke not simply of hope, as if he were referring merely to one categorical reality among others, but of the hope principle.

By the principle of mercy, we understand here a specific love, which, while standing at the origin of a process, also remains present and active throughout the process, endowing it with a particular direction and shaping the various elements that compose it. We hold that this principle of mercy is the basic principle of the activity of God and Jesus, and therefore ought to be that of the activity of the church.

"In the Beginning Was Mercy"

As we know, the loving action of God stands at the origin of the salvific process. "I have witnessed the affliction of my people in Egypt and have heard their cry of complaint against their slave drivers, so I know well what they are suffering. Therefore I have come down to rescue them" (Exod. 3:7-8). The question of choosing a term to describe this activity on God's part is, in a way, a secondary one, although it would be most adequately denominated *liberation*. Our concern here is to emphasize the structure of the liberative movement. God hears the cries of a suffering people, and for that reason alone determines to undertake the liberative activity in question.[1]

We call this activity of love, thus structured, mercy. And we find that we must say of this mercy that first it is an *action*, or more precisely, a *re-action* to someone else's suffering, now interiorized within oneself—a reaction to a suffering that has come to penetrate one's own entrails and heart (in this case, the suffering of an entire people, inflicted upon them unjustly and at the basic levels of their existence). Secondly, this activity, this action, is motivated *only* by that suffering.

The interiorized suffering of another is the first principle and foundation of the reaction of mercy. But this mercy, in turn, becomes the molding principle of the whole of God's activity. After all, the mercy under consideration is not only at the origin of God's activity: It abides as a basic constant all through the Old Testament (God's partiality to victims in virtue of the sheer fact of their being victims, the active defense mounted by God in their behalf, and the liberative divine design in their regard). The mercy in question endows with their internal logic both the concrete historicization of the demand of justice and the denunciation of those who produce unjust suffering. Through this activity (and not merely on the occasion of the same), as well as through successive acts of mercy following thereon, God is genuinely revealed. The fundamental exigency for the human being, and specifically for the people of God, is that they reiterate this mercy of God's, exercising it toward others and thus rendering themselves like unto God.

Paraphrasing Scripture, we might say that, as in the absolute divine beginning "was the Word" (John 1:1), and through the Word creation arose (cf. Gen. 1:1), so mercy is in the absolute beginning of the history of salvation, and this mercy abides as a constant in God's salvific process.

Mercy According to Jesus

It is this primordial mercy of God's that appears concretely historicized in Jesus' practice and message. The *Misereor super turbas*, "My heart is moved with pity for the crowd," is more than a "regional" activity on Jesus' part. It shapes his life and mission and seals his fate. And it molds his view of God and human beings.

When Jesus wishes to show what it is to be an ideal, total human being, he narrates the parable of the good Samaritan. The moment is a solemn one in the gospels. More is at stake here than mere curiosity as to which is the greatest of the commandments: This parable is a presentation of what it is to be a human being. The ideal, total human being is represented as one who has seen someone else lying wounded in the ditch along the road, has re-acted, and has helped the victim in every way possible. The parable does not tell us what was going through the Samaritan's head at the time, or with what ultimate finality he acted. The only thing we are told is that he did what he did because he was "moved to pity."

The ideal human being, the complete human being, is the one who interiorizes, absorbs in her innards, the suffering of another—in the case of the parable, unjustly afflicted suffering—in such a way that this interiorized suffering becomes a part of her, is transformed into an internal principle, the first and the last, of her activity. Mercy, as re-action, becomes the fundamental action of the total human being. Thus, this mercy is more than just one phenomenon in human reality among many. It directly defines the human being. To be sure, mercy does not suffice to define Jesus: He is a being of knowing, hoping, and celebrating, as well. On the other hand, it is absolutely necessary that mercy come into his definition. For Jesus, to be a human being is to react with mercy. Without this reaction, the essence of the human is vitiated in its root, as occurred with the priest and the Levite who "saw him and went on."

This mercy is also the reality with which Jesus is defined in the gospels. Jesus frequently heals those who have asked him to "have pity," and he acts because he feels compassion for persons. Even God is described in terms of this mercy in another of the foundational parables. The divine Parent goes forth to meet the prodigal child, sees him, and—moved by compassion, by mercy—embraces him and declares a festival.

If the human being, Christ, and God are all described in terms of mercy, then we must be dealing with something genuinely fundamental. Of course, we may say that love is the fundamental thing, and we have the whole of Christian tradition as our warrant. That goes without saying. But we must add that the love in question here is a specific kind of love. This love is the particular *praxic* love that swells within a person at the sight of another person's unjustly inflicted suffering,[2] driving its subject to eradicate that suffering for no other reason than that it exists, and precluding any excuse for not so doing.

The elevation of this mercy to the status of a principle may seem minimal. But according to Jesus, without it, there is no humanity or divinity, and however minimal, it is genuinely maximal, as well. The important thing to observe is that this "minimum and maximum" is the first and the last. There is nothing antecedent to mercy that might move it, nor is there anything beyond mercy that might relativize it or offer an escape from it.

Simply put, this can be appreciated in the fact that the Samaritan is presented by Jesus as the consummate example of someone fulfilling the commandment of love of neighbor. But there is nothing in the account of the parable to suggest that the Samaritan succors the victim *in order* to fulfill a commandment, however lofty a one. Simply, he is "moved to pity."

We hear of Jesus that he heals people and sometimes manifests sorrow that those who have been healed have shown no gratitude. But in no wise does it appear that Jesus performs these acts of healing *in order* to receive gratitude (or in order to have it thought that he is a special person or someone with divine power). No, he performs them only "moved to pity."

Of the heavenly Parent, it is said that God welcomes the prodigal child. But there is no suggestion that this is a subtle *tactic for attaining* what God supposedly wishes (that the prodigal confess his sins and thus put his life in order). No, the Parent acts simply "moved to pity," moved to mercy.

Mercy, then, is the first thing and the last. It is more than a categorical practice of the "works of mercy." True, the practice of mercy can and ought to include these works. But mercy itself is something far more radical. Mercy is a basic attitude toward the suffering of another, whereby one reacts to eradicate that suffering for the sole reason that it exists, and in the conviction that, in this reaction to the ought-not-be of another's suffering, one's own being, without any possibility of subterfuge, hangs in the balance.

The parable exemplifies the condition of the concrete historical phenomenon as a reality shot through with mercilessness. The priest and the Levite show no mercy, and Jesus is horrified. But the evangelists are also showing us a concrete historical reality that is shaped by the active anti-mercy that wounds and kills some human beings, then kills those guided by the principle of mercy.

Because he is merciful—not a "liberal"—Jesus prioritizes the healing of the person with the withered hand over the observance of the Sabbath. His argumentation to this effect is obvious and unassailable. "Is it permitted to do a good deed on the sabbath—or an evil one? To preserve life—or destroy it?" (Mark 3:4). Nevertheless, his adversaries—described in terms strikingly antithetical to the qualities attributed to Jesus, with their "closed minds" (literally, "hardness of heart," v. 5)—not only remain unconvinced, but take action against Jesus, and the narrative concludes with these chilling words: "When the Pharisees went outside, they immediately began to plot with the Herodians how they might destroy him" (v. 6).

Notwithstanding any anachronism that may be attributed to the passage, it makes its point. It shows that mercy and anti-mercy are real. Let mercy be reduced to sentiments or sheer works of mercy, and anti-mercy will be tolerant enough. But let it be raised to the status of a principle, and the Sabbath subordinated to the extirpation of suffering, and anti-mercy will react. Tragically, Jesus is sentenced to death for practicing mercy consistently and to the last. Mercy, then, is precisely the mercy that materializes in spite of, and in opposition to, anti-mercy.

Despite the fact that his mercy is the cause of his condemnation, Jesus proclaims, "Blest are they who show mercy." The reason Jesus gives his hearers in the Gospel of Matthew could seem to fall in the category of reward: "Mercy shall be theirs" (Matt. 5:7). But the deeper reason is an intrinsic one. She who lives according to the principle of mercy realizes—renders real—the profoundest element of what it is to be human, and comes to resemble Jesus (the *true* human being of dogma) and her heavenly Parent.

Herein, we may well say, consists the blessedness, the felicity, that Jesus offers. "Blest" and happy are you "who show mercy," you "single-hearted," you "peacemakers," you who "hunger and thirst for holiness" or justice, you who are "persecuted for holiness' sake"—you "poor." Scandalous words, but enlightening. Jesus wants human beings' happiness, and the symbol of that happiness consists in their coming together at the table of sharing. But as long as the great table of the brothers and sisters of the Reign of God is missing from history, mercy must be practiced. It is mercy, Jesus is telling us, that, for the interim, produces joy, gladness, and felicity.

The Principle of Mercy

We hope these brief reflections on mercy will help the reader understand what we mean by "principle of mercy." Mercy is not the sole content of Jesus' practice, but it is mercy that stands at the origin of all that he practices;

it is mercy that shapes and molds his entire life, mission, and fate. Sometimes the word *mercy* appears explicitly in the gospel accounts, and sometimes it does not. In either case, the backdrop of Jesus' activity is always the suffering of the masses, the poor, the weak, those deprived of dignity. Jesus' entrails wrench in its presence, and it is these wrenched entrails that shape all that Jesus is: his knowing, his hoping, his actions, and his celebration.

Thus, Jesus' hope is that of the poor, who have no hope and to whom he proclaims the Reign of God. His praxis is in behalf of the last and least, in behalf of the oppressed (miraculous cures, expulsion of demons, welcome of sinners, and so on). His "social theory" is guided by the principle that massive unjust suffering must be pulled up by the roots. His joy is the personal jubilation he feels when the poor understand, and his celebration is to sit down at table with the outcast. Finally, his vision of God is of a God who defends the small and is merciful to the poor. In the prayer par excellence, the Our Father, it is the poor whom Jesus invites to call God their Father.

This is not the place to expatiate on all we have just set forth. We have only meant to indicate what we have in mind, in the hope that it may help the reader understand what we mean by the "principle of mercy." This is what "informs," endows with their specific identity, all of the dimensions of the human being: knowledge, hope, celebration, and of course, praxis. Each of these dimensions has its own autonomy, but all can and ought to be molded and directed by some fundamental principle. In Jesus—as in his God—that principle, we think, is the principle of mercy.

For Jesus, mercy stands at the origin of the divine and the human. God is guided by that principle, and human beings ought to be, as well. All else is ancillary. Nor is this sheer speculative reconstruction, as is abundantly evidenced in the key passage of Matthew 25. Those who practice mercy—whatever the other dimensions of their human reality—have been saved, have arrived for good and all at the status of total human being. Judge and judged sit in the tribunal of mercy, and mercy alone. The one thing that must be added is that the criterion applied by the Judge is not an arbitrary one. Even God, we have seen, reacts with mercy to the cry of the oppressed; therefore is the life of human beings decided in virtue of their response to that cry.

Church of Mercy

It is this principle of mercy that ought to be operative in Jesus' church. And it is the *pathos* of mercy that ought to "inform" that church—give it its specificity, shape and mold it. In other words, the church, too, even *qua* church, should reread the parable of the good Samaritan and listen to it with the same rapt attention, and the same fear and trembling, with which Jesus' hearers first heard it. The church should be and do many other things, as well. But unless it is steeped—as a church at once Christian and human—in the mercy of the parable of the good Samaritan, unless the church is the

good Samaritan before all else, all else will be irrelevant—and even dangerous, should it succeed in passing for its fundamental principle.

Let us notice, in function of certain key elements, how the principle of
mercy informs and configures the church.

A Church "De-Centered" by Mercy

A basic problem for the church is that of determining its place with
respect to the rest of reality. The formal response is a familiar one: The place
of the church is in the world—in a reality logically external to it. After all,
it is the practice of mercy that places the church outside itself and in a very
precise locus—the place where human suffering occurs, the place where
the cries of human beings resound. ("Were you there when they crucified
my Lord?" sing the oppressed blacks of the United States, and their song is
worth many a page of ecclesiology.) The place of the church is with the
wounded one lying in the ditch along the roadside, whether or not this
victim is to be found physically and geographically within intraecclesial
space. The place of the church is with "the other," and with the most radical
otherness of that other—his suffering—especially when that suffering is
massive, cruel, and unjust.

To take its position in that place is by no means easy for the institutional
church, as we are wont to call it. But neither is it easy for the merely
progressive church, or for those within it who are merely progressive. Let
us consider a current example. Granted, it is urgent, just, and necessary to
demand respect for human rights and freedom within the church itself,
especially for ethical reasons, since these human rights are signs of siblingship—signs, therefore, of the Reign of God—and because without them the
church forfeits its credibility in the world of today. But let us not forget that
mercy *within* the church is, in a certain sense, something secondary. With
logical priority, we ought to be examining how the rights to life and liberty
are faring in the *world*. This latter focus is governed by the principle of mercy
and Christianizes the former; but not necessarily vice versa. Merciful
Christianity can be progressive, but progressive Christianity, at times, is not
merciful.

I hope I am clear about what I mean in appealing to this example. It is
surely urgent for the church to become humane within. But the most
important thing is that the church begin to "think itself" from without, from
"along the road," where the wounded neighbor lies. It is surely urgent that
the Christian, the priest, and the theologian, for example, demand their
legitimate freedom in the church—a freedom so circumscribed today. But
it is more urgent that they demand the freedom of the millions of human
beings who do not have so much as the freedom to survive their poverty,
to live in the face of oppression, or even to seek justice, be it so much as a
simple investigation into the crimes of which they are the object.

When the church emerges from within itself, to set off down the road
where the wounded lie, then is when it genuinely de-centers itself and

thereby comes to resemble Jesus in something absolutely fundamental: Jesus did not preach himself, but offered the poor the hope of the Reign of God, grasping his fellow human beings by the lapels, giving them a shake, and urging them to the building of that Reign. In sum: It is the victim lying along the side of the road who de-centers the church and is transformed into the "other" (and the radically "other") in the eyes of the church. It is the re-action of mercy that verifies whether the church has de-centered itself, and to what extent it has done so.

Historicization of the Human Cry, Historicization of Mercy

Always and everywhere, many different classes of wounds, physical and spiritual, cry out for healing. Their size and depth vary by definition, and mercy must re-act to cure them all. However, the church must not succumb to a reckless universalization here, as if all cries expressed the same wound, or appeal to that universalization in self-justification: "We have always encouraged the works of mercy." Indeed, the church has always encouraged those works. And indeed, all human suffering merits absolute respect and calls for a response. But this does not preclude some manner of hierarchization of the wounds of today's world.

Beyond a doubt, every local church has its specific wounds, physical and spiritual alike, and all these wounds must be dressed and healed. But inasmuch as the church is one and catholic—as we say of the true church—attention must be paid to the state and condition of that wound that is the world in its totality. Quantitatively, the most painful suffering on this planet of more than five million human beings is constituted by poverty, with the death and very specific indignity that accompanies it, and that poverty remains the world's most serious wound. This deep wound appears far more radically in the Third World than in the First. Theoretically, we know all of this; still, it bears repeating. Merely by having been born in El Salvador, or Haiti, or Bangladesh, or Chad, human beings have—as Ignacio Ellacuría put it—incomparably (*muchísima*) less life, and incomparably less dignity, than persons born in the United States, Germany, or Spain. This is the fundamental wound today. And—let us recall it in Christian language—what is wounded is God's very creation.

This deepest of wounds is the deepest of wounds for any local church, not only by reason of the magnitude of the fact itself, but also by reason of the shared responsibility for it that rests with any and all local instances (governments, parties, unions, armies, universities—and churches). A local church that fails to tend that worldwide wound cannot claim to be ruled by the principle of mercy.[3]

None of this militates against the importance of tending local wounds, some of which lie along the very lines we have just sketched: those of the "Fourth World" (of the "Third World within the First") and the other specific wounds of the First World (selfish individualism and crass positivism, for example, which strip things of their meaning and persons of their faith). All of this should, of course, be tended with mercy—but without relegating to secondary status that which is primary, and without ever failing to ask oneself whether a part of the root of that absurdity, a part of the responsibility for the diseased condition of culture, might possibly be, consciously or unconsciously, our own shared responsibility in having generated a planet most of whose inhabitants bear the wound of poverty and indignity.

A Mercy Consistent to the Last

It costs the church a great deal, as it would any institution, to re-act with mercy, and it costs it even more to maintain that mercy. In theoretical terms, it is costly to the church to bow to the supremacy of the Reign of God. We frequently hear a justification of the utterly un-Christian reversal of the proper order of things—the supremacy of the Reign of God over the church—to the following effect. The very existence of the church is a great good, a boon in itself. After all, the church will, in the long run, always render the world more humane, and thus speed the coming of the Reign of God. In simple terms, we might say it is costly to maintain the supremacy of mercy over self-centeredness, and self-centeredness always becomes selfishness. Hence the temptation to which the priest and the Levite succumbed: to "see and go on." But it is especially costly to maintain the supremacy of mercy over self-interest, when, in defending the wounded victim, one finds oneself in confrontation with those forgotten players in the drama of the good Samaritan, the robbers—who also act (by re-acting).

This world is ever ready to applaud, or at least tolerate, works of mercy. What this world will not tolerate is a church molded by the principle of mercy, which leads that church to denounce robbers who victimize, to lay bare the lie that conceals oppression, and to encourage victims to win their freedom from culprits. In other words, the robbers who inhabit this anti-merciful world tolerate the tending of wounds, but not the true healing of the wounded, let alone mounting a struggle to keep the latter from falling once more into their hands.

When the church does these things, it is threatened, assaulted, and persecuted—as any institution would be. This, in turn, demonstrates that the church has let itself be ruled by the principle of mercy rather than limiting itself to the mere practice of works of mercy. Contrariwise, the absence of such threats, assaults, and persecutions demonstrates that, while the church may have managed to perform works of mercy, it has not allowed itself to be governed by the principle of mercy.

In Latin America, both phenomena are abundantly in evidence. There is a church here which practices the works of mercy but is unwilling to be governed by the principle of mercy. There is another church here that is molded by the principle of mercy, which leads it to encourage the works of mercy, to be sure, but carries it beyond them—as it carries God and Jesus beyond them. Thus, to practice mercy is to strike out at the idols, the "forgotten gods," as J. L. Sicré aptly dubs them. Forgotten does not mean vanquished. The idols of death are in hiding, but they are still very real. This is what endows with its existential ineluctability the option to maintain mercy as the first and the last, regardless of whether that will entail risks, and regardless of the type and size of these risks.

Not that we should be naive. We must realistically accept the principle of subsistency that shapes the church, as it shapes any other institution. But there are times when one must show mercy with ultimacy, and this can be done only in the presence of that which runs counter to mercy. This is what Archbishop Romero did. It was not easy for him to begin practicing this ultimate mercy, and it was even more difficult for him to maintain it. The practice of this mercy meant painful intraecclesial conflicts for him, and placed at risk his earlier ecclesial prestige, his reputation, his archiepiscopal responsibility, and his very life. It also meant risking something still more difficult to risk, and something infrequently placed at risk: the institution. In maintaining this mercy, he had to see institutional platforms of the church destroyed (the archdiocesan radio and press) and the institutional church itself decimated, through the arrest, expulsion, and murder of the most important symbols of the institution: priests, nuns, catechists, ministers of the word, and so many others. Nevertheless, Archbishop Romero held firm to the principle of mercy, and in the presence of attacks on the institution, uttered these chilling words, understandable only from the lips of one ruled by the principle of mercy: "So they have destroyed our radio, and murdered our priests? Then let them know that they have done us no harm."

When mercy is taken seriously as the first and the last, it becomes conflictive. No one is thrown in prison or persecuted simply for having practiced works of mercy. Not even Jesus would have been persecuted and put to death, had his mercy been mere mercy—without being mercy as the first and the last. But when mercy becomes the first and the last, then it subverts society's ultimate values, and society reacts.

Finally, ultimacy of mercy implies the readiness to be called a Samaritan. Nowadays the word has a positive ring. But this is because it is Jesus' name for a person of ultimate mercy. In those days, it was very pejorative, and that is precisely why Jesus used it—to emphasize the supremacy of mercy over any religious conceptions whatsoever and to attack merciless religious persons.

All this is still going on. Those who practice the mercy the robbers do not desire are called every name under the sun today. In Latin America, they are called—whether they are or not—"subversives," "communists," "liberationists," and so on. They are even murdered for it. The church of mercy, then, must be prepared to lose its reputation in the world of anti-mercy. It must be prepared to be "good," even if it is called a Samaritan for it.

The Church of Mercy Bears the Mark of the True Church of Jesus

There are many other things that can and ought to be said about a church ruled by the principle of mercy. Above all, the faith of such a church will be a faith in the God of the wounded lying along the road, the God of victims. Its liturgy will celebrate the life of the lifeless, the resurrection of One who was crucified. Its theology will be an *intellectus misericordiae (justitiae, liberationis),* and liberation theology is nothing else. The doctrine and social practice of such a church will be a theoretical and practical obsession with indicating, and walking, effective paths to justice.[4] Its ecumenism will arise and prosper—and history shows that this is what occurs—in function of the wounded of the roadside, the crucified peoples, who, like the Crucified One, draw all things to themselves.

It is imperative, we believe, that the church allow itself to be governed by the principle of mercy. Everything that it is to be church can be organized—and in our opinion, in the most Christian manner—in function of that principle.

In conclusion, let us say three things. The first is that everything we have said up to now is nothing but a restatement, in other language, of the option for the poor that the church is obliged to make according to the declarations of the institutional church itself. Nothing that we have said is new, although it may be useful for understanding the radicality, primacy, and ultimacy of the option for the poor. The church of mercy is the one called in Latin America today the "church of the poor."

The second thing is that mercy is also a Beatitude. Therefore a church of mercy—if it really is such—is a church that feels joy because of its mercy, and therefore can show that joy. In this wise—a thing frequently entirely forgotten—the church can communicate *in actu* that its proclamation, in word and work, is *go-spel:* good news, news that is not only true, but productive of joy. A church that transmits no joy is not a church of the gospel. Of course, it is not just any random joy that must be transmitted. The church must transmit the joy declared to it in its Magna Carta, the Beatitudes, and among the Beatitudes is the Beatitude of Mercy.

The third and last thing we wish to state is that a church of mercy bears a stamp, a "mark," in the world of today. The mark of mercy stamps it, to boot, with the mark of credibility. The credibility of the church depends on various factors, and in a democratic and culturally developed world, for example, the exercise of freedom within the church and the proposal of its message in terms consistent with reason, endow it with respectability. But we believe that, in the world at large—which includes the countries of the First World—maximal credibility is a function only of consistent mercy, precisely because mercy is the thing most absent from the world today. A church of consistent mercy is at least credible. If it is not consistently merciful, it will seek credibility in vain through other means. Among those who are weary of the faith, agnostics, or unbelievers, such a church will at least render the name of God respectable. That name will not be blas-phemed by the church's own actions. Among the poor of this world, the church will awaken acceptance and gratitude.

A church of consistent mercy is the one "marked" and "noted" in the world of today, and it is noted as a church "according to God's command." Consistent mercy, then, is a "mark" of the true church of Jesus.

—Translated by Robert R Barr

2

Theology in a Suffering World

Theology as Intellectus Amoris

Introduction: Theology and Suffering

The intent of this 1988 annual volume of the College Theology Society is to situate the task of theology within the different realities that characterize and challenge today's world: Theology in a culturally diverse world, in a religiously plural world, and in a suffering world.

In this essay I will develop the theme of theology in a suffering world. But first, I feel it is important to make a preliminary observation that will help fit my topic into the broader framework of our discussion. The themes that make up the three foci of this volume have an identical structure: "Theology in . . . " The intent, of course, is to recognize the necessity of doing theology in relationship with the actual, concrete realities of the world. The identical grammatical structure of the topics, however, would be misleading if one concluded that these three designations—a culturally diverse world, a religiously plural world, and a suffering world—represent three realities on the same level. Formally, what the three specified realities have in common is the demand that theology incarnate itself within them. But in regard to their concrete content—if I may simplify distinctions a bit—the first two refer to a suprastructural reality that already presupposes a more fundamental reality, whereas the third reality refers to the real world as such, to the infrastructural world. In other words, I wish to assert from the very start that the theme of theology in a suffering world has a methodological priority over the other two themes because it refers directly to the reality of our world. That is to say, though cultural and religious diversity are very important realities, they are secondary with respect to the primary reality of the world as it is, characterized by widespread suffering.

The various cultures and religions are, among other things, concrete ways of understanding and reacting to the primary reality and its suffering.

Originally published in Paul Knitter, ed , *Pluralism and Oppression* (The Annual Publication of the College Theology Society, 1988)

Because of this, the theme assigned to me is not independent of the other two topics; it is in fact already present, though implicitly, in them, since they likewise have to respond, and are ways of responding, to the suffering of the world.

In what follows I would like to present a specific theology, the theology of liberation, as a theology historically necessary in a suffering world and systematically adequate for giving an account of Christian faith in a suffering world. As is known, liberation theology understands itself specifically as a theology of praxis—a praxis of eliminating unjust suffering from the world. Consequently, I wish to formally define liberation theology within the great theological tradition as *intellectus amoris*. As such, it integrates and retrieves—but in a more radical way—what is contained in theology understood as *intellectus fidei* and *intellectus spei*.

But before taking up these expressly theological considerations, some preliminary reflections are necessary in order to situate the theology of liberation in the larger theme of theology in a suffering world.

The Relationship between Christian Theology and Suffering

Throughout history, there have always existed many Christian theologies and, of course, many forms of suffering; the two realities have been related. Suffering is a perennial question for theology, to which theologians have attempted to give their various responses. In this, Christian theologies are similar to other cultures and other religions and their theologies. Such efforts to relate theology and suffering are, of course, a positive sign, for suffering is one of the "hardest" facts of the reality with which all religions must contend and stands as a problem even before it is interpreted. (Interpretations, of course, especially when given by religion/theology, can themselves become a problem and a cause of greater suffering.)

In the different ways in which Christian theologies approach the problem of suffering, we can note a certain minimal and formal agreement. At the level of reality, all Christian theologians recognize the reality of suffering, together with its natural and historical roots. At the level of meaning, they emphasize its negativity. At the level of specifically Christian revelation, they point out that suffering is unwanted by God and in one way or another is a consequence of sin. On the one hand, they admit the absurdity and meaninglessness of suffering, and on the other, its salvific possibilities. At the utopian level, all Christian theologies, in clearly different ways, hold up the possibility of doing away with suffering and propose precise formulas for doing so.

Besides these formal similarities among different Christian theologies, there are also clear differences in the concrete, actual ways in which theologians grapple with the reality of suffering in the world. Such differences tend to shape, consciously or unconsciously, the entire fabric of a particular theology and so make for radical contrasts among them. These differences are evident in two ways.

Theologies react to suffering by seeking to determine the *fundamental form of suffering*—that is, the form of suffering which, without denying other expressions of suffering, becomes a theology's focal concern. Such fundamental forms of suffering might be listed as follows: one's own suffering (centered on one's self), the suffering of others, the suffering of individuals (of the self or its equivalent, a close friend), collective suffering (of peoples, races, sexes, castes), spiritual suffering (doubts, guilt, failure, meaninglessness), corporal-social suffering (serious problems in directing one's life or basic threats to life), historical suffering (the pain that occurs within historical process), metaphysical suffering (the absurdity of history).

The fundamental way in which a theology *reacts* to suffering may be to try to *clarify* its origin (in the human condition, sin, an etiology of historical sufferings) or its meaning; or to find some kind of *meaningful co-existence* with suffering (suffering as purifying or as meritorious); or to attempt to remove suffering (eschatologically and historically); or to discover some kind of theological *justification* for suffering (various types of theodicies).

Theology Confronts Suffering in Today's World

Every theology must confront suffering, determine the fundamental form of suffering, and ask what can be done about it. I would suggest that the development of every Christian theology has been determined, explicitly or implicitly, by the way it has responded to suffering, for in one way or another, all theology claims to be a form of soteriology. This makes sense insofar as salvation stands at the heart of Christian faith. Thus, all theologies today confront the challenge of determining the fundamental form of suffering in our world and what to do about it. Unless a theology does this, its historical relevance and integral development are in jeopardy.

Let me begin by stating my claim in the form of a thesis: For liberation theology, the major form of suffering in today's world is historical suffering—suffering unjustly inflicted on some by others. Historical suffering is massive, affecting the majority of humanity, making it practically impossible for people to direct their own lives, causing a poverty that brings death slowly and violently. In the presence of such suffering, theology must understand itself as an intellectual exercise whose primary purpose is to eliminate this kind of suffering. Briefly stated, suffering in today's world means primarily the sufferings of people who are being crucified, and the purpose of theology is to take these people down from the cross.

Though this thesis expresses the self-understanding and the task of liberation theology, it *also* has valuable implications, though in different forms, for any contemporary theology. This is so for two reasons.

From a historical perspective, the causes of sufferings in the Third World are, to a great extent, to be found in the First World. To admit this is a necessary condition for the First World to know itself truthfully. Deciding to remove this suffering is essential if the First World is to carry out its fundamental ethical responsibility. To actually do away with this suffering is the way of salvation for both Third and First Worlds.

From a Christian perspective, the type of suffering specific to the Third World is in fact the same form of suffering that appears at crucial moments of divine revelation (in the Exodus, the prophets, Jesus). Contrary to the claims of personalistic and intellectual types of theology, to ignore such suffering is to mutilate Christian revelation, both quantitatively and qualitatively. It is to deprive theology of one of its central elements, for by closing one's eyes to the sufferings of the Third World, one ignores, annuls, and falsifies a pivotal part of Christian revelation. Furthermore, to decide concretely to remove the suffering of the Third World is to carry on divine revelation, for such efforts are the praxis of God's self and the praxis that God requires of human beings. If we do not take up this praxis of removing sin from the Third World, we essentially mutilate our Christian morality and our theological response to God.

Stated simply, the task of theology today, either in the First or Third World, cannot be carried out if the massive, cruel, and mounting suffering that pervades our world is ignored. If a theology closes its eyes to suffering because such suffering is not occurring massively in "its" world, that theology would disassociate itself from the real historical humanity in which we all live and which, theologically, is God's own creation.[1]

In a world of suffering, therefore, what is at stake is the humanity of human beings and the faith of believers. For these two foundational reasons, the relevance and credibility of theology is also at stake. I would now like to lay out, in thesis form, just how a suffering world specifies the place, the purpose, and the self-understanding of theology.

The Option for the Suffering World as the Place of Theology

Thesis 1: Theology finds its place in a suffering world insofar as such a world is a mediation of the truth and absoluteness of God. The determination of the suffering world as the place of theology is an option prior to theology, an option required of all believers and all persons.

Theology itself never comes first; it is always a "second act." From a theological point of view, what comes first is the reality of revelation and faith. From an historical and existential viewpoint, theology is preceded by the *objective* determination of its place and the *subjective* decision to locate this place in a concrete way.

We must try to analyze, therefore, just what constitutes this "priority" over theology. In doing so, we recognize that such preliminary considerations are rife with divergent viewpoints and heated debates.

Theology and Its Place

Before one can theologize, one has to first be situated in a specific place.

One's understanding of this place will determine how one understands theology and the theological task called for by one's place.

We can first review the different ways of understanding the place of theology and what it means for the theological task.

The place of theology can be understood in a physico-institutional sense—simply the ambient in which the theological endeavor is carried out (a community, seminary, university, and so on). Such places provide the immediate environment for the theological task by their very materiality conditioning and making possible the method and purpose of theology. But such an understanding of place does not take up the question of how theology is supposed to relate to the broader reality in which one finds these and many other "places" and where one is to find the real inspiration for the theological task.

The place of theology can also be considered the geographical-social situation, with its homogeneous cultural characteristics, which is to be served by theology. Here we have the pastoral dimension of theology, which gives special consideration to the addressees of theology. With such an understanding of place, there is the danger of thinking that theology bears a given, substantial self-constitution which simply needs to be applied in concrete ways.

Theology's place can also be understood by contrasting the historical and cultural differences between its present situation and that in which it originated and in which its faith was first formulated. This calls for hermeneutics as a means of bridging the historical and cultural distance between past and present. This view of place runs the danger of thinking that, whereas in the past there were the dual realities of revelation-faith and of place, today we have to deal mainly with place and not so much with the present-day reality of revelation-faith.

Certainly, theology must inquire about its place in all these senses. What type of institution is most conducive to the theological endeavor? How do we relate and apply the reality of faith to the present situation? How to understand what, in its origins, was experienced in a quite different world than ours today? I would argue, however, that with such considerations, we have not yet come to the fundamental place of theology.

The theology of liberation insists that its fundamental place must be that historical reality in which we can find a maximum of Truth and the Absolute and that contains both the greatest demands to act within history and the greatest promise of salvation. In other words, the place of theology is the reality which provides the greatest historical mediation of God—where one can find the "signs of the times," understood in a strictly theological sense.

From this point of view, the title of this essay, "Theology in a Suffering World," means that the preliminary task of theology is to find its place in the reality of this suffering world. This does not mean primarily finding a concrete *ubi* within a world that happens to be suffering, but rather, finding a place within the very suffering of this world. Stated graphically, the place of theology is the suffering of the world, and to stand in its place means to stand within the actual suffering that racks this world. The place of theology, then, is much more a *quid* than an *ubi*. An important problem, which we cannot take up presently, is how a concrete place (an *ubi*) can make it easy or difficult to locate oneself within the reality of suffering as it really is (the *quid*).[2] Insofar as theology is not done amid the world of suffering, as it factually exists, it has not yet found its proper place.

For the theology of liberation, theology has to be done within a suffering world because such a world is the most real world. In Latin America the hardest "fact" of reality is described as the "irruption of the poor" (G. Gutiérrez), with its capacity to reveal (*irruption* as a mediation of God's revelation) and with its historical mediation (*of the poor* signifying revelation through the reality of suffering).

The reason the theology of liberation takes the irruption of the poor as the primary reality is, in the final analysis, an option, as we shall see. But in our contemporary world, it is an option that is eminently reasonable and comprehensible. In the first place, poverty is a massive reality for most people today—to the extent that it is practically a tautology to speak about a world of suffering and a world of poverty. As Hugo Assmann said many years ago, "If the yearly deaths of thirty million poor people do not keep theology busy, nothing will." Purely from a quantitative view, to do theology in the world is to do it in a de facto suffering world.

Second, the irruption of the poor can be considered our world's primary reality because of what this irruption contains. On the human-natural level, the greatest cause of massive, cruel, and intolerable suffering in today's world is the poverty found in the Third (and the Fourth) World. In these worlds, poverty is the instrument of death—either slowly through unjust structures that make it extremely difficult to meet the most basic needs of life, or rapidly and violently through the repression that brings forth and maintains these unjust structures.

At the human-social level, death-dealing poverty is what divides the world between poor and creators of poverty, between violated and violators, between victims and tyrants. Seen as a worldwide phenomenon, poverty is the nullification of the human and of human solidarity, and by keeping the peoples of the Third World poor, oppressed, marginalized, and crucified, poverty is the generator of conflict and war.

On the ethical level, death-dealing poverty, insofar as it is rooted in injustice, stands forth as the greatest of moral evils and expresses the fundamental sin of this world: the destruction of life.

On the level of praxis, death-dealing poverty cries out for its own eradication, for as long as it endures, so will a long train of other evils—physical, moral, spiritual.

On the level of meaning, death-dealing poverty, together with its causes and consequences, poses the radical question of the meaning or the absurdity of history—the question of whether life is to be lived with hope, resignation, or cynicism.

On the theological level (and analogously on the religious or ideological levels), death-dealing poverty triggers the question of God or of the Ultimate, of whether there is any truth to God or the Gods. Any theological answer must show how God or the Ultimate is opposed to human-made idols.

Two further considerations are of extreme contemporary importance for this analysis of poverty. First, death-dealing poverty is on the increase throughout the world. The Latin American Bishops Conference at Puebla in 1979 stated that the reality of poverty was even more widespread than at the time of the previous meeting in Medellín in 1968. In his latest encyclical of 1988 (*Solicitudo Rei Socialis*), John Paul II announced that the development of peoples throughout the world not only had not improved but had worsened since Paul VI's encyclical *Populorum Progressio* of 1967. Statistics for the year 2000 indicate that poverty in Latin America is on a galloping increase. Second, there is a growing awareness of many other causes of massive poverty in our world: race, sex, caste . . . [3] But to a great extent, those who suffer the indignity and pain of racial, sexual, or caste discrimination also belong to the world of the poor, which sharpens their suffering and makes it all the more difficult for them to liberate themselves from such indignity.

Determining the Place of Theology Is an Option

To look upon death-dealing poverty as the *analogatum princeps* of suffering and the most drastic expression of the pain of the world is, in the final analysis, a pre-theological—even a pre-religious—option. Theologians must ask themselves with utter seriousness—without in any way preempting the answer—whether such poverty is not the greatest challenge confronting them as theologians, whether their most urgent theological task is to grapple with this reality, try to understand it, and save people from it. Such an option is logically prior to the so-called fundamental option for the poor in all its ethical and pastoral dimensions. It is an option whether to look at the truth of things or not.

The option is, above all, a creaturely option that puts theology squarely in contact with the created order. It is an option that every human being must make, whether Christian or religious or nonreligious. It is an option that cuts across and divides humanity into two groups: those whose feelings are lacerated by the sufferings we have described and those whose feelings are untouched.

It is an option that sees all reality from a preferential perspective—that sees suffering from the partiality of those who suffer and not from the (apparently) universal perspective of the metaphysical suffering characterizing all finite being.

Though this option is pre-religious, it is related to revelation within the hermeneutical circle. On the one hand, Christian revelation in itself does not seem sufficient to bring persons to view the world of suffering as we have described it, for there are in fact many readings of revelation that do not see such suffering or that interpret it differently. Many of the postwar theologies have viewed the world existentially or personalistically and so ignored, or not made central, basic biblical passages in which the reality of suffering is recognized and presented as a mediation of God's self-revelation. (Consider, for instance, how the Exodus or the prophets or the kingdom of God or the beatitudes have been understood.) On the other hand, the option to view the world from the perspective of the suffering has been the occasion of a revision of revelation that has done greater justice simultaneously both to the actual world of today and to biblical revelation itself. This has occurred at two fundamental levels.

On the level of content, persons have rediscovered that God has revealed God's self not only *for* but *through* the sufferings of oppressed peoples. They have discovered the transcendental correlation between God and the oppressed of this world—which means they have realized the partiality of divine revelation. Through this partiality for the oppressed, God reveals God's self as universal—but not the other way around! Theologians have rediscovered the God of justice, the God of liberation, the God of life, and through these qualities the plenitude of God as a God of love is manifest— but again, not the other way around. (Similar discoveries have been made in other fundamental areas of theology: Christology, pneumatology, ecclesiology, and so on.)

On the anthropological-formal level, theologians have rediscovered that revelation is indeed salvific—that it becomes "eu-aggelion" when (methodologically) the I and We are decentralized and forgotten and the focus is shifted to the salvation of others. From a Christian perspective, it is evident that all theology must make manifest the salvific dimension of revelation. God is *pro hominibus*. But when this salvific pro is understood mainly as "pro me" or "pro nobis"—no matter how real, necessary, or convincing this understanding may be—it is utterly different from an understanding that sees the salvific "pro" as primarily "pro aliis," "pro pauperibus." Stated more simply, to find the most pressing aspect of reality not in what happens to me but in what is happening to the suffering people of this world is a way for theology to decentralize itself and so render itself more Christian, according to the biblical admonition, "Those who find their lives will lose them and those who lose their lives for the sake of the gospel will gain them" (Mark 8:35).

The vision we have described is, therefore, an option that cannot be justified by anything outside the option itself. It is Bultmann's *Vorverstandnis*—but with a distinct content. We have already pointed out that such an option is historically reasonable or plausible. That it is also a valid Christian option is clear from what happens when it is made. It sheds more light on revelation; it reveals God as Mystery and as Parent; more simply, it produces a way of life that bears greater resemblance to the life of Jesus in his actions, his words, his attitude, and his destiny.

The Option Overcomes the "Subjection of Truth by Injustice"

The option described above may be necessary, but it is not easy. Its difficulty is evident in the simple fact that many theologians do not make it, not even in Third World countries, much less in the First World. There are weighty reasons for this, the analysis of which can lead to overcoming them.

There is, first, the difficulty of simply not being able to see the world of suffering, for in the First World, images or concepts of this kind of poverty are not available. Furthermore—and this occurs also in the Third World—one can ignore such poverty by diverting one's attention from the facticity of suffering to the problematic of the ideological or political levels, claiming that here is where worse evils are to be found. We are dealing with two very different approaches, for instance, when we view the situation of El Salvador or Nicaragua, on the one hand, as a "Marxist problem" or, on the other, as a problem of human suffering. Both approaches have their validity, but the first locates the "greater evil" (the evil that touches the greater number of people) on the level of ideology, whereas the second finds it on the level of real experience.

There is also the difficulty of *not wanting* to see the world as it is, for to look honestly at the sufferings of the world is at the same time to have to ask about their causes. Once we begin to grasp this world as the product of our own hands, we are overwhelmed with questions, uncertainties, self-incriminations. The sin of the world is unmasked, together with the lies and false values by which we seek to veil this sin.

There is also, finally, *human hubris*—the tendency to manipulate the truth and suppress it for our own advantage. According to Paul's dialectic in Romans 1:18ff., the original act of oppressing the truth results in the darkening of the heart. Then the original lie leads to the institutionalized lie.

While all of this applies to every human being and believer, it especially touches the theologian. Theology is, after all, the product of an activity—an activity that is intellectual and therefore subject to the laws of intelligence, but also a human Christian activity subject to the laws of the human. As both human and intellectual activity, theology is exposed to both noble possibility and sinful corruption. Given the nature of things, theology's basic sinfulness is rooted in our primary tendency to subjugate truth—in our case, in the tendency not to see reality as it is: a world of suffering.

Therefore, the option to view the world of suffering honestly has to be made in opposition to other options and powerful forces seeking to show there are other more "reasonable" (really more "interested") ways of looking at reality or other more important forms of suffering. More positively, the option to view the primary reality of the world as a world of suffering expresses a fundamental honesty—the kind of honesty that is necessary, though perhaps not sufficient, to find the truth of God in the truth of the world; to find the divine Ultimate in the ultimacy contained in human suffering; to find the scandalous Mystery of God in the *mysterium iniquitatis* of the world; and also, as we shall see below, to find whatever there is of promise and salvation in God within the hope and the praxis alive among the suffering people of this world.

At the end of this first part of our considerations, I would like to stress what is really at stake for theology. The problem of determining where theologians stand—that is, the reality in and from which they will develop and expand and interpret their data (revelation, Scripture, tradition, the magisterium, other theologies)—is a fundamental problem whose solution will determine all the subsequent concrete reflections that the theologians will be making. We are talking about the most fundamental truth of theology, for inasmuch as this truth is not accepted, all subsequent theological discourse will be vitiated.

From Latin America one hears the insistence that the fundamental truth of theology is the suffering of this world. As Ignacio Ellacuría states, "the primary sign of our times is our crucified people," for it is by honestly recognizing this sign or truth that the eyes of theologians can really be opened to the fullness of their task. In light of what we have been talking about, we can paraphrase Kant's questions and say, What can I know? We can know the enormous suffering of crucified peoples, and here, more than elsewhere, we can begin to grasp the fullness of truth. What am I permitted to hope for? The liberation of these people, which will lead us to the fullness of hope. What must I do? Liberate these people from their crosses, which will introduce us, more effectively than anything else can, to the kind of praxis required of all human beings: active mercy. In short, the preliminary step of all theology is—as it is for Christology—an adequate incarnation into reality as it is. And as we know from the original option of God expressed in Christology, "reality as it is" is the reality of suffering and poverty.

Theology as *Intellectus Amoris (Intellectus Justitiae)*

Thesis 2: In the presence of a suffering world, one's primary reaction is that of a compassion intent on eliminating such suffering. Like any other human and Christian activity, theology participates in this primary reaction, though in its own specific way. Thus theology will become an *intellectus amoris,* which will include the historical specifications that love assumes when confronted with a suffering people (love as justice).

Confronted with suffering, one reacts first of all with compassion (or with a lack of compassion). Confronted with the sufferings of today's world, as described above, one will react with a compassion that seeks to eliminate such suffering. In contemporary terminology, compassion becomes liberation. I am thus affirming that there is something ultimate, pre-theological, and even pre-religious in such compassion, just as there is in the suffering of today's world.

Again, this is an option. To respond to suffering with the desire to eliminate it for no other reason than that someone else is suffering is an option. *Liberation theology* participates in this option. Insofar as this option is ultimate, pre-theological, and pre-religious, we can speak about it in terms of Bonhoeffer's "etsi Deus non daretur," an expression that in its time was extolled as a graphic and rhetorical recognition of humanity's autonomy and coming of age. I make reference to this expression in order to stress graphically and rhetorically the primacy and the ultimacy of compassion as a response to the suffering of this world. Even more, when this option for compassion is carried out and experienced as an entirely correct option, it is rediscovered as a revelation of something truly ultimate that can have no other explanation than being from God.

God in God's very self is moved to compassion (parable of the prodigal son); Jesus is the one who performs miracles out of compassion; the good Samaritan, as an example of true humanity, is someone who acts out of compassion. The demand and guidance for such compassion are found in the very exercise of compassion, not in anything outside of it. It is true that in the Exodus, God wanted to make a covenant with a people. But the liberation from Egypt did not take place for the sake of a future covenant but as a primary response to oppression. It is true that Jesus was saddened when the lepers did not give thanks to God, but the healing as such was solely the result of an act of compassion. It is true that the Samaritan fulfills the great commandment—indeed, he is presented as an example of this commandment—but he acts not to fulfill a commandment but out of compassion.

Theology and Praxis

The purpose of the preceding reflections was to situate the theological task, together with all other human and Christian tasks, within the global response of compassion to suffering. More specifically, our intent was to clarify the fundamental meaning of the so-called theologies of praxis and, concretely, of the theology of liberation, and to grasp why every theology must be a theology of praxis. In other words, we now have to take up the question of what theology is really all about and how theology is affected by the fact that compassion is the primary response to suffering.

Liberation theology affirms that praxis is related to theology in two different but dialectically united ways. In the first place, the praxis (of liberation) in its historical reality is necessary in order to provide a liberative way of knowing—or more concretely, to make known the content of theology. Leonardo Boff puts it concisely: "A true theology of liberation can be developed only on the condition that the theologian make an unequivocal option for the poor and for their liberation." He explains this option explicitly in terms of "seeing" and "doing" (analysis of the causes of poverty and defense of the poor). In this, the theology of liberation is in agreement with current epistemological theory that stresses the necessary and constitutive role of praxis in bringing about knowledge. More simply, one knows reality better when one is acting within it. Or, in more technical terms, one knows reality when one not only understands reality (*hacerse cargo de la realidad*, the noetic moment) and takes responsibility for it (*cargar con la realidad*, the ethical moment) but when one takes charge of reality (*se hace cargo de la realidad*, the praxic moment) (I. Ellacuría). In biblical terms, one knows God when one does justice (Jeremias, Osea); one knows by loving (1 John); one realizes what it means to be human when one serves those in need (although such knowledge may not be explicit) (Matt. 25).

Praxis—understood as love, service, or justice—is a necessary element in the constitution of all knowledge, including theological knowledge. But the theology of liberation also stresses that theology, insofar as it is already constituted—or more precisely, in process of constituting itself—is the noetic element in all praxis. Here we have an important difference between liberation theology and other theologies that understand themselves solely as carrying out a noetic, explanatory, interpretative, or significative role. L. Boff asserts:

All praxis contains within itself its corresponding theory. This is what we see in liberation theology, which claims to be an adequate theory for the praxis of oppressed and believing peoples; it hopes to be the ingredient of clarification and animation for the road of popular liberation, under the inspiration of the Gospel.

And with even sharper precision, I. Ellacuría states: " . . . theology is the ideological moment of ecclesial and historical praxis . . . the conscious and reflective element in this praxis."

The reasons why liberation theology understands theology as the theoretico-ideological moment of praxis are varied, though convergent:

Liberation theology understands theology as a specific and autonomous undertaking insofar as it is an exercise of logos, but not as completely autonomous with regard to the fundamental human-Christian task. Within and alongside other historical activities (social, cultural, political, economic) and ecclesial tasks (pastoral, liturgical, prophetic, catechetical), the theology of liberation understands its purpose as the authentic liberation of crucified peoples. Liberation theology makes use of logos primarily in order to bring about the liberation of reality and not simply to further the clarity of theological or magisterial teaching (although such results are obtained).

Thus the end purpose of liberation theology is the liberation of reality, and this is a constant in all existing theologies of liberation. From its beginnings, liberation theologians have stressed the necessity of a *liberation of theology* (J. L. Segundo)—that is, that theology (and religion in general) must free itself from its contribution to oppression. They have insisted on a *theology of liberation* (G. Gutiérrez, L. Boff, I. Ellacuría)—that is, the need to use the social force of the religious and of faith and the churches to further historical liberation. What remains fundamentally clear is that the end purpose of liberation theology is the liberation of the suffering world. Or, in the language we were using earlier, its end purpose is to bring to fulfillment, urgently and effectively, the compassion that is called forth by the crucified peoples of our world.

In view of such an end purpose, liberation theology makes the theological determination of its fundamental object as the Reign of God; and it understands this object as something to be realized now (even though God's Reign also remains an object of hope and, eschatologically, a gift of God). The purpose of liberation theology, therefore, is that the Reign of God be realized in this world, and the specific role of the theological logos is to illuminate, promote, and direct the formation of this Reign.

In understanding God as the primary object of theology, liberation theologians always view God within the totality of the Reign, and therefore they insist that God "is to be contemplated and practiced" (G. Gutiérrez). Again, the end purpose of theology is to clarify and promote this proper relationship between God and humanity, in order to permit God to make known and make clear divine truth and (this is something new!) in order to realize within history the very reality of God (God's will, love for humanity, God's taking sides with the poor). In terms that I have developed elsewhere, the end purpose of theology is to clarify and facilitate how humanity is to *respond* and *correspond* to God within history.

The insistence of liberation theology on praxis and its self-understanding as a moment of praxis are rooted ultimately not in a theoretical discussion about the perennial question, What is theology? (although liberation theologians raise and try to answer that question) but, in the two primary options analyzed above: Before a world of suffering, the primary response must be a compassion that seeks to eliminate such suffering; and this response must be present in every human, religious, and Christian activity. Every activity will be carried out according to its specific nature, but what is specific in every activity, including theology, must be subordinated to, and directed toward (and later illuminated by), the elimination of the world's suffering. What always holds priority, therefore, is the elimination of suffering from this world, which is a praxis to which every other activity will make its specific contribution.

Theology as Intellectus Amoris

Once it is asserted that liberation theology understands itself as the ideological moment of a praxis, it becomes necessary to clarify other matters. We are talking about a praxis of liberation from massive suffering that has deep structural and unjust roots. For this reason, our praxis must take the form of justice, and our theology must find forms of historical mediation that will make it effective. We are talking about a dialectical praxis that can confront the injustice that sustains so much unjust suffering. But because the roots of this praxis are grounded in an originating compassion, this praxis must be, before all else, love—a praxis that acts both in favor of and, derivatively but necessarily, in opposition to. We are talking, also, about an ecumenical praxis that in principle is in communion with all persons who respond with compassion to human suffering, although within such ecumenism, theology, as Christian theology, will have to make its specific contributions. We are talking about a praxis that, to a great extent, originated in historical or church movements that preceded theology; but now theology must seek to clarify, enhance, purify, and energize these movements.

These and other problems need to be analyzed in detail, but for the moment I want to focus on the new theoretical insights contained in the way the theology of liberation understands itself as the ideological moment of praxis. We are dealing with a new insight—I would say the most radically new insight that liberation theology implants in the history of theology. It is an insight that touches not only the content of theology (insofar as liberation theology holds up the Reign of God as its fundamental object), but also the very notion of what theology is and what makes up the theological task. It has rightly been said that "the definition of theology is in itself a theological task; one cannot say what theology is except by doing theology" (J. Alfaro). Which is to say that the concrete way of doing theology already expresses *in actu* how the *theos* of theology is understood and how one responds and corresponds to this *theos*. I would say that the stated self-understanding of liberation theology breaks with a centuries-old way of thinking and reflects, better than other theological self-understandings, the content of revelation and faith. Let me explain.

There is a long tradition of understanding theology as *intellectus fidei*. Inversely, faith is understood as *fides quaerens intellectum*. This is not only entirely legitimate, for the inclination to know the mystery of God is innate in the human being; it is also necessary, since from the beginnings of Christianity, the divine mystery has been viewed as rational and reasonable, insofar as it is real and actual, not mythical. Therefore we must be ready to give reasons for God—"to give account of your hope" (1 Pet. 3:15). Even more, the concrete God who gives God's self to be known does so in self-revelation by grace, not solely by way of discovery by reason. Thus, as Henri de Lubac states, all theology can be, and must be, in the final analysis "apologetic"—a rational defense of something that has been given, not discovered as a human achievement. All this is clear. It means that revelation and faith are comprehensible and conceptualizable realities that can and must be shown to be true, and the responsibility for such an important task falls to theology. Theology becomes an *intellectus*—a knowing of the mystery of God and of the mystery of humanity and history before God.

But even though such an understanding of theology is clear and has been present throughout the history of theological reflection, what it really implies has not been entirely evident. What revelation seems to tell us and what theologians have recognized is that the end of God's revelation is the *real* fact of God's self-communication in history and the *real* fact that history can and must correspond to God. This real fact—naturally from the perspective of faith—is something true and therefore something able to be known and analyzed. But the fundamental announcement of revelation is that God wants this real fact to take place. Insofar as it does not *take place*, all attempts to conceptualize or comprehend God's truth will be in vain. Stated more simply, one cannot but be impressed at the way Scripture gives an absolute priority to the need for this real revelation of God to actually take place and for human beings to actually respond and correspond to God. Jesus asserts that what is ultimate and absolutely necessary is that persons follow him. Historically, he makes clear that what is most important is not to say "Lord, Lord," but to do the will of the Father. Eschatologically, he makes clear that salvation—the final realization of God's designs and the purpose of revelation—is realized when love of those in need actually takes place, no matter the explicit awareness that accompanies such love. Paul unambiguously affirms the superiority of charity over faith and hope, as does John, who adds that without love there can be no knowledge of God's truth (1 John). It is clear that it is more important for Christianity that the Christian reality take place than that it be correctly understood, and that what is most fundamental for Christians is that love happen in this world.

All this is well known, and we hear much about it from dogmatic, moral, and spiritual theologians; yet few draw any consequences for the self-understanding of the theological task. What I would like to propose here is the theoretical possibility of understanding theology according to the systematic triad of Paul. Theology can be understood as *intellectus fidei* in order to stress what in the mystery of God is the truth to be known and what in human nature is the means to know it. But theology can also be grasped as *intellectus spei* in order to stress what in the mystery of God there is of promise and of gifted love, salvation, and gospel, and what in human nature enables persons to correspond to this gift through the practice of love. In principle, we cannot say that only God as mystery and only faith as acceptance of the mystery give rise to further thought, for also the realization of hope and love can and do give rise to thought and so possess their own *intellectus* or understanding, which then serves to clarify, foster, and energize hope and love.

If we can talk about a *fides quaerens intellectum*, we can also speak of a *spes* and a *caritas quaerens intellectum*. In his theology of hope, Moltmann asserts that hope is something that seeks understanding and that the logos of eschatology functions as an *intellectus spei*. Within his theological analysis of the future as ultimate and radically new, this is entirely reasonable. But the theology of liberation affirms that it is love—the concrete liberation from suffering in the Third World and the transformation of this world into the Reign of God—that seeks understanding. Within the practice of liberating love, theology becomes an *intellectus amoris*. This, too, is entirely reasonable in view of the horrible suffering of the Third World and the essence of Christianity as consisting ultimately in the realization of love. I would say that it is the very essence of Christianity that requires theology to be, before all else, an *intellectus amoris* (scholars of comparative religion seem to agree with this when they note that Christianity is fundamentally a religion of love, though it does not ignore gnosis). But it is also the historical reality in which we are living that makes the same demand. So we must also speak of an *amor, justitia, liberatio quaerens intellectum*.

One can ask what is it, in the final analysis, that gives rise to thought and calls for reflection. Answers vary. Reality gives rise to thought insofar as it stirs admiration, promises something radically new, or displays massive suffering that cries for liberation. Each of these stimuli for thought has its distinctive perspective on how and why we are to reflect. Confronted by a world of suffering, one's thinking is affected by this suffering and responds with compassion. One's thinking is directed toward eliminating suffering and transforming it into the Reign of God.

Liberation theology, therefore, insofar as it is theology, is an *intellectus amoris*, which in our actual world is concretized as an *intellectus justitiae*. Or, in the language that we used earlier, it can also be called an *intellectus misericordiae*. But here, love, justice, and mercy are not genetives that provide a content from which we develop doctrines. Rather, they are the reality that engages the intellect and enables it to realize its own nature.

As a practical conclusion to these considerations, I would add the following. When theology understands itself as *intellectus fidei*, it tends to lay out the truth, explain it, communicate its meaning in different theological perspectives. This is surely a positive and necessary task; but, as history attests, it is also exposed to the danger of refraining from changing reality and of abandoning reality to itself. When reality is that of a suffering world, abandoning it in the name of theology's self-understanding is catastrophic for the suffering world and theology. When theology understands itself as *intellectus amoris*, it seeks to operate within reality in order to save it, incarnating itself within humanity as it is, responding from an original compassion. In this way theology realizes, in its very theological activity, the fundamental demand of God to love and save this world.

The Intellectus Amoris *as Mystagogy for the* Intellectus Fidei

Thesis 3: The practice of love and justice is not only something that theology must foster; it is also that which can become a mystagogical reality that gives access to the mystery of God. The *intellectus amoris (justitiae)* can function as a mystagogy for the *intellectus fidei.*

The fact that liberation theology understands itself as *intellectus amoris (justitiae)* does not mean that its contents are reduced to love, compassion, justice, liberation. Rather, the theology of liberation considers itself to be a holistic theology which, from its particular locus and specific self-understanding, embraces the whole of revelation. Elsewhere I have tried to show that by making the Reign of God its central object, liberation theology naturally deals with the totality of theological concerns. Here I would like only to point out, very schematically, how faith, hope, and charity are interrelated as a response to the mystery of God and what difference it makes in our approach to God when we start with a theology that understands itself as *intellectus amoris.*

In my opinion, never in the past, and certainly not today, has the theological response to faith in God been a purely doctrinal matter—that is, purely an assent to God's truth. By this I certainly do not want to deny that we need doctrines about God to make clear just what God we believe in; but on a deeper level, doctrine is preceded by a mystagogical grasp of the divine Mystery. In systematic terms, we can say that mystagogy has the role of leading the human being into the reality of radical *otherness* that is found in God, whether it is called Absolute Mystery, Origin of Origins, or Absolute Future. One effective way of maintaining what in God is mystery and the mystery of salvation is the realized *hope* or the unconditional, trusting openness to what is new, unexpected, unable to be manipulated, and salvific. But mystagogy also has the role of leading us into the reality of *affinity* with God. That is, humanity's "divinization," which consists in corresponding to the reality of God within history. This affinity becomes real through love realized within history, through making present within the world God's love and justice and compassion.

Therefore, besides being part of theology's concrete and necessary content, hope and love are also the means of being introduced into the reality of God. From this perspective, the *intellectus fidei,* in order to be true intellectus or understanding and not just doctrine, needs help from the *intellectus spei* and the *intellectus amoris.*

Furthermore, I believe that realized love is what best introduces us to the total reality of faith, hope, and charity. There is an a priori, fundamental reason for this: Love is what brings human beings close to the reality of God. Also, the practice of love is what makes faith and hope concretely Christian. What this means can be better grasped by considering the practice of love in a suffering world.

The practice of love—which, in a suffering world, is the practice of justice—enables us to "see" history's most pressing realities and questions: that sin in history is powerful and works against justice; that all too often, justice is impotent; that those who devote themselves to promoting life often are exposed to losing their own.

The practice of justice leads to many questions, and they are profound. Is hope meaningful? Or is it wiser to choose resignation, epicureanism, or cynicism? Rather than hope, are we better off embracing agnosticism or a protesting atheism? By stirring up such questions, the actual practice of justice demands that if hope and faith are to be real, they have to take concrete shape. They have to be fashioned into Christian hope and faith. On the other hand, the practice of love maintains believers in a fundamental honesty and thus in a fundamental truth. It allows them to experience personally that it is in giving that one receives, and it enables them to realize—at least in the case of doing justice to the poor of Latin America— what it means to be evangelized: to know more clearly the truth of this world, to experience conversion as necessary and possible, to be pardoned, to be inspired to carry on the pursuit of justice, to be borne forward by others.

The struggle to bring about justice confronts the believer with what is ultimate—either as something to be questioned or something to be accepted in Christian faith. Contrary to popular opinion, it is especially in the Third World that faith and hope are placed in question most radically, for it is here that the world appears to be most starkly opposed to God's will. It is here that the battle of the gods is taking place, and the idols are winning out over the true God!

On the other hand, the struggle for justice is, in fact, carried on, and this enables hope and faith to be made concrete and to take on Christian form. It is always possible to abandon hope and faith, but because this does not happen, hope becomes Christian. It becomes the hope of a people for a new heaven and a new earth (thus overcoming the egocentric individualism of other forms of hope). A people hopes against hope, not simply because of an anthropology that is open to a possible future good, but out of a historical process that continuously calls hope into question. Thus hope becomes the hope of the poor and oppressed.

Faith in the reality of the mystery of God includes all those essential teachings of revelation that are known doctrinally but are so difficult to realize outside the practice of love-justice: that the God who is the highest and most valued good is the God of life; that God is essentially a liberator; that God is partial toward the oppressed; but also that God is impotent and crucified, not only close to but the victim of humanity. More simply, the praxis of love-justice which demands an absolute decentering of self to the point of giving one's life and which at times brings forth life in some only to see it lost in others or in oneself—such praxis can be a profound questioning of faith but can also become (which is frequently the case) a way of concretizing and christianizing faith.

When the prophet Michah, in a solemn moment (6:8), announced what is good for humans and what they should strive to be, he urged two things:

first, to practice justice and second, to walk humbly with God. Taken together, both admonitions summarize what it means to lead a Christian life. But the mystagogical element in the Christian life—what is absolutely necessary to do and maintain—is the practice of justice. In this practice, one moves forward in the process of understanding historical life as a journey with God and toward God. In other words, through such a practice of love-justice, we sustain (or we question) the reality of hope and faith.

In locating love-justice in the systematic center of the triad of faith, hope, and charity, there is one more point to make. Insofar as love-justice is a matter of praxis (though it is a practice that has to be carried out with a definite spirit), it might seem to some that this praxis would not directly express—in fact, it might even obstruct or annul—an element that is essential to revelation: gratitude. Gratitude would be better preserved both by faith, which allows truth to be given, and by hope, which allows the ultimate and blessed end to be provided.

But there is no reason to reduce gratitude to a response to the gift of faith and hope. Gratitude can also imbue the praxis of love-justice. We feel overwhelmed with gratitude not only because of our "new ears" by which to hear or our "new eyes" by which to see, but also because of our "new hands" by which to do. In the spirituality of liberation, much attention is given to the gratitude that pervades the practice of liberation: We have been "freed in order to free," "loved in order to love" (G. Gutiérrez).

Conclusion

I would like to summarize everything I have tried to say in this essay. We live in a suffering world, whose suffering is rooted in a death-dealing poverty that is massive, mountingly unjust, and scandalous. Confronted with such a world of suffering, one's primary and ultimate response is, as it would be before any suffering, that of compassion. This response is an option that precedes the task of theology, as it does any human or Christian task. Given this kind of massive and structural suffering that pervades the Third World, the response of mercy must be a response of justice that will bring about liberation. When Christians reflect on such compassion and such justice, the theology of liberation takes shape.

If suffering constitutes the fundamental reality of our world taken as a whole, then every theology—even though in the First World there are other serious issues that must be confronted—must in some way be a theology of liberation. This certainly does not mean that every theology must replicate the liberation theology of Latin America, but it does mean that every theology must have the same fundamental object as Latin American theology. Yes, there needs to be a variety of theologies since there is variety in our world; but within this variety, the fundamental concern and object must be the reality of suffering that pervades our world. Every theology must seek to provide a response to such suffering.

Liberation theology is one theology; it is the historical form that responsible Christian reflection has taken when confronted by a suffering world. Although this theology may take different shape in the future, its central affirmation remains permanently valid: The most truth-filled place for any Christian theology to carry out its task is always the suffering of our world, and in the crucified people of our world, theology receives a light that it can receive nowhere else. In the crucified peoples of our world, theology finds, as part of the Christian paradox, its own salvation, its proper direction, and the courage to carry out its task. As the Puebla Conference stated, the poor of this world are to evangelize us. This evangelization takes place for theologians insofar as the poor offer them the opportunity to realize (not just conceptualize) the realities fundamental to theology: real faith and hope, real gospel values, and—something that has often required of the poor their very lives—real love. Here we have the ultimate mediation of the truth about God and the truth about humanity.

—*Translated by José Pedrozo and Paul F. Knitter*

PART TWO

3

The Crucified Peoples

Yahweh's Suffering Servant Today

In Memory of Ignacio Ellacuría[1]

Ignacio Ellacuría admired Jürgen Moltmann's well-known book *The Crucified God,* but he made a point of stressing another much more urgent theological idea: the crucified people. This was not just for historical reasons (our reality is like this), but also for theological ones (God's creation is like this). It is necessary for us to speak of these crucified peoples in relation to 1992, as well, in order to recall their historical causes. The sole object of all this talk must be to bring them down from the cross.

The Crucified Peoples: A Horrifying Fact

The obvious is the least obvious, Ellacuría used to say. And this is our starting point for talking about the crucified peoples. When what is obvious in others—the crucified peoples—shows us what we are, we tend to ignore it, cover it up, or distort it, because it simply terrifies us. So it is understandable that we should ignore the evidence of the crucified peoples, but we must at least suspect—especially in the Western world, which boasts it has been schooled by the great masters of suspicion—that this ignorance is not mere ignorance, but a will to ignore and cover up. So let us start by dis-covering the covered-up reality of our world.

That creation has turned out badly for God—another provocative phrase of Ignacio Ellacuría's—is confirmed by economists. Terrible poverty is increasing in Latin America. It is estimated that by the end of the century, some 170 million Latin Americans will be living in dire poverty and another 170 million in poverty critical to life. To this inhuman poverty, we must add the victims of repression and the wars it has caused. In Central America alone, the victims are estimated to be a quarter of a million.

The Latin American bishops have said so. What characterizes Latin America is "the misery that marginalizes large human groups," which "as a collective fact is an injustice crying to heaven," (Medellín, *Justicia*, no. 1, 1968), "the situation of inhuman poverty in which millions of Latin Americans live" (Puebla, no. 29, 1979). And John Paul II repeated it again in *Sollicitudo rei socialis* (1987).

Whether we look at it from the worldly or the Christian point of view, both agree about the tragedy. Looking at the present situation, which we can see and touch in one way or another, helps us to grasp what happened centuries ago. At the origin of what we call Latin America today there lies an original and originating sin. To give one single fact: Some seventy years after 1492, the indigenous population had been reduced to 15 percent; many of their cultures had been destroyed and subjected to anthropological death. This was a colossal disaster, doubtless due to various complex causes, but nevertheless a really colossal disaster. "For some time . . . I have felt the disappearance of whole peoples as an absurd mystery of historical iniquity, which reduces me to the most abject sort of faith," says Casadaliga.[2]

So there was a historical disaster, and we have to give it a name. Our current language calls these peoples "Third World," "the South," "developing countries." These designations are attempting to say that something is wrong, but such language does not communicate how wrong. Therefore we need to speak of crucified peoples: metaphorical language, of course, but language which conveys much better than others the historical enormity of the disaster and its meaning for faith. At any rate, it is much better at avoiding the cover-up operated by other languages.

Crucified peoples is useful and necessary language at the real level of fact, because *cross* means death, and death is what the Latin American peoples are subjected to in thousands of ways. It is slow but real death caused by the poverty generated by unjust structures—"institutionalized violence": "the poor are those who die before their time." It is swift, violent death, caused by repression and wars, when the poor threaten these unjust structures. And it is indirect but effective death when peoples are deprived even of their cultures in order to weaken their identities and make them more defenseless.

It is useful and necessary language at the historical-ethical level because *cross* expresses a type of death actively inflicted. To die crucified does not mean simply to die, but to be put to death; it means that there are victims and there are executioners. It means that there is a very grave sin. The crucified peoples do not fall from heaven. If we followed the metaphor through, we should have to say that they rise from hell. However much people try to soften the fact, the truth is that the Latin American peoples' cross has been inflicted on them by the various empires that have taken power over the continent: the Spanish and Portuguese yesterday, the U. S. and its allies today; whether by armies or economic systems, or the imposition of cultures and religious views, in connivance with the local powers.

It is useful and necessary language at the religious level because cross—

Jesus suffered death on the cross and not any other death—evokes sin and grace, condemnation and salvation, human action and God's action. From a Christian point of view, God himself makes himself present in these crosses, and the crucified peoples become the principal sign of the times. "This sign [of God's presence in our world] is always the historically crucified people."[3]

Crucified peoples exist. It is necessary and urgent to see our world this way. And it is right to call them this, because this language stresses their historical tragedy and their meaning for faith.

The Crucified People as Yahweh's Suffering Servant

In Latin America, the fundamental theological statement affirms that the crucified people are the actualization of Christ crucified, the true servant of Yahweh. The crucified people and Christ, Yahweh's servant, refer to and explain each other. This is what two Salvadoran martyrs did, who knew very well what they were talking about. Monseñor Romero told some terrorized peasants who had survived a massacre, "You are the image of the divine victim,"[4] and in another sermon he said that Jesus Christ, the liberator, is so closely identified with the people that interpreters of Scripture cannot tell whether Yahweh's servant proclaimed by Isaiah is the suffering people or Christ, who comes to redeem *us*.[5] Ellacuría said the same. "This crucified people is the historical continuation of Yahweh's servant, whom the sin of the world continues to deprive of any human decency, and from whom the powerful of this world continue to rob everything, taking everything away, even life, especially life."[6]

This theology of the crucified people has become established in Latin America, whereas in other places it may seem exaggerated, unjustified, or unscientific pious language. This is because hermeneutics seeks not only common horizons of cultural understanding between the present and the past, but above all common horizons of reality. This common reality appears clearly in Latin America. The theology of the crucified people as Yahweh's suffering servant includes not only the servant as victim—which people in other situations can understand—but also the servant's saving role in history: historical soteriology, as Ignacio Ellacuría insisted, which is more alien to the theologies of other latitudes and difficult even to imagine if the reality is not seen.

However, to grasp this theology, we need only read the songs of Yahweh's servant with the text in one hand and our eyes on the crucified peoples. So let us do this in the form of a meditation.[7]

What do the songs say about the servant? Above all, he is a "man of sorrows acquainted with grief," and this is the normal condition of the crucified people: hunger, sickness, slums, frustration through lack of education, health, employment . . . And if their penalties are innumerable in normal times, "peace time," as it is called, they increase even more when, like the servant, they decide to "establish justice and right." Then repression falls on them and the verdict, "guilty of death." Massacres occur, as at Sumpul and El Mozote in El Salvador or Huehuetenango in Guatemala and so many other places. The people become even more like the servant with "no form or comeliness . . . no beauty." And to the ugliness of daily poverty is added that of disfiguring bloodshed, the terror of tortures and mutilations. Then, like the servant, they arouse revulsion: "Many were frightened by him because he was disfigured and did not seem to be a man or look like a human being." And people "hide their faces from him," because they are disgusted, and also so as not to disturb the false happiness of those responsible for the servant, or unmask the truth hidden behind the euphemisms we invent daily to describe him.

Like the servant, the crucified people are "despised and rejected"; everything has been taken from them, even human dignity. And really, what can the world learn and receive from them? What do they offer the world for its progress, apart from their primary materials, their beaches and volcanoes, their folklore for tourists? They are not respected, but despised. And this contempt reaches its height when ideology takes on a religious tinge to condemn them in God's name. It is said of the servant: "We esteemed him stricken, smitten by God, counted among the sinners." And what is said about the crucified peoples? As long as they suffer patiently, they are regarded as having a certain goodness, simplicity, piety especially, which is unenlightened and superstitious, but none-the-less surprises the educated and secularized people from other worlds. Yet when they decide to live and call on God to defend them and set them free, then they are not even recognized as God's people, and the well-known litany is intoned. They are subversives, terrorists, criminals, atheists, Marxists, and communists. Despised and murdered in life, they are also despised in death. It is said of the servant: "They made his grave with the wicked and his tomb with evildoers." This is also the crucified people's epitaph. And sometimes they do not even have this, because though ancient piety denied no one a grave, the crucified people sometimes do not even have this. This is what happens to the disappeared: corpses thrown on rubbish heaps, clandestine cemeteries.

It is said of the servant that "he was oppressed and he was afflicted yet he opened not his mouth," that he died in total meekness. Today not all the crucified die like this. Monseñor Romero was able to speak in his lifetime, and his death shook many consciences. So did the deaths of priests and nuns, and recently that of Ignacio Ellacuría and the other five Jesuits in the UCA. But who knows the seventy thousand assassinated in El Salvador and the eighty thousand in Guatemala? What word is uttered by the children of Ethiopia and the three hundred million in India living in dire poverty? There are thousands and millions who do not say a word. It is not known how they live or how they died. Their names are not known—Julia Elba and Celina are known because they were murdered with the Jesuits. Even their number is not known.

Finally it is said of the servant that "he was taken away defenseless and without judgment" in total impotence against arbitrary injustice. Again this does not apply altogether to the crucified people. Many fight for their lives, and there is no lack of prophets to defend them. But the repression against their struggle is brutal. First they try to discredit the prophets and then coopt them for a civil and ecclesiastical society that presents them as tokens of freedom and democracy—with well-calculated risks—until they become really dangerous. Then they kill them too. Is there a real court to defend the cause of the poor, that at least listens to them and does them justice? No serious notice is taken of them during their lives, and when they die, their deaths are not even investigated.

The crucified people are this suffering servant of Yahweh today. This fact is covered up, because like the servant, the people are innocent. "He had done no violence and there was no deceit in his mouth." The servant not only proclaims the truth of the crucified people, but also the truth about their killers. All of us can and must look at ourselves reflected in the crucified people in order to grasp our deepest reality. As in a mirror, we can see what we are by what we produce.

And we have to be very aware of this in 1992. Some will recall the advances in science and democracy that the Western world has brought, and the church will remember the preaching of the gospel. Others will add that things are not as simple as that, that we cannot blame others entirely for the crucifixion. But at the hour of truth, unless we profoundly accept the truth of the crucified peoples and the fundamental responsibility of successive empires for their crucifixion, we will miss the main fact. That is, that in this world there is still enormous sin. Sin is what killed the servant—the Son of God—and sin is what continues to kill God's children. And this sin is inflicted by some upon others. In a typically Spanish turn of phrase, Ellacuría summed up what successive empires have done to the Latin American continent: "they have left it like a Christ"—they have made a Christ of it.[8]

The Salvation the Crucified Peoples Bring

The foregoing theology is fundamental, and to some extent it is usually adopted in other theologies, especially as an expression of the current problem of theodicy, "how to do theology after Auschwitz." However, in Latin America, we add a second perspective belonging more specifically to liberation theology: We must bring the crucified peoples down from the cross. This is the requirement of an anthropodicy by which human beings can be justified. This can only be done by bringing the crucified peoples down from their crosses.

This is the marrow of liberation theology. And what we want to stress now is that the crucified people themselves are bearers of salvation. The one chosen by God to bring salvation is the servant, which increases the scandal. We sincerely believe that theology does not know what to do with this central statement, unless it seeks in the servant's "vicarious expiation" a theoretical model for understanding Christ's redemption on the cross. But this model does not illuminate what salvation the cross brings, far less what historical salvation the cross brings today. Yet if we abandoned the salvation brought by the servant we would be throwing out something central in the faith. Liberation theology has tried to analyze what salvation and what historical salvation is brought by the servant, and Ellacuría did so with great rigor and vigor in his work *The Crucified People*, which he subtitled "an essay in historical soteriology." Understanding what salvation is brought by the crucified people's suffering is not only or principally a matter of speculation and interpretation of texts. It is a matter of grasping the reality.

The Light the Crucified Peoples Bring

God says of the servant that he will set him up as a "light for the nations" (Isa. 42:6; 49:6). Today this light is to show the nations what they really are. Which is no small benefit. Imprisoning the truth by injustice is the fundamental sin of individuals and also of the nations. Many evils derive from it: among others, the darkening of the heart. A light whose power is capable of unmasking lies is very beneficial and very necessary. This is the light offered by the crucified people. If the First World cannot see its own reality in this light, we do not know what can make it do so.

Ellacuría expressed this graphically in various ways. He said bluntly, using a medical metaphor, that in order to test the health of the First World it was necessary to do a "coproanalysis," that is, to examine its feces, because it is the reality of the crucified peoples that appears in that analysis, and their reality reveals that of those who produce them.

He also said that the Third World offers a great advantage over the First World in throwing light on where we ought to be going.

> From my viewpoint—and this can be one that is both prophetic and paradoxical at once—the US is much worse off than Latin America. Because the US has a solution but in my opinion it is a bad solution, both for them and for the world as a whole. On the other hand, in Latin America there are no solutions, there are only problems. But however painful it is, it is better to have problems than to have a wrong solution for the future of history.[9]

The solution offered by the First World today is factually wrong, because it is unreal; it is not universalizable. And it is ethically wrong, because it is dehumanizing for all, for them and for the Third World.

Finally he said that the Third World offered light on what historical utopia must be today. Utopia in the world today can only be a "civilization of poverty,"[10] all sharing austerely in the earth's resources so that they can stretch to everybody. This sharing achieves what the First World does not offer: fellowship and, with it, meaning of life. He proposed as the way to reach this utopia a civilization of labor as against the current civilization of capital, in all its capitalist and socialist forms.

This is the light given by the crucified peoples. If it is allowed to shine, 1992 will be a very beneficial year. Undoubtedly it will produce panic and disruption, but the light will also dispel the darkness and heal. Instead of the "discovery of America" we shall see the cover-up that has been done there and that what 1492 discovered was above all the reality of the Spanish and Portuguese empire at the time and the Catholic church at the time: a tragic but fruitful discovery. It will also produce the light of utopia: that true progress cannot consist in what is offered now, but in bringing the crucified peoples down from the cross and sharing the resources and everybody's goods with all.

The Salvation the Crucified Peoples Bring

The crucified peoples also offer positive salvation. Obviously, this is scandalous, but unless we accept it in principle, it will be pointless to repeat that there is salvation in the servant, that the crucified Christ has taken upon himself and got rid of the sin of the world. What we have to do is verify this salvation historically.

Above all, the crucified peoples offer values that are not offered elsewhere. We may discuss whether they create these values because they have nothing else to hold on to, and whether these values will disappear when their present economic and social circumstances disappear and are devoured by the Western capitalist world and its "civilization." But they are there now and are offered to all (and those who work to bring the people down from the cross also work to prevent these values from disappearing).

Puebla said it with chilling clarity, although Western countries and churches have taken very little notice: The poor have evangelizing potential. This potential is spelled out as "the gospel values of solidarity, service, simplicity and readiness to receive God's gift" (no. 1147). In historical language, the poor have a humanizing potential because they offer community against individualism, co-operation against selfishness, simplicity against opulence, and openness to transcendence against blatant positivism, so prevalent in the civilization of the Western world. It is true, of course, that not all the poor offer this, but it is also true that they do offer it and, structurally speaking, in a form not offered by the First World.

The crucified peoples also offer hope, foolish or absurd, it might be said; because it is the only thing they have left, others argue. But once again, it is there, and it must not be trivialized by other worlds. That it is hope against hope is obvious, but it is also active hope that has shown itself in work and liberation struggles. What success these have is another matter, and the Western world appears to emerge triumphant and suffocate them all. We should not hail this as a triumph but mourn it as a disaster, because it is crushing the hope of the poor and thus depriving itself of their humanizing potential. In any case, the very fact that hope arises and re-arises in history shows that history has a current of hope running through it which is available to all. The bearers of this current of hope are the crucified peoples.

The crucified peoples offer great love. It is not masochism or an invitation to suicide, nor making a virtue of necessity, but it is simply true that Latin America's innumerable martyrs show that love is possible because it is real, and great love is possible because many have shown it. And in a structurally selfish world based on selfishness and making a virtue of it—not in so many words, of course—that love is a great offer of humanization.

The crucified peoples are ready to forgive their oppressors. They do not want to triumph over them but to share with them. To those who come to help them, they open their arms and accept them and thus, even without knowing it themselves, they forgive them. In this way they introduce into the Western world that reality which is so humanizing and so lacking, which is gratuitousness: not only what you get for yourself, but also what you are given unexpectedly, freely, and without having to earn it.

The crucified peoples have generated solidarity—human beings and Christians mutually supporting one another, in this way and that, open to one another, giving and receiving one another's best. This solidarity is small, quantitatively speaking; it is only between church and human groups. But we must stress that now it is real and that it did not exist before. On a small scale, it offers a model of how people and churches can relate to one another in a human and Christian way.

Finally, the crucified peoples offer faith, a way of being the church and a more genuine, Christian, and relevant holiness for the world today, that gives more of Jesus. Again, this is more like a seed than a leafy tree, but it is there. We cannot see any other faith, any other way of being the church, or any other holiness that humanizes any better or is a better way of bringing it to God.

It is paradoxical, but it is true. The crucified peoples offer light and salvation. Both can be had in 1992 by those who declare themselves their discoverers, although they have mostly been their coverers-up. Not to receive them would be ungrateful and idiotic; it would be the most radical way of ruining the 1992 "celebrations." Receiving them and letting this gift become a new impulse to bring the people down from the cross would be the best—and the only—proper celebration. Liberated and given grace by the crucified peoples, the First World could become grace and liberation for them. And then there really will be something to celebrate: solidarity of human beings, mutually supporting one another in universal fellowship.

I wish to end with the words with which Ignacio Ellacuría concluded his reflections in 1992. He was not in the least inclined to ahistorical idealism or purely transcendental statements that could not be located in history.

I wish to state the following. Far from causing discouragement and despair, all this martyr's blood spilt in El Salvador and the whole of

Latin America infuses our people with a new spirit of struggle and new hope. In this sense, if we are not a "new world" or a "new continent," we are clearly and demonstrably a continent of hope, which is a highly interesting symptom of a future new relation to other continents which do not have hope—the only thing they have is fear.[11]

—*Translated by Dinah Livingstone*

4

Latin America

Place of Sin and Place of Forgiveness

Forgiving someone who has hurt us is an act of love for the offender because we want to relieve him of his personal failure and not definitively close off his future. It is a difficult kind of love, because the one who forgives must overcome a natural instinct to seek restitution for the offense. It is a large act of love, a form of love for our enemies. Because of all this, it is an important manifestation of the Christian spirit, a fulfillment of Jesus' simple and sublime commandment: "Be good, as your heavenly father is good" (Matt. 5:48; RSV: "You therefore must be perfect, as your heavenly Father is perfect"). It is a mediation to others of God's kindness and generosity. Accordingly, all Christian spirituality must take seriously personal forgiveness of those who hurt us.

This is well known, but there are important things we must add. We must react in a Christian way toward the *sinner* by forgiving him. But we must also act in a Christian way toward the *sin.* In regard to both, as a whole, we must react in a Christian way to the negative, evil, and wickedness in history. Sin morally destroys the sinner, but it also introduces many evils into reality, in the sinner, the sinned against, and society in general. These evils must also be confronted in accordance with the faith, and so we must talk of healing reality or, in analogical terms, of "forgiving" reality. Thus the Christian must be prepared to forgive the sinner and forgive reality, to free the sinner from sin and heal reality from the misery that sin causes. This second task is also theologal, as theologal as the first, because it is commanded by God, who not only wants sinners to repent and not die, but also the liberation of sin-laden reality. It is the mediation of God's love which hears the cry of the oppressed and decides to set them free (Exod. 3.7f). Accordingly, all Christian spirituality—not just ethics—must take seriously the forgiveness of reality.

These brief introductory reflections are important in order to speak about forgiveness in Latin America, above all because Latin America is a place where there is a great sin. Of course there are also the faults that damage personal, family, and community relations, selfishness and human weakness. There are everyday sins and sinners for whom we must go on praying, "Forgive us our trespasses as we forgive them who trespass against us" (Matt. 6:12). But in this article we shall concentrate on the great sin of the continent, which shapes its whole social and historical reality, which crucifies and kills majorities and whole peoples. In this context, we have to ask what it means to forgive the sin and forgive the sinner. Therefore we have to see, as the *analogatum princeps* of the sin, unjustly inflicted poverty which produces both slow and violent death, and as the *analogatum princeps* of the sinner, the idols which cause death and require victims in order to subsist. In this real situation we begin with the analysis of the forgiveness of sin as forgiveness of an objective sinful reality, and then go on to analyze personal forgiveness of the sinner who commits the sin. This way of proceeding is justified because the objective sin is most evident and cries out for an urgent response, as Medellín and Puebla saw; the most serious personal crimes— tortures, murders, disappearances—whose perpetrators must be forgiven in accordance with the faith, are an expression of the fundamental objective sin. The spirituality of forgiveness must take into account both dimensions of forgiveness, but ultimately with a view to a reconciliation of the reality itself, in order to make possible relationships of fellow-feeling.

This approach does not derive from a universal logic. But in the reality of Latin America, it is necessary or at least more convenient than the opposite one.

Forgiveness of Sinful Reality

Medellín and Puebla know very well that there are sinners and sins; that all sin is ultimately rooted in the human heart, which produces bitter fruits: poverty, misery, and frustration (Medellín, *Poverty of The Church* 4; Puebla 73). They add as a new point that sin is frequently transmitted in its most serious and massive form through structures "on which the sin of their makers has placed its destructive mark" (Puebla 281). As pastors, of course, the bishops of Medellín and Puebla are interested in getting rid of the sinners' guilt and procuring their salvation. However, they do not limit themselves to the exposition of a doctrine, even though it is a new one; they also pay attention to this reality. In their concentration on this, they do not begin with its causes but with its effects: the sinful reality. Although they are well known, we must repeat their fundamental statements. The Latin American reality lies in a sinful situation (Medellín, *Peace* 1), it expresses "a situation of social sin" (Puebla 28). These statements are every bit as true now as when they were made. Beginning at this point is not accidental. It does not mean overlooking the moral failure of the sinner or the means of healing him of his fault. It does not mean ignoring everyday offenses. It means beginning with what is in itself most serious and most clamorously demands an urgent solution and what helps in the treatment of the forgiveness of sinners and understanding of everyday sins. The effects of sin enable us to know the sinner's reality better. From the great sin, we can understand what is meant by great forgiveness; and from both we can understand better the little sins and forgivenesses.

This is so because the objective sin of Latin America is not just any sin but the "destitution which marginalizes large human groups . . . an injustice crying to heaven" (Medellín, *Justice* 1). It is the "situation of inhuman poverty in which millions of Latin Americans live" (Puebla 28), which enslaves them (n. 328), deprives them of dignity (n.330). It is the expression of a materialist and dehumanizing society and world order which produces "rich who keep getting richer at the expense of poor who keep getting poorer" (n. 30). This is "the most devastating and humiliating scourge" (n. 28).

The importance of these well-known statements is that Medellín and Puebla make them central because they express the signs of the times. Historically they characterize an epoch, and theologically they show God's presence or absence. All reality must be seen in terms of this reality of unjust poverty, and in this reality we have to see and live our whole Christian life. Thus it is not arbitrary partiality or merely pedagogically convenient to begin with the sinful reality of Latin America. It is necessary.

In these signs, the times are uttering a great heartrending cry of hope. The bishops merely took up this cry. They could do no less; they had to take it up because reality forced them to. "From the continent's different countries a cry is rising to heaven ever louder and more clamorously. It is the cry of a suffering people demanding justice, freedom, respect for the fundamental rights of individuals and peoples" (Puebla 87). But the bishops also take up the cry of hope, "the yearning for total freedom and liberation from all slavery" (Medellín, *Introduction* 4).

What this means for our purposes is that the Latin American reality has appeared as sin and sin is what occurs daily in this continent. This reality is the most vigorous denial of God's will, a terrible offense against God, which "cries to heaven" (Medellín, *Justice* 1). It is "contrary to the creator's plan and the honor this deserves" (Puebla 28). The heinousness of this invisible offense against God can be clearly seen in the visible offenses, the slow and violent death through daily structural oppression and the cruel repression which keeps the poor close to death; in the individual faces of the poor, each one telling its own story; and in whole peoples, crucified, as Monseñor Romero said, annihilated, as Dom Pedro Casaldaliga cried at the disappearance of whole tribes in Brazil. The transcendental relation between sin and death here becomes clearly visible in historical reality. Sin leads to the death of the sinner, but first sin causes the death of others. Sin is what caused the death of God's Son, and sin is what continues causing the death of God's children.

Above all, Christians must take on this sin, this unjust poverty, and this death. If they respond with pity, they must defend the victims. What to do about the personal guilt of the offenders is also important but, at this point, secondary. What faith demands first is liberation from this sinful reality and the humanization of the victims and then, by derivation, the rehabilitation of the sinner and humanization of the offender. This means that first of all we have to "forgive" reality. Forgiveness of reality has its own structure and goal. This is nothing less than the eradication of the sin of reality. And this must be done by fighting against this sin in order to exterminate it by bearing its weight. Fighting against sin means, in the first place, like Jesus and the prophets, denouncing it, giving voice to the victims' cry, because sin tends to hide. We must unmask it because sin tends to justify itself and even to present itself cynically as its opposite. To eradicate sin, we must begin by denouncing the crucifixion and death of whole peoples; this is intolerable and the greatest evil. We must not ideologically relativize it by saying, as frequently happens, that there are worse evils in Latin America, in particular, Marxism. We must unmask this crucifixion and death as the gravest offense against God. It cannot be justified, and even less can it be blessed in God's name, as happens in effect when this crucifixion and death is represented as a defense, willed by God, of Western civilization. We must fight against sin by destroying and building. We must destroy the idols of death, that is, we must destroy the structures of oppression and violence. We must build new structures of justice. We must provide adequate means to do this—political, social, and pastoral education and organization—everything that will help change structures. The *magisterium* of the church, theology, and the practice of Christians have said a great deal about how sin can be eradicated, and this is not the place to repeat it. Here we simply want to go over the formal structure of this eradication. Forgiving the sin of reality means converting it, setting up instead of the anti-kingdom God's kingdom; instead of injustice, justice; instead of oppression, freedom; instead of selfishness, love; instead of death, life.

But the forgiveness of reality is also a matter of spirituality. It is not just analytical knowledge of reality and adequate practice. It means beginning with and keeping hope in the utopia of God's kingdom and above all great pity and great love. Obviously it is not a question of imposing a cold and abstract justice which would restore the balance of a reality done violence to. It is a question of defending the poor, who live, or barely live, in a state of destitution. We seek justice in reality so that the poor can have life. These poor people, whose lives are threatened, are the pressing reason we can no longer be self-centered and must go out to them to the point of self-forgetfulness. Forgiving reality means loving—loving very much.

Unlike other ways of eradicating sin, Christian forgiveness of reality also means taking on its weight. This means incarnation in the world of sin, the world of the poor, letting ourselves be affected by their poverty, and sharing their weakness. This incarnation is hard, but it is a conversion which leads to solidarity with the poor and seeing reality in a very different way, overcoming the mechanisms we use to defend ourselves from reality. We tend not only to defend ourselves from God in order to manipulate him, but also from reality. We must open ourselves to it to grasp its truth and demands.

But taking on the sin means taking on its full weight, which threatens to overwhelm and destroy those who fight it, like Yahweh's suffering servant. Whatever other theories there may be on the eradication of sin and function of suffering in this eradication, in Christian terms, sin cannot be eradicated from outside ourself, simply by opposing its destructive force with force of our own, even though, of course, this must also be done. We must be prepared for the possibility—and the history of Latin America shows us what a real possibility this is—that taking on the destructive weight of sin could lead to danger, persecution, and death. Taking on the weight of sin requires courage to keep on when sin's eradication becomes extremely costly and sin turns its fury against us. It means going on hoping when we cannot see this clearly. It means being actively prepared to show the greatest love, to give our lives for the poor, whose lives we want to foster. In a word, it means sharing the fate of the servant to be transformed into light and salvation through darkness and disaster.

All this means that forgiving reality is a spiritual matter—deeply spiritual. By its nature, this forgiveness requires a fundamental spirituality of personal selflessness, radical self-giving, and radical love, hope put to the test and thus triumphant, true faith—true because it is victory over trials—in God who is the holy mystery; faith in the holy God, God who is life, who defends the poor, God of liberation and resurrection; faith in God who continues to be a mystery, crucified in the poor and those who defend them, but who still maintains hope in the future and goes on drawing history toward himself.

Forgiveness of the Sinner

In a sinful reality, there are sinners. In the first place, these are the idols who bring death. Forgiving them means fundamentally eradicating them. But these idols have particular agents who cause particular offenses: tortures, murders, disappearances, etc. The great sin takes particular shape in these forms, and the idols are personalized in torturers and murderers. These offenses are not sporadic tragic incidents; they are massive. Hence they are the *analogotaum princeps* of personal wrongdoing in sin. In this real context, we have to face in all seriousness the Christian question of forgiveness of those who offend us.

The first thing we must say is that in Latin America there is forgiveness for this type of offense as a Christian response to the sinner. Because it is forgiveness of such serious offenses, the reality of this forgiveness illuminates its essence much better than any conceptual analysis. We mention one among many examples of forgiveness, the celebration of All Souls Day in a refuge in San Salvador.

Around the altar on that day there were various cards with the names of family members who were dead or murdered. People would have liked to go to the cemetery to put flowers on their graves. But as they were locked up in the refuge and could not go, they painted flowers round their names. Beside the cards with the names of family members there was another card with no flowers which read: "Our dead enemies. May God forgive them and convert them." At the end of the eucharist we asked an old man what was the meaning of this last card and he told us this: "We made these cards as if we had gone to put flowers on our dead because it seemed to us they would feel we were with them. But as we are Christians, you know, we believed that our enemies should be on the altar too. They are our brothers in spite of the fact that they kill us and murder us. And you know what the Bible says. It is easy to love our own but God asks us also to love those who persecute us."

These words express much better than a long analysis what forgiveness is: It is simply great love. Personal forgiveness is not only or primarily the exercise of a difficult ascesis or the fulfillment of a sublime commandment. Above all, it is the showing of great love that goes out to meet the sinner in order to save him. The same love which moves us to forgive reality moves us to forgive those who offend even to this extent. It is love which wants to turn evil into good, wherever evil is present. To freely paraphrase Berdiaev's well-known words, sin is a physical evil for the victim but a moral evil for the offender. We must free him from this evil, and this is what forgiveness tries to do: convert and re-create the sinner. He must be freed by a loving acceptance from the anguish or despair he may have fallen into. Love must free him from himself and the darkness into which he has fallen. Thus the primary logic of forgiveness is love. The fact that it is a commandment does not tell us much about it, even though it may help us learn to do it. It is fundamentally doing good where there is evil, in order to transform the evil into good.

This way of forgiving presupposes a vision of life and God. Trying to convert the sinner through love means believing that love is able to convert sin and the sinner, that love has power, although history often goes against this conviction. Thus it is a utopian conviction, but it is held to, even through failures. It is not an idealist conviction, because it also admits coercion of the sinner to stop sinning and the sapiential argument that the sinner must be converted "for his own good." But what forgiveness is fundamentally saying is that for radical healing of the sinner, no other mechanism has the specific power of love. This is how Jesus acted, and this is how many Christians act: forgiving with love in the hope that this love will transform the sinner.

Thus the purpose of forgiveness is not simply to heal the guilt of the sinner but the purpose of all love: to come into communion. Of course we also forgive because of the accumulated wisdom that by strict justice alone and without any forgiveness, personal and social relations become chaos, because there are many sinners and many offenses. This wisdom requires some kind of forgiveness to break the vicious circle of offense and retaliation. But the final purpose of forgiveness is something else. It is positive reconciliation.

In the last resort, we forgive in order to build the kingdom of God, to live together in loving fellowship.

Forgiving the sinner is a powerful act of the spirit, a deep act of love, and it has specific characteristics which require a particular spirituality. If forgiveness of reality stresses the necessary efficacy of love, forgiveness of the sinner stresses the gratuity, unreason, and defenselessness of love. We do not forgive out of any personal or group interest, even a legitimate one, but simply out of love. Love is not presented as a convincing argument but simply offered.

Forgiveness of the sinner supposes a specific hope, hope for the miracle of conversion and the miracle of reconciliation. From this hope arises the attitude of forgiving up to seventy times seven, hoping for the triumph of love, or—when hope seems to be totally against hope—leaving eschatological forgiveness to God: "Father, forgive them for they know not what they do." This forgiveness may meet silence, for which we must be prepared, and surprise that the forgiveness has not been accepted but rejected and the sinner turns on the one offering it with even greater fury. But it may also have the joy of reconciliation, delight that the prodigal son has returned to his father's house, the communion of the children of God.

Forgiveness of a sinner reproduces God's act of kindness and thus shows a specific faith in God. Faith in the God of grace, tenderer than a mother, and in God's mystery, since he is also unable to transform the sinner's freedom. Faith finally in the God of the covenant, so often broken by us, which, anthropomorphically speaking, God could therefore repudiate, but which he keeps and offers again and again in a more radical way as a gratuitous, definitive, and irrevocable initiative. Forgiveness of the sinner makes plain God's saving initiative which nothing—neither sin nor sin persevered in—can change. God first loved us (1 John 4:11) when we were still sinners (Rom. 5:8). In the real history in which we live, we must make our faith in this God real in many ways. But in order to show its absolute gratuity and show that we believe in it, we must be prepared to forgive the sinner.

Spirituality of Forgiveness

Forgiving reality and forgiving the sinner are two forms of a single love, each of which requires a particular spirituality. We must also mention readiness to forgive in daily life. This means that the whole spirituality of forgiveness is a complex spirituality which has to integrate various aspects that are historically in tension: at the structural level, the relationship between the eradication of sin and forgiveness of the sinner; in daily life, forgiveness of those who hurt us and its relationship to the great structural forgiveness. The spirituality of forgiveness must take all these aspects into account and integrate them into a single spirituality, in which emphasis on one aspect does not overshadow any other.

At the structural level, the greatest tension is in the unavoidable task of eradicating sin—historically, the task of liberation—and forgiving the sinner. A familiar solution to this tension is in the old phrase, "Hate the sin and love the sinner." But this solution is not radical enough, even though what it says is true, because although we must love the sinner, we must not only hate the sin but eradicate it, and objectively this is a violent action against the sinner. Liberation from oppression also means destroying the person oppressing, in his formal capacity as oppressor. And although this task is difficult and dangerous, it cannot be abandoned for love of the oppressed.

The spirituality of forgiveness must integrate this tension between love and destruction, and this can only be done with a great love which comprehends the destruction of the sinner as love. Through love, we have to be prepared to welcome the sinner and forgive him. We have to be prepared to make it impossible for him to continue with his deeds, which dehumanize others and himself.

This spirituality is that of Jesus, who loves all people and is ready to forgive them all, but in a very precise way. Jesus loves the oppressed by being with them and loves the oppressors by being against them; in this way, Jesus is for all. Through love of the oppressed, Jesus tells the truth plainly to the oppressors, denounces them, unmasks them, curses them, and threatens them with final dehumanization. But in this, Jesus is also paradoxically in favor of the oppressors. It is a paradoxical form of love, offering them salvation by destroying them as sinners. His cry of forgiveness on the Cross movingly shows that Jesus' love was forgiveness for the person of the oppressor. That this love seeks to be truly re-creative is shown by the scene of the conversion of Zaccheus. Zaccheus was not only welcomed and thus forgiven by Jesus, but also liberated from his oppressive self and thus saved.

Monseñor Romero was a very clear illustration of this spirituality in tension. He wanted the good of the oppressors. He received them personally whenever and for whatever reason they came to him, and he forgave them at his death. But above all, he wanted them to stop being oppressors. Therefore he denounced them and exhorted them in God's name to stop their oppression and repression. He threatened them prophetically with the words of Cardinal Montini: "Take off your rings so that they don't take off your hands." In all this, he was moved solely by love, so the oppressors could stop being oppressors for the good of the oppressed and their own good.

The importance of personal forgiveness must not lead us to forget the urgency of the eradication of sin. But neither must this lead us to forget the importance of forgiveness, precisely so that the eradication of sin should take place in the most Christian and effective way.

Liberation movements—historical forms of eradication of sin—are necessary, just, and good. But they are still the work of human beings, and therefore limited and liable to sinfulness. Going beyond their limitations and minimizing their negative subproducts are the work of the spirit. In this context of liberation, an important sign of the strengthening and healing spirit is forgiveness of the sinner. This forgiveness as gratuitous love is an important way of remaining true to what is at the origin of liberation movements: love, not vengeance or mere retaliation; keeping true to the purpose of liberation, which is a just and loving society for all. Acts of forgiveness which take place within the processes of liberation have a symbolic value and force beyond themselves. They are also sacramental moments. They recall their original purpose, look forward to their goal, and in the process are profound signs of human quality, which is always threatened when one is engaged in a struggle, however just.

Forgiveness of the sinner is also a reminder—for believers, at any rate—of our own sin and the forgiveness we have received from God. Forgiving others is a reminder that we have been forgiven. This simple but profound experience is extremely important so the liberation process is not in danger of hubris. As J. I. Gonzales Faus puts it, we must "make revolution as people who have been forgiven" and remember that we carry liberating love in vessels of clay. This experience can cure any tendency to authoritarianism, dogmatism, or power mania historically inherent in liberation movements.

The spirituality of forgiveness must operate on the structural level we have described but also in daily life, in which the offense is more immediate and forgiveness warmer. Both things are related. In Christian communities, the rediscovery of the great structural sin and structural forgiveness has helped people rediscover their own worlds of sin and forgiveness. Structural oppression has helped people discover typical oppressions within communities, *machísmo*, the authoritarianism of leaders, refusal to take responsibility, selfishness, and lust for domination. Often people recognize simply: We have behaved a little like the great oppressors.

This helped people rediscover the essence of communal sin: small deaths within the community, what divides its members and sets them against each other, what is destructive of good fellowship. But it has also helped people rediscover the essence and purpose of forgiveness. Without the acceptance of forgiveness, we cannot pass on God's love. "The Lord always said that some sheep strayed, but he followed them along paths and through muddy places and did not stop till he found them." Without forgiveness, there can be no reconciliation, no community, no kingdom of God. "We know that if Don Fonso and Don Tono do not make peace with their friend Chepe, the community itself will be divided and thus we will be unable to give ourselves to one another."

The structural has helped them understand the communitarian, but the communitarian has also helped them understand the structural. These Christian communities that feel sin in themselves and are capable of forgiving are the ones most involved in the eradication of society's sin, the ones most prepared for the great forgiveness—forgiveness of those who have murdered countless people belonging to them. The communities which seek hardest for internal reconciliation are the ones most prepared to seek social reconciliation, the ones that work hardest—in the present set-up in El Salvador—for dialogue, the ones who rejoice most in the small gestures of reconciliation, exchange, or surrender of prisoners.

Forgiveness in the communities stresses—because of the closeness its members live in and the immediacy of the offenses—that the spirituality of forgiveness is communal, and although the one sinned against does the forgiving of a particular offense, it is the whole community which forgives or should forgive, and this forgiveness is for the building of the community. It also stresses—since in the communities all are more aware of their own sins—that everyone needs forgiveness and everyone is forgiven by God. Forgiving another person is thus cured of the danger of becoming a promethean gesture of ultimate superiority. It is better to respond with forgiveness to the forgiveness we ourselves have received, to let off others, knowing we have been let off.

The whole spirituality of forgiveness, in its tension and complexity, is a manifestation of the spirituality of liberation, of spiritual men and women described by G. Gutiérrez as "free to love." To forgive is to liberate, to love the oppressed through a sinful reality and thus liberate that reality; love the oppressors and thus be prepared to welcome them and also destroy them as oppressors. But the forgivers have also been liberated from themselves. They have experienced grace and forgiveness from their brothers and sisters and from God. Liberating others requires liberated human beings to do it, and those who have been liberated from themselves are the ones most able to liberate others. Forgiveness as effective and gratuitous love expresses this spirituality.

Monseñor Romero understood very well that forgiveness is love and comprises different forms of love, which have to be maintained. We must defend the oppressed and forgive reality, and so he said: "We must go to the base of the social transformations of our society. If we want violence and deprivation to come to an end, we must get to the root" (September 30, 1979). We must forgive the sinner so he said: "You can say, if they come to kill me, that I forgive and bless those who do it" (March 1980). We have to recognize ourselves as sinners in need of forgiveness, so he said: "Each one of you, like me, can see our own story in the parable of the prodigal son" (March 16, 1980). We must look to and keep as our final horizon of forgiveness the utopia of reconciliation, and so he said: "Above all God's word which he cries out to us today is: 'Reconciliation!' " (March 16, 1980).

Latin America is a place of sin but also a place of forgiveness. Sin abounds, but grace is more abounding. And let us say in conclusion that sin and forgiveness in Latin America cannot be something only by and for Latin Americans; it is by all for all. John Paul II said that on the day of judgment, the peoples of the Third World will judge the First World. What we must add is that even now they carry the weight of the whole world's sin and therefore they are the ones who can forgive and, historically, the only ones who can forgive the sin of the world.

I have said these things about forgiveness in Latin America not just to whip up emotion or admiration, but to make the First World aware of its own sin and move it to conversion. Karl Rahner said that only those who know they have been forgiven know they are sinners. The tragedy of the Third World should be enough on its own to generate this awareness of sin. But if it does not generate it, and if even the forgiveness offered by crucified peoples does not generate it, then we may ask what indeed will convert the First World.

Let us finish by putting it positively. If the crucified peoples make known the sin of the world; if these peoples are prepared to offer forgiveness and welcome the sinful world in order to humanize it in its shame; if they invite all to struggle against the objective sin and humanize reality; if this knowledge, this welcome, and this invitation is accepted, then reconciliation is possible, together with solidarity and the future of God's kingdom in history. And this in the last resort is what is at stake in humanity today in the spirituality of forgiveness.

—*Translated by Dinah Livingstone*

5

Five Hundred Years

Structural Sin and Structural Grace

Introduction

This year we commemorate the five hundredth anniversary of the arrival of Europeans in what is now called Latin America. For the first time, humankind became aware of itself as a geographical entity and, as a result, as an historical entity. But together with this opportunity there arose also, by necessity, the great human and Christian question—since the Europeans who arrived in Latin America were Christians—of how such new and different continents could relate to each other. More concretely, there arose the problem of "otherness" and how to relate to it.

From this angle, the commemoration of what happened in 1492 is important in itself, but it also serves as a lesson for 1992 because today, too, a great new development is being proclaimed—a new world unity with the disappearance of communism. History has reached such a point that the "end of history" has been announced. And, of course, the great human and Christian question still remains: how not just Europe should relate to the America which had just been "discovered," but how the entire North (Europe, the United States, Japan) should relate to the South of the planet. This is the issue which currently holds our attention—what is happening in the world today. But the events of five centuries ago cast light on the present, and for this reason we should look at the fundamental features of the past.

I should say also that we pursue this analysis from a Latin American perspective, while having before our eyes a European reality which is itself a limited and incomplete approach, because there are many groups in Europe—not very representative, admittedly—who show great solidarity with Latin America. But I think it's useful and necessary for us to discover

---

This lecture was originally delivered at Salford Cathedral, Lancashire, England, on March 21, 1992.

how, in structural terms, the European and Latin American continents relate to each other.

In order to understand this relationship correctly, the first thing we have to remind ourselves of is that the events of 1492 were not, properly speaking, a discovery. We say this not simply to avoid hurting the feelings of the natives of the Latin American continent—as if they hadn't been real before 1492 because their existence was not linked to Europe, a clear expression of sinful eurocentrism—but because of something more fundamental, as we can see from the inspired words of Ignacio Ellacuría:

> To my way of thinking, what took place is that the conquistador, the dominator, lays himself open to discovery. Thus, five centuries ago, with the "discovery" of the so-called "new world" what was really discovered was the true Spain herself, the reality of western culture and the Church as they were then. They opened themselves to discovery, they revealed themselves without realizing it, because what they did with regard to Latin America was a "cover-up" rather than a "discovery." In reality it's the Third World which discovers the First World in its most negative and truest aspects.[1]

This would seem to me to be the best perspective from which to understand what happened then and what has continued to happen up to the present day. The Spaniards and the Portuguese were discovered in their plunder and destruction of a continent and, in addition, they offered other nations, as the accepted norm, a pattern of behavior toward Latin America and toward the other continents of the Third World: "discover," "colonize," "conquer" . . . in order to plunder. In this there is a coincidence in what the Spaniards and Portuguese did in their day in Latin America, with what was done in other continents by countries such as Holland, France, England, Germany, Belgium, the United States.

After five centuries, there has been little substantial change in the basis, although perhaps in the forms, of this relationship between the countries of the North and South. The former relate to the latter fundamentally to take advantage of the spoils while passing themselves off as benefactors, as if all the evils of the world were in the South and the countries of the North were their saviors, whose only desire was to remedy those evils. Reality, however, is very different, and sometimes it is exactly the opposite. And so, although these words should perhaps be left for the conclusion, I should like to advance, from the outset, the fundamental affirmation.

Today, also, there is a will to cover up the reality of the Third World, and in this the First World shows itself for what it is. As a result, not only is the truth about most of the planet suppressed, but the First World deprives itself of the most effective means of knowing its truest and deepest self. In the reality of the South, with all of its poverty, injustice, and death, the North can recognize itself, as in a reverse mirror image, through what it has produced.

And so it is that Western, democratic, Christian civilization—with the humanism and renaissance which were in vogue in 1492, with the enlightenment and the modernity of these five centuries, and with the masters of scepticism who have set almost everything up to question—has been incapable of humanizing the Third World, although some things have been achieved. Nor, as a result, has it been capable of humanizing Europe, as the Europeans of today admit.

To recall what happened in 1492 and analyze the reality of 1992 in the end means nothing other than analyzing the state of humankind on our planet. It means analyzing whether the unity achieved, both then and now, is considered as a means of unification and growth of the human family, truly accepting and integrating the "otherness" of others, or whether it is considered as a means of shaping the world into antagonists, a unity of superiors and inferiors, of executioners and victims.

I should like to move on to address a prophetic word to the First World about its own reality, about the destruction it is causing in the Third World. We ought to do so because the First World will hardly acknowledge this by itself since—today just as yesterday—it is producing a Third World which is sin. At the same time, we should utter a word of good news for the First World. This is evangelization—offering the First World the reality of the Third World as grace. Let us allow the Third World—or at least the Christians—to be prophetic and evangelizing.

A Prophetic Word: The Unjust Denial of the Minimum of Life

Relations between Europe and Latin America have been unjust since their origins and continue to be so. They oppress and threaten life; they seek ideological and theological justifications; they hold, as an unspoken fundamental premise, the human inferiority of some in relation to others. We can call all that structural evil in a very precise sense. Five centuries of unjust behavior strengthens this way of proceeding and makes it easier, to such an extent that nowadays it seems normal for the countries of the North to live at the expense of those in the South. It is a normal premise, for instance, that scandalously allowed and facilitated the war in Iraq: The North needs the oil of the South to live well.

Life Destroyed

Very soon after the arrival of the Spaniards, the life of the indigenous people began to be destroyed. This was the founding feature in the relationship between the Europeans and the inhabitants of that new world. In 1511, on the island of Hispaniola, Friar Antonio Montesinos pronounced the following words:

You are all in mortal sin and in it you live and die because of the cruelty and tyranny with which you use these innocent peoples. Tell me, with what right and with what justice do you hold these Indians in such cruel and horrific servitude? With what authority have you waged such despicable wars against these peoples who lived meekly and peacefully in their lands and whom you have consumed in such infinite numbers with unheard of death and ruination? How do you hold them in such oppression and exhaustion, neither feeding them nor curing their ills which kill them, just to bring forth and accumulate more gold each day?

This text vigorously condemns what became a general and decisive reality for the future of the continent: the immense process of depredation, plunder, and destruction by the Spanish and Portuguese. The basic truth is that some seventy years after their arrival, a monumental debacle had been reached: The Indian population was on the verge of extinction. There were a series of causes of this, of course—wars, cruel treatment, imported ailments to which the natives had no immunity, hard labor, suicides through despair, inhumane migrations—so it would not be fair to attribute the debacle entirely to the Spaniards' desire for extermination. But we should not ignore or seek to minimize the crudeness of this fundamental truth: After the arrival of the Europeans, the indigenous population shrank to 15 percent of what it had been. In addition, many cultures, traditions, and religions were wiped out. This was no chance occurrence.

Even though direct destruction was not the intention, this was inescapably necessary. The main aim of the conquest was the insatiable quest for wealth and power, *at any cost*, even if—as now—other ideological motives are flaunted, such as Christianizing the Indians, and even though many missionaries bore distinguished witness to this. Soon they began to theorize on the existence and identity of the Indians. Do they have souls or not? But in operational terms, their existence was seen as a means to an end, a way to make the Spaniards rich. Later, when the supply became exhausted, black Africans were enslaved so they could in turn become instruments, just like modern sources of energy.

And where are we today? The methods of conquest and explanations offered to justify it have changed, without doubt, but the gross basic reality has not. The Latin American continent, which for the most part moves within the Western orbit, offers us a tragic spectacle. To illustrate this, it is sufficient to give the figures and interpretations of some economists, but it must be remembered that through these figures we are talking about how human beings live and die. In Christian terms, we are talking about the state of Creation, the sons and daughters of God. And so, by the end of this century, one-third of Latin Americans, some 170 million people, will live in poverty, or rather in normal, inhuman poverty, while another third, another 170 million, will live in dire poverty. From this we can see that as much as

60 percent of the Latin American population will live in the kind of poverty experienced in the countries of sub-Saharan Africa or Bangladesh.

If we look at the whole Third World, the spectacle is even more macabre, unworthy of a planet inhabited by human beings. From the point of view of mere chances of survival, the number of poor is frightening. Recent studies find that, in comparison with normal standards of living in Western Europe, "1,116 million people are miserably poor, another 2,000 million are poor, while only slightly more than one-quarter of humankind enjoys a living standard which is decent to good." [2]

From the point of view of fraternity, that is, of the common sharing in the resources of the planet, the abyss between humanity grows ever wider. The average per capita income in the industrialized world is "fifty times greater than the average of the 1,116 million poor of the Third World."[3] That is, although the United Nations Charter confers equality of rights on all human beings, in order to survive, it is much more important to have been born in London than in Bangladesh, in Boston than in Chalatenango. One life in the countries of abundance is worth some fifty lives of the poor.

The basic reason for this scandal is the same as it was centuries ago. The poor countries are only important for what they can provide or—if there's no alternative—for what can be plundered from them: raw materials and cheap labor. But nowadays this takes place with a number of variants which make the situation worse than it was in the recent past.

The first of these is that the "accumulation of capital depends less and less upon the extent of natural resources and labor" [4] and depends ever more on technological knowledge, with the result that the Third World is still important on the basis of its raw materials, although not quite as much, but it is no longer important because of its people. "What is no longer necessary is the majority of the population of the Third World." [5] This excess population is simply of no consequence whatsoever.

The second variant is that in the geopolitical share-out "the Third World, with its land, its air and its nature continues to be necessary if only as a dumping ground for poisonous waste." [6] A confidential document from a World Bank executive proposes the transfer of all toxic industries to the Third World.[7]

The third is the loss of power by the overwhelming majority of people in the Third World within the international order. The Third World still has relative importance but "what is no longer necessary is the majority of the population of the Third World . . . This means that the excess population suffers from a total lack of power."[8] The collapse of the socialist bloc leaves the Third World even more helpless in the hands of capitalism.[9]

The conclusion of all that we have said in the words of economists is chilling. "The Third World finds itself completely alone . . . the central capitalist countries have lost interest in a development policy for the Third World and have moved to block it as far as possible."[10] "The twenty-first century has already begun: North against South . . . never before in history, not even in colonial times, has there ever been such an extreme bipolarization in the world."[11]

> General economic activity, that is, trade and international investment, which is today set up to benefit the industrialized countries in a disproportionate and selfish way, must be arranged on a more equitable and rational footing. Unfortunately, there is still a great need for educating and motivating the leaders of the rich countries so that they give greater priority to the interest of other countries—who neither vote for them, nor can make them lose elections.[12]

All this should need no comment, but we must hammer it home. Although they are still important, for humankind in its entirety, the greatest and most pressingly urgent problem is neither European unification, nor what to do with the fall of socialism, nor the celebration of the fifth centenary, which could be regarded as scandalous in the face of the poverty here described.[13] The greatest problem in 1992 is the impoverishment of the Third World. This comes as the result of an unjust system which shows no sign of repentance. Which government, bank, or transnational corporation would even dream of asking forgiveness from the poor of the Third World? Nor do they show any firm purpose of amendment or accept any penance for reparation due. This takes place amid an objective ignorance and indifference, if not contempt, of the minorities in the North toward the majorities in the South. In the North, the capacity for life accumulates, while in the South the incapacity for survival grows.

There is a saying in the Castilian language that is difficult to translate into other languages. Ignacio Ellacuría used it in the article quoted earlier, and it expresses exactly what I have wanted to say. The conquerors of Latin America "have left it like a Christ."[14] In Christian language, where the language of statistics falls short, all the tragedy of the Third World is encompassed. In Christian language of today, again from Ignacio Ellacuría, the Latin American continent is an immense crucified people. And in the Christian language of yesterday, from Bartolome de las Casas, the reality was described thus: "I leave Jesus Christ our Lord in the Indies, scourging him and whipping him and striking him and crucifying him not once but thousands of times, such are the Spaniards who trample and destroy those peoples . . . "[15]

The Justification of Plunder

In the sixteenth century, in the face of the aberrations committed by the conquistadors, a movement of protest and defense of the Indians grew up, but there also grew up a movement which strove to justify the subjugation in which they were held, and this was the view which eventually prevailed: The conquistadors had a right to those lands and their exploitation. While they could not totally hide the ominous consequences of the real exercise of this supposed right, it was argued that such a right was one of principle. And so, the unjustifiable was justified in many and varied ways. Let us recall how it was done.

Ecclesiastically, the Bull of Pope Alexander VI was offered, published shortly after 1492, in which the domains under the rule of the Spaniards and the Portuguese were demarcated. *Theologically*, it was declared that God had granted these lands to the Spaniards as a providence or reward for their wars against the infidels during the reconquest of Spain. From the basis of *political philosophy*, it was asserted that there were no legitimate owners of those lands and therefore the Europeans could legitimately conquer them. *Anthropologically*, the human inferiority of the Indians was established, to the extent of denying them a soul or human nature. *Ethically*, the evil and perverse customs of the Indians were advanced: These not only allowed but demanded that the Indians should be subjugated, so as to be set free from them.

We cannot here analyze these arguments one by one, but it *is* important to emphasize the conclusion to which they led. A mountain of arguments were advanced, from diverse points of view, to defend what was already held in possession. It is a clear case of the use of intelligence guided by spurious self-interest. What is worse is that it was an argument of principle, without any analysis or evaluation of the "legitimate" owners which might effectively topple such a theory. That is to say, the premise of every argument was the decision that had already been taken, which was that the Europeans were going to stay in those lands and from them they were going to get rich.

On occasion the justifications reached inconceivable extremes, such as one which appeared in a document called "The Opinion from Yucay"[16] of 1571, written in Peru by Garcia de Toledo to counter the opinions of Bartolomé de las Casas. We should look at it, if only for its aberrant underlying theology.

> And so I say of these Indians, that one of the instruments of their predestination and salvation were these mines, treasures and riches, because we can see that where these exist, then there we find the Gospel has arrived, and where they do not exist, but there are only the poor, it is a form of condemnation, because the gospel will never reach there, as we can see from long experience. In lands where there is no gift of gold and silver, there is no soldier or captain who will go there, nor any minister of the Gospel. . . . Thus, these mines are good for these barbarians for God provided them so that faith and Christianity might be taken to them, and keep them there for their salvation.[17]

As further justification, he offers the parable of the two sisters, one beautiful and the other ugly. The first needs no dowry for marriage, for her beauty is enough, while the second sister needs one. God operates in this same way with regard to the evangelization of peoples. Some—and he mentions Europe and Asia—are plentifully endowed, "great beauty, many sciences, wisdom," and that is where the evangelizers are. But others—as in the case of Latin America—are "ugly, crude, stupid, clumsy and dull" and need to have some incentive—the gold from the mines—so that evangelization might reach them. It is an outstanding example of eurocentrism, the exact opposite of the option for the poor.

In the present day, theoretical progress has been made in international law as far as relations between countries are concerned, and through this, some conflicts have been resolved. But it is a process which pursues the exploitation of the Third World by the First; and what is worse is that it seems to need no justification. It is true that some were brandished in the war against Iraq, but everyone knew that these justifications were for form's sake, since the decision had already been taken.

As far as the theological justifications of the plunder of the Third World are concerned, it is understandable that these are no longer flourished in a secularized world. Besides, churches today generally adopt an official position, or at least it seems that way, of defending the Third World and condemning its exploitation by the First. I say "it seems," however, because it is not absolutely certain that the churches of the First World defend the Third World with ultimate conviction. This is certainly not the case with governments, the military, or the multinationals. While these groups do not openly seek theological justifications, they do seek the support of alienating Christian movements and sects and, above all, they react violently against those theologies which defend the poor of the world. We should recall the reaction of the First World—governments, ruling classes, armed forces, but also churches and theologies—against the theology of liberation.

From a theoretical point of view, its merits and demerits are open to discussion, but there can be no doubt that this theology—and only this one—has placed its finger in the wound of the reality of the Third World and has come out explicitly in defense of the poor. So this theology was persecuted by the report of Vice-President Rockefeller, in the documents of the advisers of President Reagan, and it has been attacked by the CIA and the armies of Latin America. In practice, it has also been harassed by CELAM, by many bishops, and by the Roman Curia. Together with the attack upon this theology, there are attacks upon basic Christian communities, Medellín, Puebla, and a whole generation of bishops (Dom Helder Camara, Bishops Proano, Angelelli, Romero, Casaldaliga).

It's not that they repeat the arguments from the "Opinion from Yucay" in an attempt to justify exploitation, of course, but we cannot ignore a strong similarity: a frontal attack upon those who defend the Indians and the poor. Exactly the same things are said today about the theology of liberation (and sometimes about basic communities, Medellín, and bishops such as Monseñor Romero) as were said in the past about Bartolomé de las Casas: that it is the root of all evils.[18]

Unknown and Despised Humanity

The words of Antonio Montesinos that I quoted earlier continue as follows: "Are these not men? Do they not have rational minds? Are you not obliged to love them as yourselves? Do you not understand this? Do you not feel this? How do you so lethargically repose in such deep slumber?"

Here there is no denunciation of the exploitation, nor is any concrete justification advanced, as the earlier ones, for the plunder, but it suggests a deeper-rooted premise for the most merciless exploitation: ignoring or doubting the humanity of the Indians. And this can be seen in the present day, in a much more sophisticated way.

To start with, there is a striking *ignorance* in Europe of the reality of the Third World. The average European seems not to know how many human beings live in the South, how many die each year of hunger, or how many blind there are in India through lack of vitamin A. There are some bits of news, but the reality of the Third World is not known. If, as a result of some hypothetical cataclysm, the Latin American continent were to disappear, or Africa or Asia, we don't know if and what the average European would miss.

But worse than the ignorance is the *disinterest.* In Europe, there are certainly ways of ensuring that the Third World is known about. There are thousands of schools and hundreds of universities, hundreds of dioceses and thousands of parishes, hundreds of publishing houses, magazines, newspapers, radio, and television stations. Yet "the interest which pro- motes *knowledge* " is not an interest in learning about the Third World. And this is probably the case, consciously or unconsciously, so as not to be confronted with the reality of what we have created.

In the north of the planet, people live in indifference, an effective post- modernism which, in the words of J. B. Metz, "removes the so-called Third World to a faceless distance." There is "a kind of cultural strategy for the immunization of Europe . . . a cult of new innocence . . . an attempt to set themselves apart in their minds from the global challenges facing humanity . . . a new variety of tactical provincialism."[19] In any case, the average European is not interested in asking about his or her own responsibility for the state of the Third World, not interested in being the target of the question "What have you done to your brother?"

In addition to the ignorance and disinterest, there exists a eurocentrism, an arrogance—even a contempt—not necessarily as explicit subjective realities but as an ever-present a priori: The reality of the Third World is already measured in terms of the extent to which it approaches that of the First World. The truth, or at least the yardstick by which truth is defined, is Europe, and the "other" human beings are only real insofar as they conform to it.

Even today, when the events of 500 years ago are discussed, the truth deals with the behavior of the Europeans. That is, it deals with European reality. The truth or reality of what happened to others occupies a secondary place. The victims—millions of human beings in the Third World—lack primary importance as far as the fundamental question is concerned, which is the European question: Whether it was the Spaniards or the English or the Dutch or others who behaved better or worse in the countries they conquered.

By the way, one Latin American author thinks that all the conquerors acted practically in the same way. The only difference would be that Spain produced prophets, which introduced some scruples into the process of conquest, while this was not the case with the other countries.[20] But we should not allow this fact to lead us to intone a kind of *felix culpa*, such as: Well, the Indians might have had a terrible time of it, but how fortunate that this brought about the appearance of people like Bartolomé de las Casas and Francisco de Vitoria. Of course, we should be grateful for them, but if it were to lead us to rejoice in the Hispanic achievements while ignoring the immense misfortune of the Indians, then it would be one more subtle example of eurocentrism.

Are things any better nowadays? Eduardo Galeano has just written some pages on "Contempt as Destiny."[21] His basic thesis is that Latin America is as if it no longer existed, that what is normal would be simply to ignore it on principle. It does not form the same kind of real entity as Europe, which *is* something real—good or bad, but real. Europe is the yardstick of what is real, against which will be measured the extent to which other human beings share in the reality of humankind.

This is what is at stake in the symbolic year of 1992, just as it was in 1492: Whether the North of the planet concedes the reality of the South and is interested in building the human family, or whether its only interest is in its own well-being, with the resulting declaration of the nonexistence of the South and of its lack of interest for the human family. This is theorized or lived out on the premise that the good life of a few in the North is at the expense of the blighted life of so many in the South.

A Word of Grace: It Is Possible to Live Meaningfully

This Europe, which Kant awoke from its dogmatic sleep, has not yet awoken from the sleep of inhumanity in which it is sunk. It has not yet recognized or felt responsible for the denial of the minimum of a just and decent life in the Third World. Nevertheless, this awakening is possible if, paradoxically, it turns its eyes toward the Third World. For there it will find a reserve of light, hope, and love which can humanize it. For this reason we speak of structural grace, because there it is for all who wish to avail themselves of light, hope, and love.

In effect, it is not a truth of reason, but it *is* the essence of the Christian faith to state that in the Suffering Servant of Yahweh there is light and salvation, and that in the crucified Christ lies the wisdom of God. This continues to be true in Latin America. Ignacio Ellacuría reflected theoretically in an article that he wrote at the time of Puebla entitled "The Crucified People."[22] In practice, a multitude of people who arrive for the first time in the Third World from the First World confirm this. I should like to offer you—from my own experience in El Salvador—what this grace for the First World consists of.

The Light of Truth

The mere fact of the existence of the Third World can help overcome not only the ignorance of the First World, but unmask falsehood, and that is no small mercy. St. Paul solemnly warns us that the founding sin which corrupts human reality and the reality of nations is "to imprison truth with injustice." It is a light that has the strength to light up the shadows and uncover falsehood and is, for that reason, very beneficial and necessary. The Third World is the light that helps the First World know itself for what it is.

This light also uncovers the fact that the solutions offered by the First World are not real solutions. They were not in the past and they cannot be in the present, for the simple reason that they are not universally applicable and, as Kant said, what is not universal cannot ethically be good. There are not nearly enough resources for the Third World to even approach the living standards of the First World. Whether it is possible or not, history shows that the solution offered by the First World is dehumanizing for all worlds.

Finally, this light illuminates a utopia, a reality relegated to the past in Europe because it was considered impossible. Nevertheless, utopia continues to be necessary, at least the utopia for which the Third World is crying out—a just and decent life for the poor which, in the words of Ignacio Ellacuría, requires a "civilization of poverty," or at least of shared austerity and the pre-eminence of labor over capital.

The Power for Conversion

Simply from a human viewpoint, changing a heart of stone into a heart of flesh—conversion—is a fundamental problem for the First World. And this is what the Third World offers it as a possibility. Above all, the Third World portrays in its own flesh the existence of an immense sin that brings slow or violent death to innocent human beings. To express it in inescapable terms, it holds the power for conversion. In another way, if entire crucified continents do not have the strength to convert hearts of stone into hearts of flesh, we must ask ourselves, what can? And if nothing can, we must ask what kind of future awaits a First World built, consciously or unconsciously, upon the corpses of the human family. There can be no reason for living, if we live this way.

There is something the First World often tends to forget: The Third World is open to forgiving its oppressors. It does not wish to triumph over them, but to share with them and open up a future for them. To whomsoever draws close to them, the poor of the Third World open up their hearts and their arms and, without realizing it, grant them forgiveness. By allowing them to come close, they make it possible for the world of the oppressor to recognize itself as a sinner, but also as forgiven. In this way, they introduce into the world of the oppressor a humanizing element which was absent grace, because forgiveness is not a victory of the executioner but a gift of the victim.

Humanizing Values

The Third World offers values which can only be found with difficulty in other places and which, frequently, are contrary to the anti-values of the First World. In other words, the Third World has a potential to humanize because, at least in principle and often in practice, it offers the following values: community instead of individualism, simplicity instead of opulence, helpfulness instead of selfishness, creativity instead of enforced mimicry, celebration instead of mere enjoyment, an openness to transcendency instead of dull pragmatism.

From a Christian viewpoint, they possess a power to evangelize, as was boldly stated in Puebla: for what they suffer, for what they are, and for what they do, for us they become the good news. They are the "poor with spirit," that Ignacio Ellacuría described.

Surrender, Love, and Martyrdom

The Third World offers a great commitment, a great surrendering, and a great love. It is not that it is masochistic or suicidal, or that the only course left to them is to make a virtue out of necessity. It is rather that, faced with the wounded man on the road, many of them have felt their hearts touched and have been moved to mercy. The accumulation of love and martyrdom in Latin America in recent years is truly impressive. And through it, love becomes a possibility for this world because it is real. In a First World which is structurally selfish, based as it is on a self-centeredness that is often gloried in, this love is a great opportunity for humanization.

The Hope Which Never Dies

Incomprehensibly for some, or for others because there is no alternative, the fact is that the Third World has hope and offers hope. It is no naive hope "against hope," as Paul would say, but there it is. It is a hope which has expressed itself in work and struggle for liberation. While the First World always tries to stifle it and appears to achieve this, this should not be interpreted as a triumph but as a defeat.

But there it is. Throughout the Third World flows this hope-filled current of humanity, which time and again strives to make life possible. Precisely because the poor do not take life for granted, they are the ones who hope for that "minimum which is the maximum gift of God," as Monseñor Romero said: life. Ignacio Ellacuría, not one for romantic statements, expressed it as follows:

> All this blood of martyrs shed in El Salvador and throughout Latin America—far from moving them to despondency and despair—infuses a new spirit of struggle and new hope in our people. In this way, even if we are not a "new world" or a "new continent," we are clearly and verifiably—and not necessarily by those from outside—a continent of hope. And this is something of utmost importance for future development in the face of other continents which have no hope and have only fear.[23]

All that I have said up to now in this section about grace has to be clearly understood. Without doubt, not all the Third World is like this. In fact, it is only minorities who actively offer those values described here—although it is majorities who suffer passively—who offer us in this way the grace of truth and conversion.

But these values and this grace are present in the Third World, and they are there in structural form. To put it in simple words, it is easier to be human and Christian in the Third World, because in it one can feel lifted along by this current of truth, commitment, utopia, and hope.

It is easier to be a prophet, to be a good Samaritan, to be a martyr, when faced with such a host of prophets, Samaritans, and martyrs. In the words of the Letter to the Hebrews, it is easier to bear witness to faith in the midst of a whole host of witnesses.

How much of this is the case has yet to be verified. But we, and many of those who visit us from outside, declare that this grace is what they have found. Fr. Jose Ellacuría, a Jesuit, the brother of Ignacio, said to us on the first anniversary of the martyrdom of the martyrs of the UCA that what he had learned in El Salvador is that "there is another way to live." That was said by someone who lived more than twenty years in Taiwan, a country which is held up to us as an example: the possibility of a material life, but without spirit.

To end, I would like to say that the solution for this world of ours is solidarity. We all need each other, and we can all help each other. The history of relations between North and South is a sad history, but it can change and, in any case, it must change. The North can and must help us make that minimum of a just and decent life possible. The South can become a reserve of spirit for the North. What is important is to recover or begin to have the idea and ideal of the human family.

When a journalist asked Monseñor Romero, shortly before his assassination, what other countries should do to help El Salvador, Monseñor listed several things, but he finally mentioned the basic premise of all of them: "that they should not forget that we are people, human beings."

This continues to be the fundamental problem and challenge. Stated in simple terms, it is a question of beginning to see ourselves as a human family. Stated in Christian terms, it is a question of being truly able to pray the "Our Father." Let us hope that 1992 does not set us further apart but joins us together as a human family in North and South.

6

Personal Sin, Forgiveness, and Liberation

The theology of liberation insists on the reality and gravity of concrete historical sin; the possibility and urgency of defeating it; and the thesis that a concrete, historical eradication is its most adequate defeat. Thereby this theology remains faithful to the core of God's revelation, which takes the negative element in history utterly seriously; which adds—as its most specific element—that nevertheless the opportunity for salvation is available; and which takes the reality of this world seriously as a world that deals death but cries for life.

The massive dimensions, the cruelty, and the growth of this concrete, historical sin requires of the theology of liberation, as it requires of all theology, that it continue to make historical sin and its eradication central to its purposes and content.[1] In this article, however, we shall also be dealing with the personal element in sin, and with forgiveness as the specific form of the defeat of sin *qua* personal.

One reason for addressing the subject would be to respond to accusations of "reductionism" lodged with the theology of liberation with regard to sin. But our main reason for addressing the subject here is that sin and forgiveness are core realities in revelation, and the acknowledgment of one's personal sin and the acceptance of forgiveness can provide enormous impetus for the eradication of historical sin.

In the first three parts of this chapter, we shall deal with forgiveness as the defeat of personal sin. In the latter two parts, we shall deal with the importance of forgiveness in the process of concrete, historical liberation. But let us begin with certain difficulties that prevail today when it comes to the recognition and acknowledgment of one's personal sin.

Current Difficulties in Acknowledging One's Own Sin

From the earliest days of the church, minds and hearts have wrestled with the meaning of liberation from sin. How can the proposition that, in

---

Originally published in *Revista Latinamericana de Teología* 13 (1988):13-31

Christ, sin is objectively vanquished, be reconciled with the notion that his victory remains to be personally appropriated by the rest of us? In our own day, we labor under another difficulty, besides, and a basic one: the crisis we experience in the problem of a recognition of our own sin. It is difficult enough to determine in what liberation from our own sin consists; it will be all the more so if we lack all awareness of that sin, or entertain only a very diminished consciousness of it.

By way of a description of the current situation where an awareness of one's own sin is concerned, we may say, speaking generally, that there is a tendency on believers' parts to move from a "totally sinful" view of themselves to a "sinless" view—from a view of life as dominated by personal sin or its possibility (and linked to a transcendent eternal damnation as its most specific consequence), to a view of diminished personal responsibility for human beings' negative acts (and thereupon to a view in which the possibility of an eternal damnation is not seriously operative).

Neither attitude does justice either to God's revelation or to human beings' experience. The first view gravely distorts the reality of God that has made its appearance in Jesus. But the logical, and experiential, conclusion ought not to be the second mentality, which deprives human beings of their capacity to recognize themselves as sinners. We make this assertion not out of any merely formal loyalty to divine revelation, let alone in the spirit of some residual masochism inherent in Christian faith. We make this declaration with the same honesty with which we must reject the totally sinful view of life. And we make it, especially, because it is a good for human beings to know and recognize themselves in their entire truth, and an evil to ignore or repress that truth. We say it because it is a good thing to build on truth, and an evil thing to build on the lie. Further, it is a good thing to acknowledge our own sin, because this acknowledgment bestows on God's revelation a specific luminosity: Forgiveness recovers its dimension as good news for the human being, a dimension screened and hidden when those human beings fail to recognize themselves for what they are.

To be sure, these are not the times—nor is there any reason why they should be—for the believer to maintain an exaggerated focus on Luther's tortured question: how to find a benevolent God (not that we are implying that it is any easier today to respond to the secularized version of the question, which is how to find a benevolent human being); or for the believer to cry out in anguish with Paul: "My inner self agrees with the law of God, but I see in my body's members another law . . . this makes me the prisoner of the law of sin in my members" (Rom. 7:21-22). These do not seem to be the times for this kind of preoccupation. Still, were our concern totally to vanish, the hope and expectation of "finding benevolence" would go by the board as well. Nor would this be without detriment both to the human and to the *go-spel*, one of whose essential dimensions is the manifestation of benevolence.

What would seem to be the causes of the difficulty we experience in recognizing our personal sin?

We are rediscovering today that *sin*—which is an "ultimate negative," at least conceptually—*is not the only expression of history's negativity*, nor indeed the only thing set forth by Scripture in terms of ultimate negativity. Death, disease, the absurd, a world of injustice in everything everywhere, are also negative ultimacies, and we are coming to grasp them as such. Were it otherwise, we should be led, if not to attempt to conjure away the ultimate negativity of sin, at least to relativize it, and to replace a view of life as shot through with sin with the notion that the only really, decisively negative element in life is personal sin. There is support for the broader view in Scripture, as well: God is determined to foster liberation from all of these negative ultimacies, and not from personal sin alone. To put it in another way: Sin itself no longer confronts the human being as the only negativity; indeed, on the existential level, other negativities may afflict that being more. We can even add that, in Christian terms, persons are called on to turn their gaze upon, and to try to resolve, the negative ultimacy to which *others* are subjected, rather than be obsessed with their *own* sin—which, in the last analysis, would be a certain form of selfishness and would fail to reproduce—although in another context—the anthropological and faith-filled "eccentrism," let us call it, of Paul: "I could even wish to be separated from Christ for the sake of my brothers" (Rom. 9:3).

This difficulty is very much a reality in the world of today. In the First World, the absurdity of life could be seen as the greatest of the negativities, with the notion that, after all, personal sin can always be corrected. In the Third World, the tragedy of the concrete historical situation makes it more than understandable that the ultimate negativity should be seen precisely in that concrete historical situation—even when trying to see history with God's eyes—with personal sin relegated to another level of values, except where it bears on the former.

It likewise seems clear that *the advance of the sciences has had repercussions in terms of a diminished awareness of personal sin*. Psychology has a tendency to dilute guilt with complex factors of human behavior, and encourages a liberation from exaggerated guilt feelings that lead to neurosis. The social sciences lay the blame for structural objective sin precisely on structures, and this tends to reduce personal responsibility to anonymity.

Theology, as well, happily, has cooperated in this process of eliminating a view of God which would see in human beings only sin or its possibility, and a view of the human being which would practically define the latter as the apt subject or agent of sin. But, while this new, and general, theological view is sound, it must be acknowledged that some of the theologies that have proliferated in the aftermath of World War II, by centering sin within human interiority and defining it, in all of its concentration, in terms of human subjectivity, can, paradoxically, powerfully formulate what sin is, and yet undermine an awareness of sin by failing to indicate it in its

historical objectification—failing to show it as something visible and verifiable, and accordingly, something of which one can and should have an
awareness. Theologies more oriented in terms of subjectivity will be able
to define sin, rightly and radically, as a closing off to God—for example, in
terms of a failure to allow ourselves to be given life's meaning by God, or
to place our ultimate trust and hope in God, and so on. These unilaterally
existentialist, personal, or "of hope" theologies, then, can formulate what
sin is, but have difficulty in pointing to real, verifiable sins. They enable
human beings to know themselves transcendently as sinners, but make it
difficult for them to know themselves historically as such. This does not
occur when theology takes its orientation from objectivity and defines sin,
historically and verifiably, as that which puts persons to death (in all the
necessarily analogous senses of the concept).

Another root of the devaluation of an awareness of sin—and perhaps the
most serious, from a strictly theological viewpoint—is the perception that,
in terms of deliverance from sin, *sin is correlative to forgiveness.* But forgiveness, unless it be understood as a bare judicial act, is neither anthropologically nor theologically an achievement of the human being. Forgiveness is
gift and grace. And here an important circumstantial difficulty arises in the
First World and even—as an inherent risk, although not of necessity—in
the theologies of praxis.

Rightly, philosophical anthropology, along with the theological anthropology that bases itself on the gospel, insist on the praxic dimension of the
human being and believer when it comes to the building of the Reign of
God. That this insistence is legitimate and necessary, lest reality be abandoned to its misery in the name of God, is evident, although an emphasis
on it is always in order, and we shall return to the point below. The danger
is that an emphasis on the praxic dimension in the life of believers might
cause them to ignore the dimension of gratuity inherent in their existence.
We shall see, shortly, liberation theology's insistence upon, and endeavor
to combine, both dimensions, that of praxis and that of gratuity. But let us
dwell for a moment on the difficulty as it presents itself, especially in the
First World.

The First World gives the impression, structurally speaking, that it does
not know what to do with gratuity. Its theology, necessarily, will continue
to speak of gift and grace and to declare that everything has begun with
God gratuitously and will terminate in God gratuitously. Conceptually, the
matter of gratuity cannot be ignored. But it is in no wise an easy matter to
integrate it with historical reality. Circumstantial mediations are lacking to
this purpose, while contrary mediations abound. The First World deems
that it has come to be what it is by its own efforts, and that this is of itself a
sign that its achievement is good. But the concept is lacking that, in order
truly to be, one must also be open to receive. In its relationship with other
worlds, the most flagrant thing about the First World is, of course, the
oppression to which it subjects them. But even in what might be conceived

as its "positive" relationship with these "other worlds," it regards its only role as to give, not receive. Thus, unilaterally, it will give—and we prescind from whatever interests it might be indulging in its "giving"—its civilization, its technology, its capital, indeed its theology. But the very notion of a gift to be received, without expectation or merit is circumstantially foreign to the First World of today. That world is open to receipt in the sphere of "having" (raw materials, foreign tourism, and so on), but not in the sphere of being—the sphere that precisely humanizes the human being. That circumstantial absence of an acknowledgment of the gift and grace whereby persons and peoples come to be, likewise renders the acceptance of forgiveness very difficult. Thereby—paradoxically, but very logically, from a Christian viewpoint—a recognition of one's own sin becomes very difficult, as well.

A final difficulty is that of *accepting the analogy of sin,* and hence of a variety of categories of sinner. The New Testament and liberation theology insist that the *analogatum princeps,* the prime analogate, of sin consists in murder: murdering the Son of God and continuing to murder the sons and daughters of God in history. In terms of this definition of sin, the most basic division among human beings—and not only from history's viewpoint, but from God's—is between the killers and the killed. In view of the gravity of the sin of murder, any sins on the part of the murdered must be relativized.

The Synoptics themselves distinguish three kinds of human beings, and Jesus makes specific demands on each kind. First, there are the *oppressors,* those sinners par excellence whom Jesus denounces and exposes for what they are, calling for their radical conversion (which consists in ceasing to be oppressors). Then come the *poor and oppressed,* whom Jesus defends, calling upon them to submit to a *metánoia* that, at bottom, consists in a radical change of their view of a God who is against them to a God who is for them, although it also adds the requirement that they overcome their "regional" sins, the fruit of human weakness. Finally, there are *Jesus' followers,* whom he calls to commit themselves to mission.

As for a consciousness of sin, in terms of these categories, it is as plain today as it was in Jesus' day that the oppressor-sinner will attain to that consciousness only with the greatest difficulty. Let us recall that, in the Synoptic presentation, Jesus achieved success only in the case of Zacchaeus.[2] When it comes to the poor, it is they, paradoxically, who maintain the keenest awareness of their own sin, whether this be due to their traditional piety or to their new liberation piety. With Jesus' followers, it is obvious that, in their self-awareness—with the humility appropriate to each case—they see themselves as moving in the right direction, battling with the fundamental sin, the one that kills.

What we wish to stress here is that, in the presence of the greater sin of the oppressor, with the suffering it causes in its victims, and in the midst of a struggle against it, an understandable tendency arises to relativize one's own sins. Although even the poor and the most honest of Jesus' followers recognize and acknowledge their own sinfulness, the terrible disproportion between the sin they suffer at the hands of the oppressors and their own sins can incline them simply to disregard the latter.

Recognition of Personal Sin through Forgiveness

The difficulties of recognizing one's own sin are varied and abundant. Some of these difficulties are rooted in things themselves sinful, while others have their root in things that are good. But whatever the difficulties, it is no good thing for human beings to fail to recognize themselves in their truth, which includes the truth that they are sinners. Therefore some kind of *mystagogía*, or initiation to mystery, is needful, that human beings may be introduced, not into the mystery of God as yet, but into that of their own littleness and darkness. The point, of course, is not to encourage the return of a "theology of blackmail" or to champion the "killjoy God" Bonhoeffer denounced. Nor are we concerned to universalize, without hierarchical differentiation, the sinful condition of all persons, which would lead to a neglect or softening of the tragic wickedess of the *analogatum princeps:* the murder of human beings.

Delivered from the old *mystagogíai* that proceeded from an "utterly sinful" view of human beings (reinforced with the threat of eternal damnation), we have to wonder what the fundamental *mystagogía* would be from a strictly theological standpoint (be its ulterior pastoral concretions what they may). This could seem an easy task. It is not, however, not even methodologically. Beyond a doubt, from a Christian standpoint we shall have to have recourse to God's revelation if we are to find our "mystagogy," but we must do so with an openness to allowing God to tell us what sin is and how it is possible to recognize it, rather than regarding these things as already known. We make this statement because "sin" is not a sheerly regional reality—in principle, something already adequately known. Rather, it is a "limit reality," which, of course, is objectified in the concrete. Formal theological definitions of sin call it "offense to God" or "transgression of the will of God." But then the element of God in the definition necessarily invests the very reality of sin with a certain "indefinition," inasmuch as the indefinable, transcendent God now comes into the definition of sin, and concretely, precisely in relation to sin.

We do not mean to suggest, of course, that we know nothing of sin and its gravity antecedently to God's revelation. What we mean is that, antecedently to God's revelation, we possess no definitive concepts of sin, however important and necessary the ones that we do possess may be. The situation is analogous to our concepts of humanity and divinity in Christology. We have antecedent concepts of them both, but what they truly are is only knowable in terms of Jesus' manifestation of true humanity and true divinity, which concretizes and modifies our antecedent concepts of the same. And so it is, analogously, with sin: In order to know what sin is and what to do about it, one must be actively open to what God says of sin and does about sin. One must be open to the surprise that this may entail.

Let us see, then, very succinctly, what God's revelation in Jesus says of personal sin. On the one hand, it says that human beings are capable of sin—able to have a heart of stone and of oppressing, even killing, others, so much so that they actually do put to death the Son of God. It says that we have the innate tendency to hide from ourselves and repress our truth as sinners (what Paul universalizes in Rom. 1:18ff.), to the point of being able actually to think that we give worship to God when we send our siblings to their death (see John 16:2). It says that we produce human traditions in order to justify the voiding of God's will, or in order to act in a manner contrary to the divine will, although we may spuriously think we are acting in God's name (see Mark 7:1-13). God's revelation, then, is anything but naive when it comes to human sinfulness.

On the other hand, that revelation asserts that sin as human beings' radical failure is not their ultimate potential—that for the sinner, too, there is good news, a future open to possibilities—and it expresses this now in terms of salvation, now in terms of forgiveness or redemption.

Both things are clear, then, and pertain to the core of Christian reality, which thereby takes its distance from naïveté and despair alike. But what we wish to emphasize now is God's own *mystagogía*, which is calculated to communicate both truths. We mean the concrete manner in which, through Jesus, God exposes sin and proclaims salvation. In the form of a thesis, we might assert that, in God's revelation in Jesus, the immediate word is the one pronounced upon salvation to the effect that (as we have shown a number of times, citing Rahner) God has shattered forever the symmetry between being potential salvation and potential damnation. What is properly God's is salvation. Therefore the unmasking of the truth of our sin is performed with a view to salvation and, furthermore, precisely in terms of salvation. What sin is, understood from a concrete point of departure in Jesus, is understood in terms of forgiveness, rather than the other way around. This by no means deprives the reality of sin of its seriousness. But the divine *mystagogía* into a recognition of sin in all its seriousness operates from a point of departure in forgiveness. Nor let it be thought that this is somehow an easier, softer way. Human beings may well prefer to cling to that which is of themselves, be it their sin, rather than be delivered from it, if the price to be paid is to be forgiven gratuitously.

This, very briefly, is what appears in concrete form in Jesus' dealings with sinners. And we have previously alluded to the fact that Jesus stands in a different posture before the sinful oppressor and the sinful oppressed, demanding conversion and reparation of the former and faith in God's goodness of the latter. We may also add that Jesus' *mystagogía* to a recognition of one's own sin takes various forms. He uses a sapiential *mystagogía* (wealth serves no purpose at the moment of death), and he uses an eschatological *mystagogía* (it is better to enter the Reign of God minus a hand or an eye than to go to eternal fire). But his basic *mystagogía* is strictly theo-log-ical: God is essentially inclined to forgiveness. God goes in search of the sinner, and it is in finding that sinner that God's joy consists. This holds true, in principle, for every kind of sinner, as we observe in Jesus' behavior with various persons and in his parables. What remains to be analyzed is the meaning of forgiveness in Jesus' dealings with sinners.

In two Synoptic scenes (Mark 2:5, Luke 7:48), Jesus is seen forgiving sins. Exegetes, it is true, do not recognize these forgiveness accounts as historical. But Jesus' welcome for sinners is historical. This is a historical finding. Furthermore, this finding—in our opinion—helps us to a better under-standing of the forgiveness granted by Jesus and God's *mystagogía* of the sinner. After all, the scenes in which Jesus forgives sins could shift the accent to Jesus' power to *pardon* sins, thereby suggesting that the forgiveness Jesus grants is a forgiveness of *pardon or absolution.* That aspect of Jesus' forgive-ness is important enough in itself, but it does not introduce us into the heart of the matter, since pardon could present Jesus (and God) ultimately as a judge—a just and understanding judge, but still a judge—from start to finish. In this conception, sinner and judged, pardoned and pardoner, would remain in their mutual alienation. However consoling it might be to find a judge who pardons, the symmetry in God that we have rejected would abide, and we should very likely abide in our "antecedent" concep-tualization of sin and forgiveness.

But in the gospels, rather than pardon—rather than a mere quasi-jurid-ical absolution—it is Jesus' *welcome and acceptance* of the sinner that stands forth. The difference is crucial. Jesus' acceptance includes the pardon of absolution, but it goes much further. The acceptance that is Jesus' (and God's) forgiveness is their primordial love in going forth to seek the sinner instead of waiting like a judge, even the most just and benevolent of judges, for the sinner to come to them; in showing mercy rather than justice; in offering dignity and a future to one who had seemed so helpless and abandoned.

What this means for our purpose of offering a *mystagogía* into the mystery of sin is that, in the dialectic of sin and forgiveness, the prior theological pole is forgiveness. To be sure, an antecedent notion of sin can and should of itself say a great deal about forgiveness. But the New Testament has a logic of its own. In Rahner's words, "Only the forgiven know themselves sinners." It is the acceptance that is forgiveness that adequately and wholly discloses the fact that I am a sinner and gives me the strength to acknowledge myself as such and change radically. The conversion demanded so radically by Jesus is preceded by the offer of God's love. It is not conversion that requires God to accept the sinner; rather, just contrariwise, it is God's acceptance that makes conversion possible. Nor let it be thought that this trivializes human beings' sinful reality. Like the religious leaders of Jesus' time, human beings would rather cling to what is theirs, though it be sin, than be delivered from it if liberation is granted them freely and not ascribed to them as a deed of their own.

This, which appears in concrete, historicized form in the gospels, is also the ultimate meaning of the most sophisticated propositions of the other New Testament writings. The theologies that present the cross of Jesus as forgiveness of sin may seem very lofty, and they have been highly esteemed by later theology because they seem to be trying to explain what sin is, what forgiveness is, and the conditions under which the latter can be granted. Jesus' cross could be understood as an expiatory sacrifice, a vicarious death for the sins of humankind. But as explanations, these propositions fail to go to the heart of the matter. They can be deceptive and entail the risk of haling God into the court of human reason—the danger that God be told how one is to forgive.[3]

The only "explanation" for forgiveness that the New Testament gives, when we come right down to it, is God's love. The surrender on the cross is the expression of that love. If God has loved human beings to this extreme, then God's last word must not be damnation: It must be salvation. At bottom, the assertions of the other New Testament writings do no more than express in the language of transcendence what the gospels say with such consummate simplicity and clarity: God has come to this world of sinners to save, and not to condemn. And thus, God comes to this world on the divine initiative alone, not in response to any action on human beings' part. This free approach to our world is what makes God's love credible, as well as—and this is what the transcendent propositions of the New Testament say—what places that love "at the mercy" of human beings.

On Jesus' cross, seen in the transcendency of the event, are revealed at one and the same time the consummate gravity of sin—which can actually murder—and God's consummate love, which has found no better avenue to its manifestation than through maintaining God's loving nearness to the very end, to the very death of the Son. Jesus of Nazareth's "acceptance" of persons appears here as an absolute "nearness" to human beings to the very last. This God absolutely near, who makes not even the cross a pretext for withdrawing, is the God who can pronounce an irrevocable word of love for human beings. And when men and women truly hear that word of love, they no longer need anyone to speak to them of any pardon, any absolution, on God's part. They know that they are loved by God unconditionally. They know that they are accepted by God. They know that they have drawn near to God in God's absolute nearness to them.

In sum, revelation says that human beings are sinners and that sin is supremely grave; but it also says that the opportunity for forgiveness is available. Indeed, revelation tells us that to be forgiving is not merely one characteristic of God among others, but the very expression of the divine essence. And it says that, through forgiveness, human beings can come to a knowledge of themselves as they really are: as sinful, and as saved.

Forgiveness as Liberation

What we have said so far shows not only that forgiveness is central to the New Testament but that, in its quality as acceptance and not mere absolution, forgiveness is formally liberating.

The *forgiveness of acceptance* bestowed by Jesus in the gospel accounts is something *not merely beneficial, but liberating*. An important expression of liberation appears in those accounts. The context is the contempt and social ostracism (at times deserved, one could think, but often hypocritical) to which sinners are subjected. The fact that Jesus addresses sinners, receives them into his company, and takes his meals with them is a forthright expression of victory over social segregation. But especially, Jesus restores sinners their lost dignity. Here is how Joachim Jeremias describes what must have happened to Zacchaeus. "That Jesus should wish to be a guest in his home—in the home of this despised person shunned by all—is inconceivable to him. Jesus restores to him his lost honor by entering his house as a guest and breaking bread with him."[4] The forgiveness that is acceptance opens up a new, positive future to sinners. It opens social space to them in the sight of others, and inner space to them in their own sight. Truly Jesus can tell them, "Go in peace."

There is another element in the liberation bestowed by the forgiveness that is acceptance, one that has been observed by exegetes with raised eyebrows. In a number of the incidents of healing, and in one of the scenes of forgiveness, Jesus pronounces these surprising final words: "Your faith has healed you" or "has been your salvation." Jesus is saying that *acceptance of the sinner has sparked an authentic interior renewal* in the person. He is saying that forgiveness is more than something merely good but external to the person. In the declaration "Your faith has been your salvation" appears the salvific power of the God who wishes to effect, and is able to effect, a person's real, interior transformation. And there appears what we may call God's consummate delicacy, which says "You can." Doubtless that delicacy implies that God has *forgiven* the sinner; but in *accepting* sinners, what is of interest to God is not winning some kind of triumph but encouraging sinners to change and convincing them that they *can* change—that their potential is greater than they had thought.

Conversion, then, is not a Pelagian affair, but an enabled one. More than anything else, however, it is real. It is really the human being who is now changed, justified, and liberated.

The conversion that is acceptance delivers human beings from their sin, surely. But more than that, it *delivers them from themselves*—from what they regard as being their truth. As we have said, it is no easy thing to come to the recognition of one's own sin. It is not easy because sin has the innate tendency to hide from itself and even to try to pass for the contrary. Thus, in John, the sinner is a "liar." And it is not easy because a forthright acknowledgment of one's own sin—without the possibility of forgiveness—would logically lead a human being to paralysis, anguish, and despair. However, to know oneself a sinner in the act of knowing oneself to be forgiven facilitates the acknowledgment of one's own sin, since now the latter is perceived no longer only in its dark, enslaving side, but under the light of forgiveness, as well. This is what can shatter human hubris, which had rather retain its own than retract itself, rather cling to the negative than enfeeble the keenness with which persons cleave to themselves (the hubris overcome by Christ in the transcendent declaration of Phil. 2:6). Forgiveness, then, is liberation from the lie about oneself, with which human beings seek to oppress their own truth.[5]

Finally, forgiveness liberates the human being *to recognize God as God actually is*—to recognize God in the essential divine dimension of gratuity and partiality. Standing in correlation to our tendency to wish to appear just before God is the view of God shown in justice. But to accept forgiveness is also the way in which one asserts God's authentic reality as gratuitious and partial. What theology emphasizes with respect to the relationship between God and the poor must also be emphasized with respect to the relationship between God and the sinner. Both relationships introduce us to the authentic reality of God.

Not to accept efficaciously the possibility of God's forgiving acceptance—to ignore it or regard it as of lesser importance—would mean failing to recognize God. Not to accept, as something central in God, the ultimate joy of God's acceptance of the sinner, would be tantamount to not believing in God. Conversely, allowing oneself to be accepted forgivingly by God is believing in God and making it plain in what God one believes.

The forgiveness that is acceptance, therefore, is something good, and also something formally liberative. Forgiveness is a benefit because it is liberation from the lie with which we seek to conceal forgiveness from ourselves and exclude it from our view of God.

Liberation from Personal Sin and Eradication of Historical Sin

All that we have said is a central truth in God's revelation and, furthermore, in a surprising way. The difficult recognition of one's own sin, and the difficult actualization of conversion proceed, in the last analysis, from forgiveness in its quality as light shed upon one's own truth and strength for one's own conversion. Since forgiveness is truth, it cannot be opaque to itself, nor can it establish itself through a logic proceeding from any source beyond the fact itself. Simply, God is thus.

Theologically, however, we are responsible for reflecting on the manner in which this central truth is integrated into theological reflection and, in the present instance, into the reflection of the theology of liberation. More concretely, what does this truth say to a theology that takes as its specific finality the eradication of structural historical sin? What relationship obtains between allowing oneself to be personally forgiven by God and the practice of the Reign conducted for the purpose of uprooting the anti-

Reign? Let us state from the outset that there is no question here of manipulating either truth in favor of another. Our concern is to assert both truths as central, in terms of the premise—a faith premise, to be sure, but a premise maintained on the basis of reflection, as well—that both truths converge in the truth of total liberation, that of the interior human being and that of human history, to comprise what is called integral liberation.

If we ask ourselves how personal liberation from sin supports historical liberation, a number of critical questions may arise. It can be alleged that what we have been saying, while true enough, is too utopian (not even Jesus, we shall hear, enjoyed a great deal of success in this area) and excessively individualistic; historically, it can actually foster an escapist attitude. And we basically agree. We grant that our proposition entails its danger. We admit that no truth, however central or "key," must be elevated to the status of sole truth. This would be just another manifestation of human greed. But we also believe that the plural truths in which the single truth of God is manifested, converge. We hold, a priori, that a positive, mutually complementary relation must obtain between personal forgiveness and the eradication of concrete, historical sin. A posteriori, this relationship will be observable in the light of concrete, historical reality.

A priori, we must assert that the logic of revelation forbids us to make anything of our "own" as central and sole, even something as important as our own forgiveness and salvation. Not even God makes anything of "God's own" the central thing. The divine self-revelation is that of a God-for-others, and more specifically, a God-for-the-weak. Hence the logic—the logic of reality, rather than the logic of sheer concept—that one forgiven, a person who has allowed herself to be accepted by God, would not make that acceptance the core thing, the ultimate fact. Rather, a person accepted by God would become accepting of others: The forgiven person would become a forgiving one.

This is the logic of the first letter of John: Being loved by God issues in love for one's siblings. It is the logic of the theology of liberation, as Gustavo Gutiérrez has enunciated it: "Loved in order to love," and "liberated in order to liberate."[6]

Let us now formulate this in terms of concrete history. We must inquire not only into the *what*, but also into the *for what* of our own forgiveness, our own liberation. Were there to be no *for what* that transcends the forgiven individual as such, personal forgiveness would remain shut up in that forgiven individual, and this would run counter to the ultimate logic of God's revelation. If the forgiven person were to focus exclusively on this personal forgiveness, he would be transformed once more into the selfish human being. He would become—in Christian logic—the ingrate, and we should even have to doubt whether this person had actually permitted his forgiving acceptance by God.

That *from* which forgiveness delivers the forgiven one has now been sent forth. *For* what it delivers him or her is next in order of analysis. Forgiveness frees a person, in the first place—in virtue of the concrete, historical nature of forgiveness—*to* accept and forgive others. But more generally, it sets a person free to engage in a positive effectuation of God's love with regard to the world, of which this created person has had a personal experience. One of the essential elements of the divine love is that it sees the world as it really is, in its truth and not in its lie, and that it effectuates, in the truth of that world, the divine will. Liberation from personal sin, experienced as letting oneself be accepted by God's love, thereupon leads one to render present in the world the love of God that has now been experienced. The only essential further specification is that, on the level of the concrete, historical world, to *forgive* the sin of the world is to *uproot* it.

Concretely, one must ask precisely what personal forgiveness contributes to the eradication of historical sin. Substantially, it contributes the possibility of an enhanced liberation praxis, one superior in its direction, its intensity, and its values—all of which can have an influence on persons and groups committed to liberation.

As we have seen, the forgiven one is delivered from her own lie. But according to John himself, while "lying" is the formal anthropological assertion with regard to the sinner's sin, its material content is "murderous." The words are harsh (and must be understood analogically). But this must not detract from the importance of the basic intuition, which is the following. The sinful human being simultaneously wreaks a double vitiation: of the *verum,* and of the *bonum*—a twin subjugation of truth through the lie and goodness through murder—a double rejection of his creatureliness, so as to be (falsely) more than what this being is before God (Adam's original sin), and so as to be (wickedly) more than his sibling (Cain's original sin). It will be open to theological discussion which of these two poles enjoys anthropological priority, but in any case we must accept their dialectic, the reciprocation that prevails between the "lying" and the "murderous," between defending oneself from God and offending one's sister or brother.

In other words, sin is "lie," but it has a content: "to kill." In forgiveness, human beings become *knowers of their lie and of the content of their lie.* They become aware of the gravity of the one as of the other. And while this may appear minimal, it is not, for now one's eyes are opened to know what one is and what one does—the supreme wickedness of one's hubris and its historical product. And as these "knowledges" are offered in forgiveness, it becomes possible to attain to them and to maintain them in all their raw realism, and thus to live in truth. We live in a world that murders, and in this is the most radical truth of that world.

Traditional theology and piety have always maintained that, in order to know what sin is, one must gaze on Christ crucified. Christ is the forgiving one, but he is also the offended one, and in a precise way: It is he who has been put to death. Today, as well, those who forgive open their eyes and know just what it is that is being forgiven: responsibility in the continued crucifixion of entire peoples.

To be able to see with new eyes the genuine reality of the world, to be able to stare it in the face despite its tragedy, to be able to perceive what it is to which God says a radical "no," is (logically) the first fruit of allowing oneself really to be pardoned by God.

The freely forgiven one is the grateful one. And it is *the gratitude of knowing oneself to be accepted* that *moves a person to a de-centering from self,* to generous action, to a life of eager striving that the love of God that has been experienced may be a historical reality in this world. The logic of the forgiven and grateful one—with all due caution when it comes to the enthusiasm of new converts—is what opens the heart to a limitless salvific, historical practice. The prototype here is Paul, who feels so loved by Christ that he makes of his life a total, absorbing apostolate in behalf of others, to the very point of neglecting his own salvation in order to concentrate on the salvation of his brothers and sisters. The phenomenon recurs in Ignatius Loyola, who is so overcome with gratitude for being accepted and forgiven that he can only ask himself, as he stands before Christ crucified, "What am I doing for Christ?" and "What ought I to do for Christ?" These questions are the most complete, the most adequate, concrete historical expression of gratitude. Here is not only a grateful responding, but a generous *corresponding* to the reality of the one who has accepted me and forgiven me.

Hence it is that the experience of the love of God moves a person to render that same love real in the world, and to do so with limitless generosity: in the language of Ignatius, to act for the *greater* glory of God.

These experiences of Paul and Ignatius have their historical translation today. Forgiven persons, who have had their eyes opened to the death that reigns in today's world and to their own shared responsibility in the same (analogously, depending on the case), are impelled to produce their gratitude, and this they do. Like Ignatius before Jesus crucified, they ask themselves before a crucified people, "What have I done to crucify them? What am I doing to take them down from their cross? What ought I to do that a crucified people may rise again?"[7]

Forgiveness, then, does not remain shut up within the forgiven one but overflows in gratitude in the historical practice of mercy (with all conjunctural and structural mediations of objective transformation, of accompaniment in suffering and hope, and so on).

The contribution to liberation made by the forgiven is the memory of their own sinfulness, the real, and still possible, sinfulness of those who steer their lives in the direction of a liberation practice. This recollection, once more, is not masochistic. It is a salvific recollection, just as is the "perilous memory of Jesus." Demanding though it be, it pulls us back to the truth, back to honesty with the real. The recall of one's own sin engenders a fruitful humility. It makes it easier to recognize (and remedy) the limitations to which liberation processes are subject, however necessary, good, and just these processes may be. It makes it easier to perceive (and remedy) the dogmatisms, chauvinisms, and reductionisms that constitute the inevitable by-product of these processes.[8] In a word, the memory of one's own sin—a memory that, being honest and not neurotic, has only been made possible by forgiveness—helps minimize the hubris that comes into the practice of liberation. To "wage a revolution as one forgiven," as González Faus puts it so well,[9] is a boon for the practice of liberation. It renders that practice more humane and more humanizing; it tends to preserve it from the dangers that lurk along its path; and it even makes it, in the long run, more effective.

The Poor and Oppressed: Historical Mediation of a Forgiveness That Is Acceptance

An emphasis on the fact that sin is rediscovered precisely in the light of a forgiveness that is acceptance obviously calls for a reflection on the concrete, historical mediation of that forgiveness. Otherwise, everything we have said up until now will have been said in vain. From the standpoint of liberation, it calls for a reflection on whether any role in that forgiveness falls to the poor and oppressed, and what that role would be. That is, we must reflect on whether, as the offended, they are "forgivers," and whether, as forgivers, they reveal the magnitude of the offense that afflicts them.

What we wish to state here is that, throughout the history of the church and theology, many historical mediations of *pardon,* of the forgiveness that is absolution, have been developed, but the question of the mediation of the forgiveness that is acceptance remains open, especially in the case of those sins (as also structural sin in itself) that oppress and deal death on all sides. And our thesis (obvious in its formulation, but by no means obvious in its corresponding practice) is that those who offer the forgiveness that is acceptance today—structurally, and in concrete expressions—are the poor and oppressed of this world.

The elevation of the poor of this world to the status of mediators of the forgiveness that is acceptance has nothing of the rhetorical about it; nor, in principle, ought it to cause any astonishment. In the reflection maintained by biblical theology, and in current systematic theology, the presentation of the poor—including their collective presentation—is a constant in crucial aspects of revelation: God's self-manifestation, immediate and with partiality, to an oppressed people; a salvation emerging from this same people, as it takes on the sin of the world; the basic ethical requirement of serving the poor; the right of the poor to demand conversion; and, in the beautiful, unprecedented words of Puebla, their evangelizing capacity. To these familiar core affirmations, John Paul II has added another very important one: On the day of judgment, the peoples of the Third World will judge the peoples of the First World. To put this in theological language: The Son of Man, still present today in the poor, will preside at the last judgment through the poor.

This actual *theologoumenon* of John Paul II can and must be completed in the following manner. It is the poor of this world who take on the sin of the world. It is they, therefore, who are the genuinely offended, and the plaintiffs. But further, it is they who *already* judge the world and can grant their oppressors the forgiveness that is acceptance. The truth of this last proposition does not rest on anything subject to speculation. It must be verified through observation. What we are concerned to add, however, is that, unless there were to be such a thing as the forgiveness that is acceptance on the part of the poor, in vain should we seek forgiveness, as we have described it, in this world. We might continue to receive notice of God's attitude of a forgiveness that is acceptance, but we should be lacking a historical mediation for it in the case of the gravest of sins, and not merely some sin of lesser import.

Is this *theologoumenon*—that it is the poor who offer us the forgiveness that is acceptance—a sound one? That will have to be decided in concrete, historical reality, and it is the latter that must be examined. In our opinion, there is sufficient historical experience to verify the truth of the *theologoumenon*, although we do not know whether the forgiveness in question, the forgiveness that is acceptance, is offered everywhere in the same way. In the Central American experience, there are examples of this kind of forgiveness that we should like to present in the following phenomenology.

As you approach a peasant refuge, a village devastated by war, or any community that has suffered persecution and martyrdom, one of the things that will strike you most is the difference between what you might logically expect in your encounter with the poor and oppressed here, and what actually occurs. Logically—in the logic of natural reason and the logic of an absolving pardon—it might happen that the poor would reject a visit from persons belonging structurally to the world of their oppressors, or that they would receive them with recriminations for having arrived so late (years late, centuries late) and for coming so casually (without having made a total decision of commitment to themselves, the victims). It might happen that they would receive them with a purely pragmatic attitude, hoping to reap whatever advantages they can by way of their services; or with an attitude of the pardon of absolution, in terms of the rule of condignity according to which one's sins are remitted in proportion to restitution offered. But this is not what usually occurs. Elements of it can be present, but by and large, what happens is just the opposite. The poor in these localities fling wide the doors of their homes and their hearts to receive these strangers. They tell them of their afflictions, give them of the little that they do have, and show them how glad they are that they have come. They ask them not to forget them and to tell of what they have seen when they have returned to the places whence they have come.

What has happened in this encounter between persons who belong, structurally, to different worlds, the oppressed world and the oppressive? The answer is plain to see. The poor have welcomed those who belong to the world of their oppressors, and—without saying so, indeed without explicitly thinking of it in these terms—have imparted to them the forgiveness that is acceptance. In this encounter, as so many have acknowledged who have been a part of it, the visitors have had the experience described above: They know themselves simultaneously sinners and forgiven. They know themselves in their truth and in their possibility, and they reorientate their lives in terms of "what I ought to do."

Our phenomenology may seem idealized. But it is not. No mellifluous lyricism marks the experience described. Utter gravity and seriousness prevail between welcomed and welcomers. We might have been thought not to be describing sheer reality, but to be making some unjustifiable extrapolation from what might be called "pious examples" of forgiving and forgiven behavior. Such is not the case. Be the magnitude of the particular situation what it may, this experience occurs almost *ex opere operato*, that is, on the basis of the structure of reality, and not of pure intentionality. The experience described is no mere example. It is a *typos*, an intrinsically repeatable experience. It may seem paradoxical and scandalous to say so, and this it is—but no more than other propositions that theologians repeat: that God is in the poor, that the poor are the vessels or vehicles of salvation, and so on.

The poor, then, are the concrete, historical mediation of God's forgiveness that is acceptance. And if it is true that, on the basis of forgiveness, the recognition and acknowledgment of one's own sin becomes possible, and strength is gained for a practice contrary to sin, then what this says is that today, as well, we have the possibility of recognizing the sin of the world and deciding on its eradication. Just as in the case of personal sin, however, we must add that here, too, the recognition and acknowledgment of the sin of the world is not easy to come by. The world of oppressors does not wish to let itself be forgiven, and therefore it is consummately difficult for it to know itself in its truth.

This basic truth, that the forgiveness that is acceptance proceeds from the poor of this world, also serves to solve—or at least shed light on—a strictly ecclesial problem that is rarely broached. Who forgives the sin of the church as such? We well know that, ever since it came into being, the church has acknowledged the presence of individual sinners in its midst and has designated various forms of pardon to be bestowed upon the individual sinner. But with the rediscovery of the sin of the church-as-such, in the process of taking seriously that the church is structurally holy and structurally sinful (the "chaste whore")—as Rahner shows it to be on the basis of Vatican II[10]—the question arises of what to do about this structural sin of the church, since for purposes of examination and repentance of the same, satisfaction for it and absolution from it, the Sacrament of Penance or Reconciliation does not suffice.

This question is no rhetorical one. Were the church to fail to address it, it would be admitting that it does not take seriously the structural dimension of sin, and the timid words it occasionally pronounces regarding its own sin would only be routine and vain. That is, it is vain to repeat that there is sin in the church without indicating the offended who, because they are the offended, would be the potential forgivers.

In Latin America, it must be said that the church as a whole has made considerable advances over its previous secular activity, which has been performed objectively against the poor. But the failure to make a consistent radical option for the poor continues to be the church's most serious sin, and the eradication of that sin its heaviest responsibility. But in order to do both, it must be prepared to let itself be forgiven by the poor.[11] Puebla says, beautifully, that the poor evangelize the church: They issue it a challenge, summoning it to conversion, and they bring to it the concrete realization of important evangelical values. What we propose here is that the church take one more step: that it regard the poor as forgivers, as persons and peoples who proclaim to it the gospel of the forgiveness that is acceptance. This step is both a crucial one and a very difficult one. It is crucial because, unless it is taken, unless the poor are regarded as the forgivers, neither will they be actually looked upon as the offended, and the church will continue to conceal from itself its own sin. The step will be difficult because it requires a victory over the hubris of the church, a hubris as real as that of other social groups and as real as that of the individual. Here is a hubris that will make it impossible to stand before God as God really is: as accepter and forgiver. Historically, church triumphalism will endure: No one need teach the church anything really important, and no one need forgive the church anything really grave.

But if, instead, the church not only forgives, but allows itself to be forgiven by those whom it has offended, then it will be able to acknowledge itself as it is, not only in its chaste dimension, but in its sinful dimension, as well. It will be capable of a radical "eccentrism" toward the "other," toward the poor. It will be able to stand before the true God, God the demanding and merciful, letting God be God, without its hubris dictating to it in advance the manner of God's self-manifestation. Amid hard reality, it will have the joyful experience of knowing that it is accepted. And it will have the gladsome experience of living in communion with God and the poor of this world.

Conclusion

In Latin America, the *mysterium iniquitatis* reigns, and it is amid that reality that the *mysterium salutis* must be proclaimed. There is sin in a thousand forms—as hubris and as oppression, as lying, and as murder. And in that reality the go-spel must be proclaimed that victory over sin is possible, and its eradication absolutely necessary. What we have sought to say in these pages is that sin, in all its forms, is an evil, is that which puts to death the spirit and flesh of human beings. Besides being an evil, sin is also enslaving, and therefore its defeat is formally liberation. Among all the various *mystagogíai* for the recognition of the reality of sin and the motivation for its defeat, there is one that must not be lacking, inasmuch as it is central to God's revelation: the readiness to be accepted and forgiven.

This last is more readily grasped in the case of personal sin and forgiveness, but it must be introduced as one of the structural elements in the the historical eradication of the sin of the world. This task demands other elements, obviously—for example, practices of liberation. In order to motivate oppressors to cease to be such, all persuasive and coercive means must be employed, with an appeal to political conveniences and the warning that the situation of the Third World can lead to the disaster of all the Worlds. But as a specifically Christian contribution to liberation, the opportunity of forgiveness must be proposed, as well—the forgiveness that God continues to exercise through the oppressed of this world. Historically, it might be thought that such an effort will not meet with a great deal of success. But like any utopian principle, it can "principiate"—be the principle of, initiate—positive realities: a recognition of the sin of the world, and a readiness to take the crucified down from their cross.[12]

—Translated by Robert R. Barr

PART THREE

7

Toward a Determination of the Nature of Priesthood

Service to God's Salvific Approach to Human Beings

Problems of the Nature of Priesthood, and the Manner in Which Theology Ought to Address Them

There is a priesthood in the church, common, and ministerial. This priesthood subsists in concrete realizations, and there is a doctrine concerning it. A great deal has changed since Vatican II and Medellín, and the changes are variously judged as positive or negative. Priestly practice itself, honestly discerned, sheds light from within on the goodness of what is new here, as well as its potential dangers. But we believe that, besides, a theoretical explanation of the reality of the priesthood is necessary, since there remain a series of problems in its regard.

If we focus on what has occurred in Latin America since Vatican II and Medellín, reality itself stirs powerful questions concerning the priesthood, be what it may the manner of their solution in practice. With regard to the ministerial priesthood, there can be no doubt that the priest faces hard questions, and that these questions go to the very heart of his person.

In the first place, what does it mean to be a priest in a world of misery and injustice, of hope, and of movements of liberation? How can the peaceful priestly existence of yesterday be integrated into a world convulsed? How can the old priestly functions be creatively translated so as to be relevant and credible in this new reality?

In the second place, what can it mean, within the church, to "direct" a community, to have "responsibility" for it, when the laity (encouraged, in principle, by the church) are gaining an awareness of their place and mission within the church and when—an even more recent phenomenon—priests repeatedly experience that they not only give, but receive, that they

Originally published in *Revista Latinoamericana de Teología* (1984): 47-81 not only teach, but are taught, that they not only encourage and inspire, but are encouraged and inspired by their very communities, and this on the deepest levels of Christian faith, hope, and love? While the formal need of a ministry of intra-church direction and leadership abides, the content of that ministry is changing very substantially.

In the third place, what are the consequences of sharing in the priesthood of the church in the ministerial form of that priesthood, under the direction of the hierarchy? After all, ministerial priests are seen more in terms of their relationship to the episcopate than in their relationship to the priesthood of the faithful—which doubtless has its advantages when it comes to their apostolic effectiveness, but which can also raise questions for them, including questions of conscience, when the hierarchy is seen not as salvific but as oppressive, just as they experience the joy of sharing in hierarchical power when the latter is exercised in the service of the poor.

Finally, what is the meaning of priestly spirituality when today—in addition to its traditional demands, which still apply—it must reconcile things as disparate as the hierarchical element in the church and the church of the people at the base, the religious and the secular, personal work and work integrated into an entire theoretical and practical network of pastoral activity?

Along with these problems, many other practical ones beset the ministerial priest and his office or status. Among them: how to determine and prioritize priestly functions; which are "strictly" priestly and which are convergent and/or accompanying; where the priest stands in relation to the world, politics, and revolutions; what the priest may do and what he may not; how to maintain a dialogue with the communities and with the hierarchy; when the point is reached at which a prophetical denunciation within the church becomes legitimate for a priest, seeing that he is also a representative of the institutional church as such. To cite a matter of a different order, what about the problems involved in the training of future priests in the seminaries? This is currently a most serious problem. Who will determine the form and content of that training? What share will priests and faithful have in its shaping, evaluation, and so on? All of these problems can be expedited in administrative terms, but that is no guarantee that they have been fittingly solved.

As for the common priesthood of the faithful, it must be acknowledged that lay participation has grown in the church. At the same time, it remains unclear what the "priestly" element of lay participation might be. The laity have been given more pastoral responsibility and a greater share in the liturgy, but little progress has been made in the direction of their acknowledgment as the ecclesial locus of faith (see *Lumen Gentium*, no. 12), to whom the hierarchical church must also pay attention in the development of church doctrine. On the level of the practice of charity, the church encourages the faithful—partly lest ministerial priests become involved in it—to enter the world and work there, and this includes the slithery world of politics, parties, and popular organizations. But then, not infrequently, they find themselves abandoned by their hierarchy and their priests. (Few bishops have consistently called for a pastoral ministry of accompaniment in these difficult areas, as Archbishop Romero did.) And so the faithful begin to wonder why they were encouraged to get into these things in the first place. Is the world of history and politics really included in the field of their priesthood, after all?

Along with these more immediate problems, other more theoretical ones have arisen, even since Vatican II. A theoretical tension arises between the exclusive sacred power bestowed on priests by the Sacrament of Order—which would seem to refer the element of the priesthood directly to the sphere of public worship—and the practical primacy ascribed to the ministry of the word (*Presbyterorum Ordinis*, no. 4). Still in need of a theoretical explanation is why some secular activities can be required of, or at least permitted, priests, while others are not. Still without an explanation is what is authentically common to the ministerial priesthood and the priesthood of the faithful, in such wise that the differences between them may be understood from a point of departure embracing both. Still without an explanation is the relationship between the priesthood and the religious life, in the case of ordained religious, and a theoretical tension persists between the essential prophetical element of the religious life and the "ministerial" element of the priesthood.

All these problems, and many others, could be listed in a treatment of the concrete nature of priestliness. To be sure, such a treatment ought to be theological. But it ought also to be spiritual, pastoral, and "historical" (sociological, cultural, political, and economic).

What we should like to emphasize, however, is that, with the myriad problems we have mentioned, we have not yet cited what, in our opinion, is the fundamental problem. This is none other than the simple question: *What* is the "priestly," the "sacerdotal"? *What* is the essential nature of the priesthood? All other questions (as to origin, functions, differentiation, and so on) are important, and a response to them will be helpful. But they leave the basic question unanswered. Unless the basic question is answered, not only will the others persist, but we shall be without the fundamental criterion of discernment in the complex replies they receive. This is what we seek to do in these pages (with the modesty indicated in our title): determine the concrete nature of the priesthood. But to this purpose, we think it will be important to clarify two antecedent problems: the finality of the priestly element, and the theological method of an approach to the nature of priestliness.

Though still by way of introduction, it is important to remember what the finality of priesthood is. To what human, concrete, historical reality has priesthood responded? What has made it necessary? That finality is nothing other than salvation—that which human beings have always sought. It is not important that we analyze here whether the historical religions in which a priesthood has arisen have responded well or ill to this problem. But it is indeed important to recall the fact that priesthood has expressed the reality of a humanity in need of salvation and hoping to attain it. Thus, questions of priesthood have always been comprehensive rather than "regional," and priesthood has always corresponded to humanity's most important series of questions: those bearing on salvation.

The question of salvation, whether formulated explicitly or implicitly, in religious terms or secular, has always been with us. When expressed in religious terms, it has always had a relationship with God. In Jesus' times, the poor looked for the coming of the Reign of God. Paul speaks of a humanity impatient, a humanity that harbors the hope of seeing its liberation from slavery—the hope of a future in which it would be revealed what it is to be children of God. Many centuries later, at the dawn of modernity, Luther wondered how to find a benevolent God. Needs, or an awareness of them, have managed to change over the course of history, but the framework of salvation has always involved a reference to God. In these terms, the basic notion of priesthood has changed repeatedly, as we see in the examples we have cited (from the New Testament and Luther).[1]

In the Third World today, there can be little doubt that whole peoples look for, await, hope for salvation. In Latin America, the need for salvation has been expressed in a historical and religious fashion, through an indication of the most crying need from which a salvific deliverance is required, and an appeal to the God of that salvation. A single, familiar passage from Medellín will be worth a dozen from elsewhere: "We are on the threshold, on our continent, of a historical era charged with a deep aspiration for total emancipation, for liberation from all slavery, for personal maturation, and for collective integration." All of this is interpreted, in religious terms, as "an evident sign of the Spirit who guides the history of human beings and peoples toward their calling" (Introduction, no. 4).

Our point is that the priestly problematic (whether or not it be thus denominated) is very much alive in Latin America, and that the priesthood must be understood in terms of that overall problematic. We have said next to nothing, as yet, *about* salvation—about how it ought to be understood, or about how it may be attained. Our sole purpose has been to restore the question of the priesthood to its comprehensive matrix, that we may understand it in terms of that and not in function of its "regional" realities and problems. Let us say, albeit in passing, that the bishops and communities who have taken a comprehensive need of salvation most seriously, such as Dom Hélder Câmara, Bishop Pedro Casaldáliga, or Archbishop Romero, to cite just three, have also been the most priestly: they have restored genuine value to the common and the ministerial priesthood alike.[2]

In the official consciousness of the church, while theology has moved ahead,[3] priesthood is still treated as a regional, rather than comprehensive, object of reflection. The salvation mediated by priesthood continues to be understood as something already known, rather than as something always to be learned. Vatican II, which brought a new outlook to so many points, left this one particularly out of account. An explanation of the reason why can be useful for a determination of the concrete nature of priestliness.

True, the Council bases all priesthood on Christ (*Presbyterorum Ordinis*, no. 2), and, less "traditionally," restores to its place of honor the priesthood of all the baptized (*Lumen Gentium*, no. 10; *PO*, no. 2) and the ministry of the word, without reducing the ministerial priesthood to a ministry of public worship (*PO*, no. 4). But in a concrete analysis, the nature of the priesthood is addressed regionally, in subordination to a consideration of what the ordained priest is in the church, rather than comprehensively.[4] Paradoxically, comprehensive salvation is better expounded in *Lumen Gentium* and *Gaudium et Spes* than in *Presbyterorum Ordinis*. When *Presbyterorum Ordinis* speaks of God's total salvation, priesthood does not come in for a great deal of consideration; and when it addresses priesthood, any very meaningful consideration of God's total salvation is missing. There may be a number of reasons why the Council approached the reality of the priesthood in this fashion.[5] But our intent here is to observe its theological *modus procedendi* on this point, an approach so different from the one it employs in other important areas. If the reader will permit us a brief excursion, we might recall that the church already possessed important systematic concepts with regard to the church itself, as with regard to revelation. Nevertheless, the Council plumbed the depths of these things and included them in its renewal, by way of the deep-reaching theological method it employed: that of an understanding of both realities from a point of departure in Christ, and in the God who became concretely present in Jesus. The reason the church itself is regarded as a sacrament of salvation is that Christ is such a sacrament (see *LG*, no. 1). The reason the church has the mission of proclaiming and inaugurating the Reign of God among all peoples is that Jesus proclaimed and inaugurated it (*LG*, no. 5). The reason the church adopts a new concept of its relationship with the world—a concept practically contrary to its old one—as a relationship of service is that Christ came "to serve and not to be served" (*GS*, no. 3, citing Mark 10:45 and parallels). The reason an incipient ecclesial option for the poor already appears in a call to poverty (*GS*, no. 1; *LG*, no. 8) is that Christ "was sent by the Father 'to bring good news to the poor, to heal the contrite of heart' (Luke 4:18), *'to seek and to save what was lost'* (Luke 19:10)" (*LG*, no. 8). The same can be said of the Council's systematic understanding of revelation. The reason a more doctrinal conception of revelation as consisting of a series of veracious enunciations is replaced by a revelation of God as God, God who engages in a self-communication to human beings through works and words, is that Christ " 'speaks the words of God' (Jn. 3:34), and completes the work of salvation" (*Dei Verbum*, no. 4).

Paul VI used the same approach in speaking of revelation in *Evangelii Nuntiandi*. He appeals to Christ, as this more authentic theological method requires. The reason he asserts that evangelization constitutes the church's deepest identity (no. 14); the reason why he makes such advances in the definition of evangelization, calling it "bringing the Good News into all the strata of humanity, and through its influence transforming humanity from within and making it new" (no. 18); the reason he adds to the traditional modes of evangelization—proclamation and testimonial—a new one, that of liberation (nos. 29-31)—the reason for all these things is that his analysis of the church's evangelization has been preceded by an analysis of Christ's evangelization, and of course that of Jesus of Nazareth (nn. 6-12), "the very first and greatest evangelizer" (no. 7). The reason Medellín and Puebla speak of the solidarity of the church with the poor and of its preferential option for them, is that these synods have first analyzed Jesus' work, in which they discern the relationship between the poor and God (see Puebla Final Document, nos. 1141-42).

This brief survey shows that it is possible to rework systematic concepts of realities of the highest importance for the church, and that the church has done so. This reworking preserves the best elements of church tradition, but enriches it in a way that had not been anticipated. These new systematic concepts are richer, have more content, generate more intra-church creativity, have more historical relevance, and endow the church with greater credibility than the old ones. But we must remember that this new enrichment has emerged from the church's humble, honest confrontation with Christ and God. That is, it has emerged by way of a theological *modus procedendi* willing to reach beyond the church and ecclesiology to christology and theo-logy—a manner of proceeding that takes the signs of the times seriously and is guided by an interest in the human being's salvation.

In an explanation of the concrete nature of the priesthood, we do not think this theological procedure has been consistently followed. Granted, it is asserted that the sole true priesthood is that of Christ. But when it comes to a concrete analysis of the priesthood, the premise of Christ's priesthood remains without any impact on that analysis. To put it very simply: Can we assert that, in its determination of the nature of priestly reality, in its verification of whether or not priestly reality is at hand, the church has consistently appealed to the high priest of the Letter to the Hebrews? Do we not, instead, gather the impression that what priests are and what they ought to do, what the manner of their existence ought to be, which virtues they should cultivate, and so on, is already sufficiently known, antecedently to a reading of the letter?

Somewhat the same thing must be said of the systematic determination of the nature of priesthood. Granted, the Council offers a comprehensive definition of this reality on two occasions. It says that the mission that priests are to "pursue by their ministry and life is the glory of God the Father as it is to be achieved in Christ." And it adds that "that glory consists in this: that men knowingly, freely, and gratefully accept what God has achieved perfectly through Christ, and manifest it in their whole lives" (*Presbyterorum Ordinis*, no. 2). In speaking of the priesthood common to all the baptized, it says that "through all those works befitting Christian men," all of the baptized "can offer spiritual sacrifices and proclaim the power of Him who has called them out of darkness into His marvelous light (cf. 1 Pet. 2:4-10)" (*Lumen Gentium*, no. 10; cf. *PO*, no. 2). But these determinations are still merely generic. They do not analyze in depth, or in relation to the signs of the times, what "God's glory" or "spiritual sacrifices" actually are. Once more, an adequate analysis of the reality of God is missing in connection with a discussion of the nature of priesthood. But we shall have need of such an analysis if we hope to specify a concrete relationship of priesthood to God.

In the following pages, we shall attempt to determine the concrete nature of priesthood from a point of departure in its deepest roots—in theo-logy and christo-logy. We shall not thereby solve all the concrete intra-church problems we have mentioned (some of which cannot be solved by theological argumentation alone, since they depend on historical decisions legitimately taken by the church—although some of these, in turn, may be open to revision). But if we explain what it is to be a priest, we shall then be able to shed some light on concrete problems, and at all events shall have presented the minimum—or maximum—which must not be missing in any historical configuration of the exercise of the priestly office, whether ministerial or common.

We shall now attempt to develop a theoretical concept of the nature of the priesthood, taking account both of the bases of the faith—the reality of God and Christ—and of the current signs of the times. Accordingly, while theoretical, our efforts will be guided by the concrete reality of the priesthood as we see it in Latin America (and we shall subjoin a few concluding words about this).[6]

The Theo-logical Dimension of the Nature of Priesthood

Let us begin with the theo-logical dimension of the reality that is priesthood, which will mean answering this question: To what concrete reality of the God in whom the church believes does priesthood correspond? It is strictly impossible to give a direct answer to this question without taking Christ into account. But let us begin by analyzing the theo-logical dimension, with the understanding that we are guided by the manifestation of God in Christ. Our purpose in starting out this way is to present the nature of the priesthood, in the most radical and ultimate terms possible, within a framework of theo-logy and anthropology. For that matter, the reality of Christ, as well, including his priesthood, ought to be understood in terms of a relation. Furthermore, the customary analysis of the presentation of the priesthood of Christ in the Letter to the Hebrews has (rightly) borne on a demonstration of the historicity of Christ's priesthood and his sacrifice, in the presence of a church priesthood understood more in terms of public worship. That presentation of Christ's priesthood is necessary for polemical purposes. But because it is polemical, it has been able to ignore, by and large, the question: In the service of what was the priesthood of Christ placed? And this is what we seek to investigate in our theo-logical analysis of priesthood.

With a view to determining the nature of priesthood on a theo-logical level, let us begin with an altogether traditional proposition: There is a need for mediation between God and human beings. The proposition rests on the premise that God and human beings are distinct, separate realities, the distance between whom culminates in sin and separation, which is the absence of salvation, or positive damnation. The problem confronting the human being is how to bridge this distance—how to reach God and thereby find salvation.

The solution given to this problem by the religions of the biblical world and, in part, by the Old Testament itself, is a ritual solution. Human beings need to approach God. But, to that purpose:

> Moral perfection does not suffice, for this kind of perfection leaves human beings in their merely human world. The key to approaching God is to enter a different world, a sacred world, the world radically distinct and detached from the profane, the sphere of the divine and supernatural. But human beings have access to that sphere and that world by way of rites and ceremonies, which withdraw them from *the profane* and afford them access to the sacred.[7]

In this way of reaching God, the priest is the key, crucial piece, since it is he who effects the mediation in question. The premise here is that the priest is the person of the sacred, the person set apart from the profane. The orbit of that mediation is public worship; within that, at the center, is sacrifice, especially expiatory sacrifice. With varying nuances in the various religions, at least in the case of those of the biblical world, the be-all and end-all of priesthood is to bring it about that human beings be purified of their sin, reach God, and attain salvation. The nature of priestliness is "mediatory" in this precise sense.

The Old and New Testaments both maintain the anthropological premise that the human being is separated from God and in need of salvation. The Old Testament proposes the cultic solution to the problem, although in tension with another type of solution represented in the various covenants into which God enters with the chosen people. The New Testament proposes a radically different, contrary solution to the human being's problem, because the God who appears in Jesus is radically different. What priesthood is or is not, what a mediator is or is not, will have to be discovered, in the first place, in function of the radical difference, the novelty, of that God. Let us see what fundamental characteristics attach to that God when it comes to the human being's problem of access to God.

The transcendent God is now no longer a separated, remote God, but is a God close and near to human beings. This divine proximity is more than a condition sine qua non of the divine manifestation: It is the very content of the reality of God. God reveals the divine reality by drawing near to human beings, and seeks to reveal the fact that (part of) the divine reality is approach to the human being. That coming, that drawing near, belongs to God's reality, and not merely as one more element in the content of this mysterious reality, but as central content. The fact that drawing near to human beings is central to the reality of God is uttered radically and systematically in the Incarnation: God no longer *is* without this divine coming. The transcendent God—who does not cease to be such, and therefore will have to be understood in terms of a Trinity—*is* the God who has come near.

This drawing near of God's is free and gratuitous. It does not depend on (nor can it be forced by) the will of human beings, nor do the latter need strive that God may desire to approach them. It is an active approach that seeks to reach an actual encounter with the human being, and not merely to "be there." It is an ongoing approach, not just a transitory one, in Christ. It is an unconditional, irrevocable approach, independent of the will of the human being.

God's coming is good *for* the human being, and *is* the supreme good. Superfluous as it may seem to recall this, it is central for an understanding of the nature of priesthood. God draws near because God is good; and God draws near as that which is good for human beings. God's approach to the human being is not for the sheer purpose of being closer and thereby finding it easier to pass judgment. No, God approaches, the better to save. God has heard the cries of the people, God is mindful of the people. The sheer fact of God's coming means that God has shattered for good and all the symmetry between a potential salvific divine approach and a potential condemnatory one. Thus, God approaches *in order* to save, and approaches *as* savior: God draws near *for* love, and *as* love. Hence it is that Jesus presents God's approach as the human being's supreme good: God comes in a "Reign" and approaches as a "Father"—expressions of a God who is good for human beings—a God who forgives their sin, heals their heart, humanizes them, and fulfills them.

This approach, this coming of God's, as it has de facto occurred, manifests a partiality to the weak element of this world. It is partial to the poor, the despised, to sinners who are weak, partial to all those for whom living is a heavy burden. This partiality, as concrete fact, is open to no further analysis or argumentation. Simply, this is the "way things are," as the Old and New Testaments show, and this "way things are" forms part of the core content of actual faith in God. But the partiality of God's coming evinces the congruity of the fact that God's love should be present as mercy and tenderness, in being addressed to the little, and as justice, in being addressed to those who are little precisely because they are oppressed. This does not militate against God's salvific universalism. It does, however, require that God's saving universalism be understood in terms of God's saving partiality, and not the other way around.

While the partiality of God's approach is not open to further analysis, it might nevertheless be reinterpreted as God's pedagogy—as a way of convincing human beings that it is true that this coming is a salvific one. After all, God has approached precisely those whom none approach, those who would seem to have the least title—in the mind of the persons regarded as "just" in Jesus' time—to God's approach.

The orbit or field of God's approach is human beings' life and history, with all the needs therein comprised: the need for forgiveness and healing, for bread and hope, for truth and justice. God draws near not in separation and disjunction from that life and that history, but within them. Nor does God bestow salvation by way of removing human beings from that life and that history. Rather, God heals human beings, humanizes them, factors their capacities exponentially, and grants them the divine self-communication.

The God who comes is still the holy, transcendent God. But God's holiness is not distantiation from the historical. Rather, God's holiness is maximal incarnation, as its purpose is to enable human beings to be "made perfect as their heavenly Father is perfect" (cf. Matt. 5:48). Nor does the divine transcendence consist only in being beyond history, thereby relegating history to a level of relative unimportance, as some think. God's transcendence of history also consists in an active drawing of that history onward and upward, in the direction of God, that history may give more of itself.

The opposite pole of God's salvific coming is the world of sin. This means not only that there are those who do not welcome the divine approach—the wealthy and cowardly youth who stood before Jesus—nor only that there are those who are not grateful for it—the ungrateful lepers who had been healed—but that the world of sin acts positively counter to it. Why this is, is history's ultimate mystery. Why this active rejection and battle to the death with the human being's supreme good? There is no other explanation—nor is even this any explanation, since it merely calls the scandal by a new name—than the hubris of human beings, who ultimately would fain decide for themselves what is good for them.

But this action mounted against God's coming is actually assumed, taken on, by God in the divine approach itself; both the evil action and its divine assumption culminate in Jesus' cross. On the one hand, the cross shows there is deadly opposition to God's coming, that the divinities of death—scandal and foolishness, yesterday as today—will ever put to death the God of life. On the other hand, it shows that God's approach is absolutely real and unconditional, that God would offer not only salvation, but the divine being itself, for the sake of that salvation. Once more, the fact cannot be further analyzed, but it can be reinterpreted as the pedagogy God uses to evidence the absolute seriousness and absolute love of the divine coming.

Because this is "the way God is," a radical change occurs in the problem of our access to God and the structure of our encounter with God. It is not we who reach God in quest of salvation, but God who bends down to us to offer it. Our encounter with God indeed has the structure of active response, but not of Promethean exploit. And that response is offered in a double dimension. On one side, we ought to respond to God in thanksgiving, as well as in faith and hope, whose central content is precisely an acceptance that God has freely drawn near as salvation. On the other, we ought to "correspond" to the reality of the God who has come near, being ourselves transformed into good news and salvation for others, being ourselves an expression of God's approach to human beings. To state it in John's programmatic formula: "Love, then, consists in this: not that we have loved God, but that he has loved us" first, and that, "if God has loved us so, we must have the same love for one another" (1 John 4:10-11). In acceptance of, response to, and correspondence to the God who comes, salvation is accomplished.

All that we have said demonstrates that the nature of priesthood has changed radically by comparison with what it was in the ancient Palestinian religions and the Old Testament. The basic premise has changed, and this automatically abolishes the ancient priesthood, even though the Letter to the Hebrews does not mention that. To put it briefly, nothing created can cause, as efficient cause, God's salvific coming; nor is it necessary that it do so. To claim to do so—as the self-styled "just" of Jesus' time claimed to do—would be, strictly speaking, to commit blasphemy, since it would be an attack on the profoundest element of God and the divine holiness. The ancient priesthood is superfluous and assaults the reality of God.

In these terms, can theo-logical discourse upon the nature of the priesthood any longer have any descriptive, specifying meaning? An affirmative answer has actually been given by God, and therefore one which cannot be elucidated a priori. In order to draw near human beings salvifically, God has personally adopted an expression of this coming: Jesus. There was no other way to reach human beings in their history and their historicity. Jesus is the historical expression par excellence of God's saving approach to us. Hence, all that Jesus is is priestly. This is what the gospels describe, without appealing to the terminology of priesthood, and this is what the Letter to the Hebrews makes explicit, now employing that terminology but reinterpreting it on the basis of the reality of Jesus.

A theological reflection on that priestly reality is still possible and necessary. It is possible because it is possible to follow in Jesus' footsteps and—in the conviction of faith—because there will always be, in one form or another, real followers of Jesus. This is a condition sine qua non of the priesthood today—a reminder that might seem unnecessary, but one that is important nonetheless. Otherwise the only necessary condition of priesthood today might be the existence of an uninterrupted priesthood coming down from Christ, a condition certain persons do indeed think sufficient. No, the authentic following of that true priest is also a necessary condition.

It is necessary because God means to keep on approaching human beings and keeps on needing historical expressions of that salvific coming.

Accordingly, we can offer a theo-logical determination of the priestly that will stand in need of concretization on the basis of christo-logy but has the advantage, we hold, of proposing a systematic concept in terms of which the actions, persons or groups, fields of activity, spirituality, and verification of the actual nature of priesthood can be specified.

Priesthood is essentially related to that concrete reality of God that we have denominated God's "salvific approach to human beings." In these terms, at the theological level, priestly service is anything that helps to express, concretely and historically, that coming of God's. Priestly actions will be all actions that thus express it. Priests will be all persons and/or groups performing these actions. Derivatively, pertaining to the nature of the priesthood will be everything that helps persons respond and correspond to the God who comes.

In using the word *derivatively,* we surely have no intention of belittling the dimension of priestly service just indicated. It is in human beings' responding and corresponding to God that salvation is accomplished. We have spoken in this way in order to maintain the logical primacy of God's coming, which has a profound practical consequence. In priestly service, various means will have to be used, and various arguments employed, but the supreme argument of the goodness of God must neither be missing nor be relegated to secondary status. Rather, it must be human beings' ultimate motive. This of itself imposes an obvious demand on priestly existence: that of rendering the goodness of God present, in order that that goodness be present in all liturgical, doctrinal, exhortatory, admonitory, secular, and so on, functions, without any of these functions acquiring complete autonomy on the basis of their structure. When all is said and done, priestly service is helping human beings respond to and correspond to God, and doing so in the very manner in which God acted in Jesus—convincing or persuading them from within, on the basis of a great love.

This determination of priestly service is systematic and theoretical. It does not explain many concrete things about that service. But as a theo-logical determination, it is important and crucial. Let us list the consequences deriving from this systematic determination. We shall set them forth in positive form, although they could be presented polemically, as well—in which case we should have to maintain the discussion on the theo-logical (and christo-logical) level, without admitting disqualifying arguments based on premises outside theo-logy and christo-logy. If these consequences are correct, they ought to be applied to any and every form of concrete priestly practice. In our opinion, at stake here is precisely an understanding of priestly service and its concrete practice.

Primarily and directly, priestly service is *apostolic:* Its addressee is the world, as the ultimate correlative of God. Negatively, this precludes a methodological point of departure in the exercise of the intra-church priesthood—important and necessary though that priesthood be—in order to arrive at an understanding of the essence of priesthood. No, the starting point must be the mission to the world expounded by Vatican II in its presentation of the priesthood of Christ (*PO*, no. 2). The apostolic nature of priestliness flows from the very nature of the matter under consideration. It flows from the very reality of God, and cannot be determined on the basis of certain texts (many as there are in the New Testament that insist on it), as if the apostolic nature of priestliness were the function of an arbitrary decision by God.

Positively, taking into account the Latin American situation, three things must be said of the addressee of priestly service. The first is that, of its very essence, this service ought to be addressed to the world of the *needy*, those who are most in need of salvation, in terms of a judgment from the standpoint of God as to who are needy and why, and in terms of a hierarchy of needs drawn up from a point of departure in God. This judgment and hierarchy will be an expression of the partiality, the preferential character, of God's approach. On the basis of this partiality, it will be possible to arrive at the universality of the addressee.

In the second place, priestly service ought to be addressed to the needy not only as individuals, but as a world of needy, as well—that is, as having needs that shape an entire world, in the sense in which one speaks of the "sin of the world." This world could be millions of human beings in the so-called First World, which has been dehumanized by abundance and is unconscious of any responsibility for the misery of humanity or for the by-products of that misery in terms of absurdity or anguish. In the Third World, there can be no doubt that millions of human beings live in a world of misery and oppression. Here are the worlds that lie open to priestly service. The reason we mention them is that we must defeat the understandable temptation of intraecclesialism, when these worlds—whether in virtue of their novelty, their danger, their antagonism, or a failure to understand them, depending on the case—imply a serious difficulty for the church. To abandon them for any reason whatsoever would be profoundly "unpriestly." To seek refuge in the church in order to be safe from them would be anti-priestly.

In the third place, there are other sociopolitical groups in the Third World who present themselves as saviors. Some propose a concrete, historical salvation within the Western world, in terms of what have been regarded the traditional values of that world. Others, the "revolutionaries," propose a different kind of historical salvation. This is not the moment to analyze a problem this complex. But it will indeed be in place to offer certain reflections on a priestly attitude to be taken toward these groups. On the one hand, one must analyze, on the basis of the reality of God (and not on the premise that one particular world—the Western—is God's world), the affinities and convergences, as well as the differences, between the salvation offered by these groups and the salvation of God. To whatever extent it may be possible, the priestly task will include an effort to bring it about that the salvation offered by these groups be convergent with God's salvation. On the other hand—and this tends to be the more frequent problem—the church must not ignore or divorce itself from groups committed to liberation or revolution; least of all may it do so with an appeal to the nature of priestliness. The church may be dismayed at the presence of these groups, by reason of their novelty, their radicalism, and indeed, their denunciation of the church. But none of this implies that a greater priestly service will emerge from paying less attention to these groups. An effort to evangelize their projects from within is also priestly. For concrete, historical reasons bearing on its credibility, the church has a great deal at stake here. If these groups were to be regarded as evil (if they are dubbed Marxists, they are automatically regarded as the worst possible peril for the church), then we might at least recall the example set by Jesus in going in search of the lost.

It is not our intent to address the series of problems involved here. We only wish to shed some light on the apostolic character of priestliness. At least it ought to be clear that one is not more priestly the less one ventures into the world. One is not holier the less one is willing to face the dangers of the world. One is not closer to God the less one is contaminated by the world. At least it ought to be clear that, on the theo-logical level, the *analogatum princeps* of priestly service is service to a world in need of salvation, lest, in the name of priestliness, one be anti-priestly or, in the words of Charles Peguy: "Because they have not the courage to be of the world, they believe that they are of God . . . because they love no one, they believe that they love God."

The *vehicle of priestliness*, at the theo-logical level, is anyone (man or woman, individually or collectively) who expresses, concretely and historically, God's salvific coming. In this sense, in strict logic one could even speak of an anonymous priesthood, just as we speak of anonymous Christians. Prescinding from the questions arising here, it remains to emphasize that the vessel or vehicle of the priestly is the one who approaches God by pursuing the work of Jesus. This profound consideration entitled Vatican II to reassert the common priesthood of all the baptized, although it did so only after differentiating it from that of the ordained.

Two important conclusions follow. The first is that the bearer of that which is priestly, at this theo-logical level, must be understood in terms of what this person actually does in the service of God's coming, and not the other way around. The second is that the church ought to posit the nature of the priestly in terms not only of priests as individuals, but of itself as community and as people of God. A priestly church is not the same as a church with priests, although the specific reality of the priests will have a great deal of influence on that church as such. Priestly activity, as we have seen in the case of the church of El Salvador in Archbishop Romero's times, will depend on the activity of the whole church. It is the activity of a whole church—and this is how peoples grasp it—that determines whether God has drawn near.

Priestly service is *evangelical*, in the etymological sense of the term: bearing on the communication and concretization of good news. To serve God's approach to human beings is to concretize the good and the supreme good. This reminder may seem superfluous, but it is important for an understanding of the formality of priestly service. Priestly service means doing good by communicating that good which is God's and is God. That this God who comes is good for the human being appears in two key words used by Jesus: God approaches as "Father," supreme goodness, mercy, and tenderness; and God approaches in a "Reign" whose content is humanity's utopia—justice, peace, liberty, siblingship. To bring God near is to bear the good to the heart of the individual and society, healing them, humanizing them, and multiplying their being and their capacities to the nth degree.

But it is also good for the human being that the Father draw near precisely as God, and that the Reign that comes be precisely the Reign of God. The goodness that approaches is unlimited, therefore it cannot be adequately received. In its fullness, however, it endlessly encourages and inspires human beings not to strike a compromise with their creatureliness but to give ever more of themselves. The transcendence of God and the utopia of the Reign continually stir us to larger fulfillment. It is this coming of a *Parent* God and a Reign *of God* that heals, empowers, and fulfills human beings. It is this that humanizes them, and arouses them to an ever greater humanization—stirs them to receive the good and concretize it, placing no limits on either the reception or the concretization.

This service to God's "good coming" is the formality of priestly service. Of course, this good God's tremendous demands abide. Indeed, it is precisely in function of such a God that greater demands are made on the human being. After all, what is required of us is that we be good, as our heavenly Parent is good (see Matt. 5:48). But priestly service inspires the human being to comply with these demands, trusting ultimately in the goodness of God. We see it in the gospels, with their programmatic presentation of priestly service in the scenes in which Jesus forgives sins—the scenes in which, vanquished by God's love, sinners change, are converted.

Neither does this formality of priestly service—service to God's "good coming"—mean anything like a softer prophetical denunciation and condemnation of oppressors. Rather it requires an even more powerful denunciation and condemnation of those who stand against and act against that goodness, since they are assaulting the profoundest reality of God. Denunciation and condemnation are a service to the goodness of God. They are a defense of the weak whom God so loves; they are good news, *sub specie contrarii*, to the oppressors.

In the last analysis, the proposition that priestly service is formally evangelical means ultimately that God seeks to communicate the divine goodness, and that that goodness is God's ultimate argumentation and motivation. Whether it succeeds or not is another matter. But if the service is to be priestly, the communication of God's goodness must be present in its pastoral, exhortatory, liturgical, and theological activities.

The *field* or fields of priestly service must be determined in function of the field or fields in which God, too, draws near. Least of all on this point must we allow ourselves to be guided by the logic of the field of the priestly as we find it in the religions and public worship. A priori, it could be said that this field is comprehensive, since it is precisely God who comes; and this is indeed what we find a posteriori. An emphasis on the totality of that field is of the highest importance, lest we succumb to the temptation to reduce priestly service to some regional element or consideration, perhaps even to understand its essence in terms of the regional.

By way of description, we may draw upon what we see in the Old and New Testaments: God's saving approach occurs in the field of the personal, the sociohistorical (the concrete social fabric), and the whole. God approaches a person by forgiving the sinner, changing a heart of stone into a heart of flesh. Synthesizing, we may say that God endows the forgiven person with a likeness to Jesus, thus divinizing her. God comes socially and historically by liberating a people: exchanging structures of oppression for structures of liberation (that they may "live in the houses they build, and eat the fruit of the vineyards they plant; they shall not build houses for others to live in, or plant for others to eat," Isa. 65:21); structures of war for structures of peace (that they may "beat their swords into plowshares and their spears into pruning hooks," Isa. 2:4); structures of ostracism for structures of siblingship ("The wolf shall be a guest of the lamb," Isa. 11:6); impotent religious structures for other, effective structures ("Before they call, I will answer," Isa. 65:24). God draws near the individual, social, and cosmic totality by striking an alliance with a people and with all humanity (see Zech. 11:10), creating "new heavens and a new earth" (Rev. 21:1), coming at last to be "all in all" (1 Cor. 15:28).

The fields of God's approach, then, are all those areas in which God seeks to bring about the realization of the divine salvific will. God is known to have drawn near in any of those orbits when that will has been realized. However, we may wonder whether there is some hierarchy among the fields of God's coming. This is no theoretical question, since it is on the basis of such a hierarchization that the "priestly" actually is specified, and the hierarchy of "priestly" activities determined. The premise of a possible hierarchy lies in the duality, or plurality, of the dimensions of the human, since it is the human that stands in need of salvation and has the capacity to give more of itself.

The diversity in question can be understood dualistically. In that case, history has demonstrated a frank preference for prioritizing God's approach to the spiritual, personal, and transcendent element of the human being. In the gospels, however, no provision is made for any such dualistic focus on God's coming. Rather, a complementarity prevails. To take Jesus' key symbols: "the Reign" is a concrete social reality, surely. But besides this, it is the locus of the realization of spiritual values, such as siblingship and reconciliation, and is to be built of spiritual values. "Father" is the symbol of God's approach to the human heart: but more than that, God comes healing the infirmities of the body. One must ask the "Father" for the forgiveness of sins, but for one's daily bread, as well.

We shall understand the complementarity prevailing between the two orbits of the human if we recall God's partiality toward the poor. Were we to permit ourselves a conceptual universalization (and thereby a dehistoricization) of the addressee of God's coming—which, in Jesus' time and place, was the corporeal and the social—then the corporeal and the social, wherever their reality were to be sufficiently supported and guaranteed today, could seem to constitute mere preparatory fields for the "true" coming of God in the human heart. But if God approaches the poor *in directo*, then the orbit of the corporeal and the social acquires far greater importance. God's salvific approach to the poor can neither be proclaimed nor occur unless that coming occurs also for the purpose of saving the poor from their poverty—as we see that coming in Jesus, with ultimacy, and as we have heard this criterion acknowledged in Latin America, in the proclamation of an absolute need for liberation.

The intrinsic reason for this need resides in the fact that poverty corresponds to death and salvation to life. "Life," here, refers not only to the corporeal, in contradistinction from the spiritual. It bespeaks the human being's most primordial reality, our primary participation in the reality of God our creator, from which sharing we can and must accede to other states of fulfillment, but without which the very existence of a creature of God is threatened and vitiated. Can a loving God, a God who is parent and liberator, really come to the masses of poor, oppressed, and crucified, and leave their misery, ostracism, and death intact? Is God's approach for the purpose of healing these things merely secondary, provisional, tactical?

In terms of God's approach to the poor, the problem of a hierarchy of fields becomes more complex. At the same time, one of its aspects is clarified: The problem cannot be solved simplistically, by way of a prioritization of the spiritual and the individual over the corporeal and the social. Viewed from the standpoint of the poor to whom God draws near, it is obvious that the poor grasp God as their defender and liberator, as the one who fosters their life—although it is also the poor, often enough, who provide us with the best example of a salvation of God effected in the depths of the human heart, when these poor are converted from their past resignation and their sins, to embrace a hope, a solidarity, a generosity, and a commitment that extend to the surrender of their very lives. Viewing the matter from the standpoint of God, one could ask, by way of a purely speculative exercise, whether God approaches in a Reign that liberates the material and the concrete historical *in order that*, subsequently, the poor may be able to accept God as Parent, or whether, *because God is God, God must come personally and in substance* jointly with a divine Reign of deliverance. In the gospels, no such disjunction appears: Both "alternatives" are set forth with simplicity and ultimacy. Why? Because this is "the way God is" and this is the way human beings are—in need of Reign and Parent, summoned to respond to that Parent and to build, and live in, a Reign.

Priestly service to the coming of God, then, is effected in various complementary fields, all of them dialectically interrelated. The ultimate finality of priestly service is that absolute coming of God when Christ will deliver the Reign over to the Father (1 Cor. 15:25) and God will be all in all (1 Cor. 15:28). Then will occur God's full approach, and the absolute salvation of the whole human being and all human beings. But in history, priestly service is composed of partial services. God must be brought to the human heart, and God must be brought to human material and social reality. The signs of the times suggest the profound pedagogy of this service. In Latin America, it will obviously be difficult to speak of the approach of God without positing any signs to the effect that that God wishes the life of the poor and not their death. And the poor grasp and feel that God has drawn near to them when they see those signs. Thereupon, further, they feel with greater depth their need that this God enter the inmost recesses of their hearts. Many examples could be adduced in favor of this proposition. Suffice it to mention what occurs in the refuges of the church in El Salvador when the poor receive both bread and Eucharist, literacy and catechesis, physical presence and hope. In this comprehensive experience, they grasp that God has drawn near them, and the concrete elements of the experience reinforce one another to communicate this coming of God. It is this approach to them—that of the good God—that moves them to wonder about (and accomplish) their own goodness, that motivates them to seek to be wholly good. Here the various fields of God's approach appear in unity. But the key thing is the conclusion: The poor feel that God has drawn near them indeed, that this coming is good for them, and that it is moving them to be good themselves.

The *locus* of priestly service is real history, not a place apart from that history, as the gospels show and as the Letter to the Hebrews elucidates in polemical fashion. God draws near human beings in their concrete life and history. This holds for their material and social reality, but it also holds for their personal and spiritual reality. In these terms, priestly service must not be "religious" in the sense of fostering some kind of mechanical communication with God; nor must it be performed through "worship," in the sense of fostering that communication in a place apart. However, it may and must be religious and expressed in a liturgy.

The meaning of these terminological specifications—prescinding from any consideration of the felicity of the terms selected—is the following. The bringing of the God who is good for human beings can be effected only through concrete "goodnesses"—things and actions that show that there is goodness in God. In priestly service, therefore, one must bring God. God is approached conjointly with historical realities: forgiveness and bread, the signs of mercy and the practices of justice, examples of faith and the invitation to and demand for one's own conversion, new life, and so on. Without this "concrete historical," God's salvation cannot be communicated, and therefore priestly service must be historical and "worldly." On the other hand, inasmuch as it is not just any goodness or just any salvation that seeks to be communicated, but precisely the goodness and salvation of God, the concrete good must be effected in such a manner as to ever lie open to the "more." And so the need arises that the concrete good be accompanied by some word or deed calculated to express this openness. To do and offer good, from a priestly standpoint, means to do and offer good in its quality as open to a good ever greater and open to all the fields or orbits in which God seeks to approach. This is the historical form in which, through the concrete, a greater goodness can be rendered present— one which points asymptotically to the goodness of God.

This is what we mean when we say that priestly service must be religious. It must bring a God who is Parent, and therefore good to the human being, but a Parent who continues to be God and therefore always greater than the concrete "goodnesses" in which God must necessarily approach. This is why priestly service must be historical and not "religious," in the sense of piety divorced from reality. But that same service must be religious in the sense of an openness to the ever-greater goodness, and must place no limits on the good in the name of concrete "goodnesses."

For this same reason, priestly service must not be a service of "worship" in the conventional sense of isolation and insulation from the rest of life; but it may and must be expressed in a liturgy. By *liturgy* we understand here the locus of explanation of, gratitude for, and celebration of the approach of the good God, accompanied by an emphasis on the fact that it is the approach precisely of God. Therefore the liturgy is also the locus of petition for the coming of that "more," and the place of repentance for having diminished it. Liturgy is not opposed to history. Rather, it sup-poses history—rests on it as on its proper foundation—and dis-poses it to the "more." Liturgy is not divorce from history, but a plunging into history for the purpose of explicitating its deeper meaning and its capacity to give more of itself. Therefore priestly service can and must be effected in liturgy, as well.

Priestly service as we have described it makes possible, and requires, a determinate *existence and spirituality*, which must be concretized from a point of departure in Christ, but which follow from what has been said.

Priestly spirituality must be formally apostolic and missionary, in order to bring God to human beings, with the important nuance that it must be a spirituality that goes forth to seek the neediest of human beings. "I am ruined if I do not preach [the gospel]!" says Paul (1 Cor. 9:16). It must be mindful of those most in need of salvation—of the poor, of the lost of the house of Israel, or the pagans of Paul's time, with today's translations of "poor," "lost," and "pagans." Negatively, it must overcome the temptation of intraecclesialism, not to mention that of abandoning the world to its misery, whether out of incapacity, cowardice, or a fear of contamination with the real world of politics, conflicts, and revolutions. When this fear arises—naive or hypocritical, as the case may be—we may recall the example of Jesus, who took his meals with tax-collectors and prostitutes, those paragons of sin.

Priestly spirituality must be founded on the deep conviction that God's coming is good for the human being and for history, that with God, the humanization of both of these is enhanced, in quality and intensity. But all of this must be done not out of routine, but from conviction. Hence, on the one hand, follows the decentering of the priestly individuals or group themselves, since they desire to communicate not themselves (as it has always been said, the priest acts not in his own name, but *in persona Christi*) but God. On the other hand, we see a single-minded striving that the supreme good that is God really draw near to human beings, to the point indicated by Paul in his extravagant overstatement, "I could even wish to be separated from Christ for the sake of my brothers" (Rom. 9:3).

Priestly spirituality must be a spirituality prepared for conflict, inasmuch as the good news cannot be told and done without a denunciation of wicked reality and its champions, or therefore without the reaction of these latter against priestly service. Hence the priest's readiness for prophecy— with the conviction that this, too, is good for the human being—and persecution. Hence, again, the priest's need for fortitude, in order not to flag in the fight but rather hold firm to the very point of making a sacrificial offering of life itself in martyrdom.

Priestly spirituality must be a spirituality of witness, in such a manner that the vessel or vehicle of the priestly will personally evince, in all modesty and humility, that it is a good thing that God should have drawn near; and in such a manner that the priest will generate credibility (be ever more a "touchstone" of priestly service), and thus help bring it about that the God who draws near is accepted and "corresponded to"—help to bring it about that this God is able to invite (and demand) that response. An important part of that witness is creativity and freedom, as a condition for expressing that it is precisely God who approaches, God who comes by pathways divinely chosen, old or new: creativity and freedom as expressions of the all-consuming desire that God really come.

Priestly spirituality must be a spirituality that will kindle a priestly service to concrete persons, and not only individuals as such, but whole worlds in need of salvation. It is a spirituality that, accordingly, ought to enable its subject to gaze upon human beings with a regard of mercy and make an effective response to their needs—once more, not only individuals, but whole peoples, as well. Hence also the importance of being willing to work not in isolation, but as a member of the priestly "college"—in the narrower sense of the ministerial priesthood, as well as in the broad sense of an entire priestly church—in order to "bring God" more effectively. Hence, finally, the greatheartedness and magnanimity that enable priestly individuals and groups to relativize their own successes and failures, all of which are seen to pale alongside the success, or basic failure, of an entire priestly church.

Priestly service requires *historical verification*. When we say *verification*, we are referring to what occurs de facto and a posteriori in consequence of the performance of a priestly service. A priori, it can be said that the desire to bring God near will be unconditional and indefectible—as expressed in, among other things, the *ex opere operato* theory. A priori, one can say that priestly service requires a call and mission from God. Priestly existence, spirituality, and activity can also be determined a priori. All of this is important to keep in mind, but it does not solve the problem of verification. To put it very simply: The saving approach of God occurs when it occurs. When Jesus blesses his Parent because the little ones have heard of the Reign, when he sends the healed invalid or forgiven sinner away in peace, when he declares that salvation has come to Zacchaeus' house, his priestly service has been efficacious.

The importance of recalling something this obvious lies in the fact that priestly service can fail. The failure may be due to a shortcoming in the addressees, in the vehicles of the priestly, or in both. But it is important to ask oneself *why*, in each case, the failure has occurred. This is extremely important for pastoral theory and practice. Prescinding from any potential failure due to a shortcoming on the part of the addressee, one must ask oneself whether a determinate priestly activity met with success or failure owing to some factor on the side of the priest or the priestly activity itself. But the first thing to be done is humbly to recognize, to *verify*, whether there has been success or failure. By this we mean that, along with the effort to meet the a priori conditions of priestly practice, we must conduct an in-depth analysis of the results of that practice.

To begin with the negative side, it may occur that, either because of a sinful practice of priestly service, or simply by reason of incompetence, with all good will, the church fails to bring God to human beings. This has in fact occurred in Europe among intellectuals, in the world of laborers, and now more and more even among the middle classes. To put it positively: One observes that various local and particular churches in Latin America have brought God to many of the poor and have shored up the faith of the doubting, or at least have managed to bring it about that the problem of God be taken seriously among alienated intellectuals or agnostics.

Granted, God alone knows whether and when this divine approach to human beings has occurred. But we are not entitled to refrain from a judgment indefinitely, even though that judgment must be made "from without." It cannot simply be presupposed that all the right methods of bringing God near—all the right approaches to "pastoral practice," in the broad sense—are already known. One must learn what really happens.

Viewed from the opposite direction, there are novel pastoral approaches that are frequently judged risky and dangerous and yet bring God to human beings. The worker priest movement, Archbishop Romero's novel homiletic style, a pastoral accompaniment of base communities and popular organizations, and so on, are indeed seen to have brought God near. These pastoral approaches have been novel, to be sure, and at times they have been regarded as heterodox; yet they have proved effective.

It follows from all of this that the success of priestly service must be verified in the event, and not simply presupposed to be automatically at hand, as if one already knew how to attain it. It would be a sad thing—indeed, it would mean disaster—if the church were to apply to the priestly the ancient dictum: "*Fiat justitia, pereat mundus*"—"Do justice, though the world perish"—whose translation today might be, "Practice the priestly as you already know, regardless of how irrelevant it may become for the world."

As with any verification, the positive is discovered from a starting point in its contrary, as well. In order to ask oneself whether effective priestly service is at hand, one must look to see whether an unpriestly or antipriestly service is being performed, even among many conventional priestly activities. If interest in God and the coming of God is on the wane, if the proclamation of God is not grasped as good news, then—with the best or worst of intentions—service has been unpriestly. And if, still worse, the reaction to a service were to have been that of which "Scripture says, 'On your account the name of God is held in contempt among the Gentiles' " (Rom. 2:24; cf. Isa. 52:5, Ezek. 36:20)—then that service will have been antipriestly.

We repeat, a verification of the success or failure of priestly service must include an investigation into the attitude of the addressee, but it must not exclude that of the vehicles of the priestly. Persons who seek to be genuinely effective in their priestly activities will not be satisfied with defining the reality of these activities a priori, or offering their various activities to God by way of "intention," in order that their actions may be "priestly." An a posteriori verification is of the highest importance, both out of honesty with God and for the development of an effective priestly pastoral practice.

With the foregoing reflections and specifications in mind, we may offer the following synthesis. Priestly service at the theological level is a service that expresses, concretely and historically, God's saving coming to human beings and human beings' response to the God who comes. As this determination is a theological one, it goes further, and embraces the conventional distinction between universal and ministerial priesthood. Individuals or groups whose actions meet the criteria for a verification of priestly service actually perform that service, and any other priesthood, common or ministerial, must be understood in terms of this.

Priestly service must be performed in all of the fields or orbits in which God approaches the human being and the human being responds to God.

In the areas of God's approach to the human being, this service will be realized in several ways: (1) Through the word, which enunciates and announces—defines and proclaims to be imminent—God's saving reality, rescuing persons from their doubt concerning God, from any anguish or desperation they may be experiencing with regard to God, and laying bare their innate tendency to fashion their own gods. (2) Through an actualization of the content of that word, which content is the love of a God approaching as Parent and approaching in a Reign. (3) Through the liturgy, in which the word of the God who comes, that word ever ancient and ever new, is explained.

In the areas of the human being's response to God, this priestly service will be realized in several ways. (1) In the *mystagogía* that leads persons to accept this new, unexpected, and scandalous, but also transforming and good, news of God. (2) In the invitation-and-demand that human beings respond to, and correspond to, God's love in love for their siblings, at all of the levels on which the latter stand in need of salvation. (3) In fostering a liturgical response to the God who draws near, with gladness when this coming has occurred, with repentance when it has been vitiated by human beings' fault, and with humility, asking that it come.

Both services—to God's approach and to human beings' response—must be performed in partiality toward the poor and weak, which is the manner in which God actually comes. And they must be performed with a readiness to enter into the historical conflicts stirred up by such service, as well as with the fortitude needed to hold firm in the persecution unleashed by the gods of the wicked realities against those who render present the God of the good news.

Christo-logic Dimension of the Priestly

All that we have now said presupposes, of course, the reality of Christ. At this point, however, a specification of Christ's priesthood, the christo-logic dimension of priestly reality, is important for a concretization and elucidation of all that has gone before. It is likewise important for a verification (and correction, if need be) of whether what we have said thus far has been correct, or whether it has been excessively aprioristic, in terms of the reality of God. More concretely, a christo-logical analysis of priesthood is important for a normative determination of priestly existence, in order that the intra-church priesthood be understood in terms of the priesthood of Christ, and not in terms of the religions—that perennial temptation of the church.

As we know, the term *priest* (*hiereus* and derivatives) is not used in the New Testament to describe Jesus' person and mission, except in the Letter to the Hebrews. When the term appears elsewhere in the New Testament, it refers, with very rare exceptions, to pagan and Old Testament priests. One of the exceptions is Paul's explanation of his apostolate. "God has given me . . . the priestly duty of announcing (*hierourgounta*) the good news of God"

(Rom. 15:16), he says, thereby reinterpreting the priestly along the theo-logical lines set forth above.

The gospels present Jesus as a lay person of the tribe of Judah, not a member of the tribe of Levi. Of greater significance is the fact that, in their theological interpretation of Jesus, the gospels do not give Jesus the title of priest, although various other honorific titles are applied, and in Jesus' time the hope of a Messiah included that of the appearance of the definitive High Priest.

Nor in the rest of the New Testament, with the exception of the Letter to the Hebrews, is Christ denominated a priest, even though, in the reinterpretation of his salvific work, there is an allusion to the conceptual structure of Jewish worship ("Christ our Passover has been sacrificed," 1 Cor. 5:7); the typology of the "lamb" of reconciliation is used (Rev. 5:9); and the "blood" of Christ is mentioned in such a way as to imply the offering of a sacrifice (Rom. 3:25, 5:9; Eph. 1:7, 2:13; see the gospels, as well: Mark 14:24 and parallels). But on the whole, it was possible for Jesus and his work to be understood without an appeal to priestly concepts and terminology.

Nevertheless, Jesus' reality was priestly—fully priestly. Indeed, it was the only absolutely priestly reality, as the Letter to the Hebrews says. Before analyzing this letter, we think it would be good to go back to the gospel narratives, because what the letter says systematically of the priesthood of Christ and what we have called "theo-logical priestly service" will appear in the gospels concretely. Familiar as they may be, let us offer a brief résumé of Jesus' person and mission from the theological priestly perspective.

Jesus comes forward proclaiming the approach of the Reign of God as good news, and the approach of God as bountiful Parent. This approach occurs graciously, that is, by God's pure initiative. Jesus insists that that is the very nature of God, and demonstrates this: He demonstrates it positively in the parables of God's love and in his concrete approaches to the poor and sinners. He demonstrates it negatively in his controversies with those who do not wish that God should draw near gratuitously as Parent, and in his denunciations and exposés of them, as well as of those who act against the Reign of God by oppressing persons economically, politically, and religiously. In word and work, Jesus emphasizes that that approach of the Reign and the Parent is for the poor and little, and for those who are sinners in terms of the law.

All of Jesus' activity is governed by service to this approach on the part of God. Hence his miracles and exorcisms, his forgiveness of sins, his activity of preaching and guiding, his concrete approach to the poor and sinners; and on the other hand, his activity of denunciation, exposé, and controversy. In a word, Jesus strives passionately to show that God is drawing near in the divine Reign and is drawing near as Parent.

Jesus' activity is also ruled by the desire to help human beings respond to and correspond to God's approach. Hence his requirement of conversion, of following or discipleship, and of the practice of prayer. Hence also the commandment of love, of corresponding to God in the spirit of the Beatitudes, and so forth. All of this not as pure, cold requirement, however, but as response to the God come near—response costly but gladsome, being the response of the one who has found the pearl of great price or the treasure hidden in a field.

Jesus celebrates the fact that this is "the way God is," and that that God is drawing near. He rejoices when the little ones have come to know this, or when salvation has come to Zacchaeus' house, and he celebrates this coming in festival, when he takes his meals.

Throughout, Jesus refuses to differentiate between the secular and the cultic, between worship and actual day-to-day living. In the concrete reality of his time, as we know, Jesus saw public worship not as the locus of a privileged access to God, but rather as a suspect thing, a vitiated thing. Jesus fought a ritual conception of the human being's relationship with God, he fought an extrinsic conception of sanctification: "It is mercy I desire and not sacrifice" (Matt. 9:10-13; cf. Matt. 12:1-3, 15:1-20; John 5:16-18, 9:16; etc.). His obsession, if we may call it that, was with an approach to human beings, in whatever manner and whatever area that approach might be possible. And so we can say that he was priestly when he forgave the woman taken in adultery and restored her peace to her, when he approached lepers to show them that at least God had not abandoned them, when he taught prayer by calling God "Father," when he gave the hungry to eat and healed the sick, when he attacked oppressors in order that they might stand aside and no longer block the way to God, and so on. It was priestly for Jesus to make God's love present to persons, so that persons might know God and feel God's saving proximity. And he was also priestly when he invited and required human beings to respond to God, and not do as the ungrateful leper who had been healed or the cowardly rich young person—let alone as the powerful, who manipulated God in their own interest.

All of this activity shaped the interior of Jesus' person—his priestly existence, we might call it. In order to bring God to persons, Jesus himself approached persons, and the weakest of them. He himself approached God in prayer and in obedience, keeping faithful to the end. It was in this fidelity to God and human beings that he spent himself, and his life thereby became a sacrificed life. This is what, in the end, led him to the sacrifice of his own life—to being himself the victim.

After his resurrection, that life was believed and theologically interpreted as a life of authentic mediation, and as salvation. After all, in Jesus' life God has approached in fullness and forever, forgiving, healing, saving, and fulfilling human beings.

The gospel narratives are positively open to a priestly reading of Christ. In systematic terms, they are sufficient to establish Jesus' priestly reality and existence without any mention of the Letter to the Hebrews at all. However, an analysis of this letter continues to be important for a number of reasons. Hebrews is the only New Testament writing that analyzes priesthood systematically, therefore it will be important to examine the meaning of priesthood in the letter, as well as the methodology the letter uses to determine this. As for content, it will be important to observe whether and to what extent the content of the letter coincides with our own systematization, although we can scarcely expect an exact parallelism, nor ought the texts to be forced in such a way as to produce such a parallelism. As for methodology, it is important to observe that, although already aware of the intra-church ministries, the sacred writer appeals to the life of Jesus in order to establish priestly reality. That is, the writer does not state that Jesus is a priest as if he already knew, a priori, what priesthood is. He approaches the matter from the other direction: What is a priest? A priest is what Jesus is. Objectively, this ought to be obvious. And yet, it is scarcely obvious in the eyes of those whose argumentation for the purpose of determining the nature of the ministerial priesthood draws so much more on intraecclesial tradition than on Hebrews; and so it will be in order precisely to emphasize the "obvious." Furthermore, the letter expounds priesthood not only positively, but polemically, as well. That is, it explains priesthood not only by asserting what priesthood is but, in order to explain it even better, also by forthrightly expounding what it is not. Finally, Hebrews presents Christ's priesthood in the face of the temptation of the community to return to a more cultic, pietistic understanding of Christian faith. The readers of the letter were Christians who were weary, afflicted, and discouraged. Faith in Jesus seemed too much for them, and they preferred to return to a more traditional piety. Worn out by the sufferings they had to undergo as Christians (Heb. 10:32-34, 12:3-13) and disillusioned with the Parousia, which had not occurred (Heb. 3:14, 6:12, 10:36-39), the old religion, especially its worship, exerted a great attraction for them. In this context, the letter is no pacific dissertation on the priesthood of Christ, but a polemical one. It inveighs against the innate tendency to "pietize" (and thus dehistoricize) the Christian life and exposes any comprehension of the priestly that, coarsely or subtly, seeks its orientation in the model of the religions.

For all these reasons, the letter continues to be of great currency for a determination of priestly reality. Presently we shall analyze, systematically and not exegetically, some very important points in the letter that shed light on what we have said. More concretely, we will analyze the vigorous systematization in the letter itself of priestly existence and priestly sacrifice. But it will likewise be important to analyze priestly service at the theo-log-ical level, since this is what has guided our analyses thus far.

The most familiar point in the letter is its declaration that the old priesthood is null and void and its reinterpretation of priestly existence, worship, and sacrifice. However, our analysis will need to indicate the *object of service* of that new priestly existence and that new sacrifice. That is, we shall have to analyze the *constitutive relationality of Christ as priest*. In the letter, as in the rest of the New Testament, this is a basic presupposition. But we shall have to render it explicit, lest we confuse priestly service with priestly existence, important as the latter is for the former.

That priesthood is service is clearly stated in the letter in terms of the formal concept of *mediation.* That in which the mediation in question consists is determined, in a number of ways, from a point of departure in what it causes. Hence the general assertion that this mediation effects "eternal salvation" (Heb. 5:9; cf. 2:10), "sanctification" (cf. 10:10), "our entrance into the sanctuary," and our access to God (10:19-20). More concretely, the letter tells us that Christ "cleansed us from our sins" (1:3; cf. 10:11-14), "cleanse[d] our consciences from dead works to worship the living God" (9:14), so that we might have "our hearts sprinkled clean from the evil which lay on our conscience" (10:22).

The formality of priestly service is clear, then. Priestly service is Christ's service to God's salvation. We may wonder, however, whether the letter does not reduce God's salvation to the forgiveness of sins, ignoring the breadth of salvation we have described as the finality of priestly service. In order to reply to this question, let us keep in mind that throughout the New Testament, the forgiveness of sins is essential to salvation, and even a way of denominating salvation in its totality, although it does not exhaust it. More concretely, given the thematics and polemics of the letter in speaking of the new priesthood, it certainly had to be made plain that this new priest forgives sins. But this being said, we shall need to do some further investigating before we can determine the nature of the salvation in whose service the priest is. We must not try to force a mechanical parallelism with what we have already said, but neither may we ignore any affinity we find between the two explanations.

In the first place, let us remember that the letter presents salvation as the new, definitive covenant, as well—superior to that of Sinai (Heb. 8:5), and foretold in Jeremiah (Jer. 31:31-34) in a text cited in Heb. 8:6-13 and 10:16-17. While *covenant* can be understood in terms of public worship, so that rites of worship can go with a covenant, per se a covenant is salvation and forgiveness of sins. It is also more than that, however, as the text from Jeremiah shows. The nature of the salvation bestowed by the covenant in question may be gathered from what the letter says of the new manner of life of those who have received the grace of that salvation. In the passage immediately following his mention of the new covenant, the author proposes to sum up our new Christian existence as "the fullness of faith," "our profession which gives us hope," and "love and good deeds" (Heb. 10:19-25; cf. chaps. 3, 4, and 11, on faith; chaps. 12, 13, on hope; 12:14-13:21, on charity). Observing as a whole the response made possible by the new covenant, we can gather the constitutive elements of the salvation it bestows.

Furthermore, we must ask whether comprehensive salvation appears in the letter—what the gospels express with "Father" and "Kingdom of God," the key we are using for our own theo-logical interpretation of priestly reality. That the letter manifests a great affinity with the gospel narratives is evinced in its descriptions of Jesus' important traits: his obedience, fidelity, humaneness, and so on. Does the letter make an allusion to anything equivalent in content to "Father" and "Kingdom of God"? Without forcing the texts or looking for mechanical solutions, we can nevertheless answer in the affirmative. Baena[8] maintains that Jesus' service to the coming of the Father and the Reign of God finds its equivalent, in the letter, in the *mercy* of the high priest. This mercy is described skeletally and systematically, but at central moments. It is said of the high priest that he "sympathize[s] with our weakness" (Heb. 4:15), and that therefore we may trust that we shall "receive mercy" (4:16); that he is "able to deal patiently with erring sinners" (5:2); that he is "merciful" (2:17). Jesus' mercy can be characterized as an antecedent condition for the exercise of his priesthood, but it is also more than that. An active mercy is what moves Jesus to bring salvation, and the exercise of mercy is the realization of that salvation.

If the letter calls Christ a "priest," it is because it sees in Jesus the person of mercy. In the gospels we encounter the mercy of Jesus at every turn, and the texts there show us that they are presenting something central in Jesus. Jesus sympathizes with all in need. He "saw a vast crowd. He pitied them, for they were like sheep without a shepherd" (Mark 6:34, par. Matt. 9:36). He "was moved with pity" at seeing the widow of Nain mourning her dead son (Luke 7:13). "When he saw the vast throng, his heart was moved with pity" (Matt. 14:14). We read that he had compassion for a leper (Mark 1:41), for two blind persons (Matt. 20:34), and for persons who had nothing to eat (Mark 8:2, Matt. 15:32).

In all these passages, the verb translated as "pitied," "[his] heart was moved with pity," the like, is *splangchnizomai*, which comes from *splagchna*, meaning "innards," or "entrails." A com-passionate person's entrails wrench at the sight of keen suffering in others. The compassion of which the gospels speak flows from the furthermost depths of Jesus' "insides," and is not just one aspect of his psychology on a par with others. Mercy becomes a criterion of action, of mediation of the will of God, since Jesus acts in accordance with the dictates of that compassion. When Jesus would portray the human being who truly fulfills the law—the Samaritan of the parable—he defines him as the one who has been "moved to pity" (Luke 10:33). Even God is described as being "deeply moved" at the approach of the repentant sinner, who is represented by the returning prodigal child (Luke 15:20). The Greek verb we have just seen continues to be used in each case. And Jesus requires of human beings that they "be compassionate, as [their] Father is compassionate" (Luke 6:36).[9]

The letter calls Jesus a priest because of the mercy he feels and practices. Herein is the service of mediation between God and human beings. Jesus "is expressly understood as the very mercy of God, coming in concrete form to this world."[10]

The field of that mercy is comprehensive, not regional. Indeed, in Jesus' times, mercy is the condensation of all the great expectancies of the messianic era.[11] It is mercy, systematically speaking, that relates Jesus with the divine Parent and the Reign of God. Jesus forgives sins in the gospel and comforts the weeping, lowly adulteress (Luke 7:50); but it also is out of mercy that he heals infirmities. In at least four miracle accounts (Matt. 9:27-31 and par., 15:21-28 and par., 17:14-29, Luke 17:11-19), Jesus heals on the occasion of the petition, "have pity!" In the first controversy in Mark—although here it is the controversy that is emphasized, rather than Jesus' mercy—Jesus heals a paralytic and forgives his sins (Mark 2:1-12, Matt. 9:1-8, Luke 5:17-26). In that mercy, Jesus renders God's coming real. "Mercy is the love typical of God, who humbly stoops to the weak to raise them up."[12]

It is in this comprehensive context of mercy that we must understand forgiveness of sins as salvation. To be sure, without forgiveness of sins there is no salvation, and a very important part of salvation is forgiveness of sins. But seen from the standpoint of God's actual saving reality, forgiveness of sins is but one moment within the totality of salvation. Speaking systematically, and taking account of the whole of the New Testament, the salvation process could be described as follows. God has had pity on human beings and has come near them in Christ. God vanquishes the sinner from within, by approaching that person with incredible goodness. This goodness is manifested visibly, through the healing of the human being's bodily element, as well. Then that human being who has experienced God's mercy is transformed for the exercise of mercy toward others.

This, we hold, is a valid approach to an interpretation of mercy in the letter to the Hebrews in its relationship with the essence of priestly service. It may be that our approach ought to be complemented with certain exegetical nuances; but on the systematic level with which we are concerned, we have at least shown that the exercise of mercy is by no means secondary for priestly service, and that it explains a good deal of that service, even in the letter. Jesus' priestly reality, then, can be described in this way:

> Jesus is God's mercy in person, which comes to this world and approaches human beings concretely and physically, touching them in their temporality and their flesh, that they may trustingly and unconditionally deliver themselves over to that same action of God and be transformed into what God is, mercy. Forgiven persons, in turn, are capable of mercy.[13]

The letter presents the fundamental characteristics of *priestly existence* in the service of God's salvific coming. That is, it explains how the priest is basically to be and act, how the priest is to relate to God and human beings.

Regarding the priest's relationship with God, the priest is chosen by God, called to the priesthood by God (Heb. 5:5-6). The priesthood is communicated not through the flesh, but through the call of God. "It is clear that our Lord rose from the tribe of Judah, regarding which Moses said nothing about priests" (7:13). This familiar, repeated assertion is of the greatest importance, since it configures the priest not only in terms of origin, as one called, but in terms of existence. That existence is, before all else, theological: The priesthood is realized, rendered actual, in responsibility to God, and ultimately to God alone. Hence the letter's description of the relationship between the priest and God not only as response to a first call, but as obedience (5:8, 10:5-10)—ongoing availability to the will of God, which is novel and unmanipulable and subject to no limits or preestablished channels, not even in the area of the priestly. Thus, the letter asserts that Christ was a true priest because he was faithful to God (2:17, 3:2)—because he remained obedient to God's will, as the gospel narratives show us in their accounts of Jesus' prayer and temptations.

With regard to the priest's relationship with human beings, the priest must be close to them, and thus cut through the category of separation that was fundamental in the old priesthood. The letter describes this intimacy, systematically, in terms consonant with the data of the gospel narratives. It programmatically states of Christ that he was in all things equal to human beings except sin (Heb. 4:15). That there may remain no doubt of this, it makes the astounding declaration that God made him "for a little while lower than the angels" (2:9). This assertion echoes the unanimous conviction of the New Testament concerning Christ's true humanity, but in a precise, polemical context which sheds light on that authentic humanity. It would seem that the devotional environment of the letter's addressees included a certain Christology of the angels, strongly motivated by soteriological interests. The angels are close to God and therefore can work salvation: hence the popularity of a cult of the angels, "a seductive mélange of false mysticism and religious formalism."[14] Over against this conceptualization, the letter makes a twofold declaration. First, Christ's action is more powerful than that of the angels, since he is closer to God than they: He is at God's right hand (1:4). But second, he works salvation in virtue of being closer to human beings than they: He is "less than the angels." Christ manages salvation not from above, as do the angels, but from below, from the fullness of his humanity. Thus, the letter rejects the temptation of any priestly "angelism," whether in the raw form we have just analyzed or in its substitutes down through history.

While not a sufficient condition for the effectuation of salvation, the priest's authentic humanity is asserted to be a necessary one. Christ's humanity is part of priestly existence in the quality of that humanity as related to the rest of human beings, and this in a precise way: He is not only a human being, but a sibling. That is, he is not only similar to human beings, but intimately akin to them—a co-sharer in their human condition. "Therefore he is not ashamed to call them brothers" (Heb. 2:11). In fact, the letter shows that Christ shares that which is weak and imperfect in what it is to be human: It mentions his anguish (5:7), his suffering (2:10, 5:8). In this wise, his intimate kinship with human beings becomes solidarity with them, for he has been tried and tested ("tempted") "in every way that we are" (4:15). Because he, too, suffered, he can aid those who suffer (2:18). Because he, too, was "beset by weakness, he can feel compassion" ("deal patiently," *metriopathein*, 5:2). Thus, emphasis is laid on the constitutive partiality of priestly existence toward, and from amidst, what is weak in this world.

These two characteristics—Christ's fidelity to God and solidarity with his siblings—are historical not only in their describable content, but in their processuality, as well. The letter is at pains to assert that Christ *attained* to the status of priest. To this purpose, it declares that Jesus "had to become like his brothers in every way" (Heb. 2:17), that he had to undergo a learning process ("he learned obedience from what he suffered," 5:8). Christ is presented as a priest from eternity to eternity ("You are a priest forever," 5:6), but this "forever" has a history: Christ was made perfect (2:10) and came to be the cause of salvation (2:10). Accordingly, priestly existence is not something given once for all, nor can it be defined in the abstract. One comes to be a priest through a process, in fidelity and solidarity, and the process has its culmination in the surrender of one's own life. The actualization of this "coming to be" is what makes Christ not only our sibling, but the firstborn among us—the actualized potential of the priestliness of every human being. Thus, the high priest is also described as "our forerunner" (6:20), the pioneer on whom we ought to "keep our eyes fixed" (12:2). Priestly existence, then, becomes exemplarity.

Priestly existence as we have described it stands opposed to traditional priesthood. The priesthood of Hebrews is realized and verified in history, not in the detached ambit of public worship. The letter sets that difference in relief when it points to the difference between the priests of old (who were set apart, rigorous with human beings, sinners incapable of entering into intimacy with God) and Christ (who is near, merciful, "holy, innocent, undefiled," Heb. 7:27). Hebrews shows the difference between the sanctuary of the temple and the city where Christ dies, between fleshly rites of worship and the existence of Christ.

The greatest difference between the old and new priesthoods, however, and the highest degree of historicization of the true priest, occurs in the determination of *sacrifice* and *victim*. For the logic of the letter, it is evident that there can be no priesthood without a sacrificial offering (Heb. 5:1, 8:3). The only problem is in the relationship between the two. In the old priesthood, a distinction prevailed between priest and victim, between personal priestly existence and the rites of sacrifice that this existence implied. Now this distinction has been abolished. The offering presented by Christ is inseparable from his own existence. Christ enters the sanctuary "not with the blood of goats and calves, but with his own blood" (9:12). He "offer[s] himself up" (9:14; cf. 9:25), and not something distinct from himself. The rites accompanying his sacrifice are his own life and lot (5:7-8, 9:15,26).

In the letter, therefore, Christ's sacrifice is the most historical element of his priesthood, and the most priestly element of his historical life. We may well ask, however, why this is so. What relationship obtains between Christ's self-sacrifice and theo-logical priestly service? In other words, why and how does that sacrifice bring God near? The letter does not directly pose itself this question, since, in its theological conceptualization, sacrifice is precisely the essence of mediation. But with regard to this or any other theological conceptualization, we ourselves must inquire into the relationship between sacrifice and priesthood, in order to methodologically avoid their simple identification.

Obviously, service to God's coming is historically a service of sacrifice. Paul speaks of the hard work (*kopos*, 1 Cor. 15:58) of preaching the gospel. Although it cannot be decided a priori whether this service leads or may lead to the sacrifice of one's own life, this is what actually occurs. The gospels narrate the fact and adduce its historical causes. The letter observes and theologizes the fact, as well as indicating its de facto historical causes—fidelity to God and solidarity with human beings. From a historical standpoint, the possibility that the priest may have to lay down his life cannot be excluded. On the contrary, it is included. Availability for this act is part of priestly existence.

But this is not yet an answer to the question of the deeper, constitutive "why" of the relationship between priesthood and sacrifice. First, why is this sacrifice necessary in order to bring God to human beings? Second, why is it efficacious for this purpose? The first question ultimately has no answer—although the fact is observed time and time again, and the New Testament itself uses this argumentation to compare Christ's death with that of a prophet. The assertion that this is God's design elevates the scandal to the status of a mystery, but does nothing more. Negatively, one can only say that the servant of God is vanquished by the gods of death, and that, in very God, there is a moment of helplessness before these other gods.

The second question—why the sacrifice of Christ the priest is effective—can be answered in terms of various soteriological schemas. At bottom, however, these, too, fail to convince, since they leave it unexplained how destruction in itself can be reconciled with the reality of a God who means to approach salvifically. We shall find the answer only if we can relate the negative in sacrifice with the positive of the God who comes. And this we can do. From this viewpoint, what Christ's death says is that in God there is a great love (an absolutely simple phrase, but irreplaceable); that this love is so great that, in human language, it delivers up the Son (Rom. 8:31, John 3:16); and that Christ's death out of concrete, historical love for human beings is the expression of God's love. The actual power and efficacy of that love of God's will appear only in the Resurrection, but Christ's sacrifice evinces the truth of that love and endows God with credibility. One thing, at least, is clear: It is true that God approaches human beings limitlessly and unconditionally.

Sacrifice is but the consequence of a genuinely "proexistential" priestly existence, an existence in behalf of human beings. To hold firm in sacrifice is nothing but to say in human fashion that one really loves human beings and seeks their salvation. According to Christian faith, it is the whole of the Paschal event that expresses salvation and the coming of God. It is the death/resurrection of Christ that generates hope and the practice of charity, that expresses God's definitive, total approach to human beings, in the firstborn, Jesus. Jesus has been raised because he has been our savior; and the letter says, beautifully—once more, in a determinate conceptual structure—that he is still savior as the one who has been raised, that he is still intercessor (Heb. 7:25, 9:24). The sacrifice does not of itself constitute the intercession, although it accompanies it. What constitutes the intercession, and thereby the intercessor, is being "on behalf of human beings." In the last analysis, sacrifice is to be explained by love: historical love for human beings to the point of sacrifice, that unconditional expression of God's absolute, unconditional love.[15]

We are now in a position to sum up the christo-logical dimension of the priestly—that is, of priestly service *in actu*. The priesthood of Christ is at the service of God's coming, and the kernel of that service is the exercise of the mercy of God, who bends low to the weak in that which makes them weak, sinful, anguished, tried, and so on.

This priestly service is realized in a theological and anthropological existence, in faithful obedience to God, and in solidarity with one's siblings. That priestly existence is historically sacrificial in virtue of this double characteristic: It leads one to give of one's own life, and to the supreme sacrifice of giving up one's life. The fact cannot be deduced a priori, but once verified, it can be reinterpreted as the maximal expression of fidelity to God and human beings alike, and on the other hand as that which endows with credibility the God who comes.

Is There Priestly Service in Latin America?

By way of concluding these reflections on priestly service, we should like to state once again what it is that we have attempted to do. We claim to have analyzed neither the concrete problems of the ministerial priesthood today nor the technical meaning of the common priesthood. Each of these deserves a separate treatment. We have only attempted to set forth the substance, as it were, of priestly service—that which will be absolutely required in any form of its ecclesial exercise. We have sought to understand the priesthood from a starting point in God and Christ, and not in the intraecclesial element of the church, necessary and legitimate though that element may be. We have taken as our guide the method of the letter to the Hebrews, which knows the intra-church ministries (as exercised by those who proclaim and bear witness to the faith: Heb. 2:3-4, 12:1). It praises the leaders of the community and regards them as being of great importance (13:7,17), inasmuch as it is they who have "spoke[n] the word of God to you" (13:7) and who "keep watch over you" (13:17). It even elevates them to normative status: Those ministers are to be obeyed, and their faith imitated (13:17,7). But it does not list priests (not a very important omission) or attempt to deduce from them the nature of priestly reality (which it is indeed important to remember). This article, then, suffers from the obvious limitation of not having considered the ecclesiological dimension of priestly service. But it does claim to have overcome a more basic limitation and more common temptation: that of a failure to understand priestly service consistently from a starting point in God and Christ.

We have also sought to offer a systematic concept of priestly service and existence. It might be argued that this systematic determination is excessively deductive, and even that it "proves too much." As for priestly existence, we do not think this to be the case, since a deduction from a starting point in Christ is indispensable, and is the only way to determine priestly existence as *Christian*. As for priestly service, it might be objected that it "proves too much," since what we have said of this service could also be applied to evangelization, or to the entire mission of the church. To be sure, it will be of prime importance to determine the essential nature of the service to be performed by the church, whether that service be called priestly, evangelizing, or simply ecclesial. But it is also important to determine the nature of the priestly. In the first place, the church makes abundant use of the language of the priestly, and some theo-logical content must be assigned to that language. If our systematization were to seem inadequate, then another should have to be sought out, but it would still need to be one that indicates the relationship between priestly service and God, and that does so concretely enough to account for the denomination of this service precisely as priestly. Neither, in the second place, must we overlook the fact that, in our own day, as well, the nature of the priestly is not infrequently appealed to as one of the ways of glossing over deviations from the gospel and attacking novel and risky actions undertaken by the church with a view to defending oneself from these actions. It is sometimes customary, in the name of the priestly, to disparage authentically Christian actions. Thus, it has seemed important to us to describe these activities as genuinely priestly and thereby defend them. Finally, and positively, we have seen, in the language of tradition and the religions, the priestly in relation to God's salvation. Therefore we have tried to reinterpret priestly service in terms of this salvation of God's, although this reinterpretation ought to be present as well when we speak of evangelization, revelation, God's self-communication by grace, and so on. The concrete analysis that we have applied has succeeded in helping us concretize the specificity of priestly service in its relationship with God's salvation, which salvation is comprehensive, and therefore whose conceptualization must be present in the treatment of any theological theme.

This article has sought to provide priestly reality with a theoretical explanation. Not that the origin and finality of this article are purely theoretical. At its origin is the observation of what has been done by the church in Latin America, and this is what has guided our theoretical analysis from its starting point in a basic premise: What makes the church authentically priestly is service to salvation. That premise, known and accepted theoretically at the outset of our argumentation, has thereupon ceased to be a mere premise and been transformed into something central, in view of the reality of the church's activity. The finality of this article has been none other than to inspire and encourage the church to be more priestly.

Let us conclude with a few words about all that we have said in conceptual form, from the standpoint of Latin America. Latin America offers an optimal locus for priestly service, and its concrete historical reality makes that service an absolute necessity. In Latin America today, as in Jesus' time and place, whole peoples stand in urgent need of salvation and await the same in active hope. The collective misery, the injustice and oppression, the annihilation of indigenous cultures and peoples, the repression, the torture, the "disappeared," the murdered, the massacres, the refugees, and so forth, on this continent show how urgent salvation is. This reality has become a mighty cry of the peoples, who have a great hope: to be able to live, and to live with dignity.

These peoples are able to describe their hope of salvation in nonreligious terms, but they express it in religious language, as well: God wills not that human beings die, but that they live, and this God is capable of giving them life. Furthermore, the poor have turned to the church, as well, in their quest for salvation—an expression (implicit, perhaps, but effective) of their sense that salvation is from God, too. Indeed, they have made an option for the church before the church has made an option for them.

It is this reality and this hope that have made priestly service and a fundamental challenge to the priesthood of the church necessary and possible. Priestly service must extend to all of the orbits or fields described above, but its great field, within which all concrete fields acquire their relevance, is the field of life: " . . . That they might have life and have it to the full" (John 10:10). Apart from or independently of this field, the partial exercise of the priesthood would be vain, since it would not be nourished by its deepest vital theological sap.

Not all persons concerned, of course, have responded to that priestly demand, and among those who have responded at the beginning there may be some who have withdrawn from their response. But neither can it be doubted that many—from cardinals and bishops to ministers of the word and members of communities, as individual Christians and as church groups, as communities, dioceses, and even bishops' conferences—have reacted in the manner of the high priest of the Letter to the Hebrews: with a great mercy. They have been touched by misery and the hope of living and have assigned genuine primacy to that misery and hope. They have changed their eyes, to see this world with God's eyes; they have changed their hearts, to feel the pain of this world as God feels it. In consequence, their feet, as those of one who proclaims good news, have traversed new paths that lead to the poor, and their hands have been put to work in defense of those poor. It is this great mercy that underlies the church's movements of insertion among the poor, its work in the defense of human rights, its struggles to foster justice, its dogged endeavor to create communities that are alive. Mercy has sprung from and fostered that which is fundamental: "We must defend God's minimal gift, which is also the maximal—life," Archbishop Romero said.

This is the basic priestly attitude, and indeed this is how the poor have interpreted it. The poor, with the unblurred vision of those who live and suffer reality, and antecedently to any ideologization, have grasped that, in this ecclesial movement, salvation has drawn near, and with salvation, God. Whether or not they verbalize it—frequently, they do verbalize it—they grasp that the God of the Exodus has descended again to deliver them; that the God of the forty years in the Sinai accompanies them still; that the God of the prophets has come forward once more in their defense; that the God of Jesus offers them a new Reign; that the God of the cross is with them to the end; and that the God of the Resurrection is working once more the wonder of hope and life.

That the poor have found "salvation" and "church" once again is something supremely important, both for the poor and for the church. That they actually grasp these in the reality around them means that the church has become genuinely priestly and that, in order to become priestly, it has had to return to the most fundamental element of its faith: faith in a God who truly wills to save and faith in the power of that God to save. This might have simply been assumed to "be there." After all, it is elementary. But we cannot simply assume that it will "be there." A routine, doctrinal rehearsal of the salvific will and power of God is one thing, and the conviction that this is the way things are actually observed to be in history is another. It is this deep faith in a saving God that has moved the church to render God present in history and the human heart. There is no "reductionism" here— the accusation we so frequently hear—in service to God's coming. Why? Because one really believes in a saving God and works to establish the Reign of God, but works that that Reign be precisely of God. One has worked for siblingship, but also for human beings' discovery of their Parent. In many communities, especially those of the poor, along with work for liberation, there is also an honest, joyful standing before God to be converted—to open to God, to ask God to fill them with the spirit of the Beatitudes, in order to accomplish things as important and difficult as reconciliation or forgiveness, in order to become ever more and more, in Jesus' footsteps, the daughters and sons of their heavenly Parent.

Priestly service seeks really to bring God's full salvation. But its premise is the conviction that God is good for human beings. It is this sort of practice of the priestly that has restored faith and hope in God to their pristine value.

The Reign of God and the God of the Reign, the Parent's love and the Parent who loves, are once more in their proper place in the order of things. The recovery of these values is historical verification that priestly service has been performed. Beyond any doubt, when the church has performed that service, faith has grown among believers, has gained strength among the doubting, and has obliged unbelievers at least to take seriously what they had formerly seen as being of little moment, or even as alienating. God, through the work of bringing God's salvation near, has been made to "come alive" again.

This priestly service has engendered a priestly existence that reproduces the traits presented in the Letter to the Hebrews. On the one hand, it generates openness to God and the quest for the divine will. The enormous efforts being expended to discover the will of God today cannot be ignored or reduced to a simple doctrinal function. Among the results: magnificent, existentially meaningful insights, from the grand discernments of Medellín to the lights that flash in meetings of the base communities; the search for the signs of the times, discovered in the misery and hope of the people, but also in things as concrete as the popular organization of the peasants, as Archbishops Romero and Rivera acknowledged in a pastoral letter; days of reflection; countless meetings; theology itself; and so on. From the standpoint of the priestly, all of this demonstrates openness to God and fidelity to God's will as continuously sought and discerned; openness to new mechanisms for finding that will, such as dialogue between hierarchy and grassroots, or among theologians, social scientists, and pastoral agents. And so on. These activities, which are public and visible, presuppose prayer to God, as well, personal or collective, joyful or anguished, and are expressed in liturgy, in the celebration of the word, and so forth. In this wise, the church has become a faithful priest.

But on the other hand, priestly service has generated the church's approach to human beings. After long years, the church has surrendered a certain "exteriority" vis-à-vis our continent and has become "Latin-Americanized." This has meant not only sharing in the nature or culture of the men and women of the continent but, above all, sharing in their weakness and need. The church's insertion among the poor, solidarity with them, and option for them, is the priestly solidarity of the Letter to the Hebrews, that simultaneous effect and cause of priestly mercy.

This priestly existence in the exercise of priestly service has produced countless martyrs. It is a priestly existence consummated with the sacrifice of one's very life, even as the life of the high priest. For one thing, millions of human beings die a slow or violent death: whole crucified peoples, who resemble more the servant of Yahweh than the high priest, but crucified peoples who—in the difficult faith-assertion—"shall justify many" (Isa. 53:11). But alongside this more generalized phenomenon, thousands of Christians accept death as the lot befalling them in their priestly service.

Many have been threatened, arrested, "disappeared," tortured, and murdered.

This new, massive fact in Latin America is of the highest importance for verifying that there have been priestly service and existence. At times, a casuistry is applied to determine whether the persons who offer this sacrifice are actual martyrs or not, just as it was applied to the death of Jesus, who was sentenced as a blasphemer according to some, and a subversive according to others. If the casuistry is applied in good faith, then the conclusion is reached that abundant priestly blood has flowed. And if it were to be applied in bad faith, then not only would a most serious injustice be done so many martyrs, but methodologically—with the methodology of practice, a mightier one than the purely theoretical—we should be once again steaming down the wrong track when it comes to determining priestly reality, a track running counter to its deepest essence. If all of this bloodshed is ignored—if we fail to learn from the priestly terminus of the process the priestly element in that service, if we fail to discover in this generous surrender of life that which is great priestly mercy and fidelity to God—if we do not make of all this something enlightening and central for a determination of the priestly, then I fail to see how we can manage to understand what is priestly; but then neither shall we be able to appeal to the Letter to the Hebrews for this understanding. If, when Christians more resemble Jesus, this resemblance is not discovered, then the explanation must be—despite so many protestations to the contrary—that the essence of the priestly is regarded as already established, with logical anteriority to an analysis of the concrete priesthood of Christ.

Can priestly reality be summed up in one word? Vatican II recalls that priesthood means seeking the glory of God. By coincidence or good fortune, in Latin America, too, this language has been used. Archbishop Romero quoted the familiar text of Irenaeus: "*Gloria Dei, vivens homo; vita autem hominis, visio Dei.*" "The glory of God is a human being alive; and the life of the human being is the vision of God." He vigorously reinterpreted the first member: The glory of God is the poor when they come to life. He actually paraphrased the second member, without explicitly alluding to it, when he declared: "None know themselves, so long as they have not met up with God." Archbishop Romero's entire mission, like that of so many others, consisted in bringing God near by bringing life to the poor and enabling everyone, especially the poor, to draw near to God and thereby to life in all its fullness.

This had the effect of rendering an entire local church a priestly one and even effecting the renewal of the intraecclesial priesthood in terms of apostolic priestliness. But the source of it all was the great mercy Archbishop Romero felt toward the poor of this world in fidelity to God, which meant seeking salvation for those poor, and in his interior, crucifying self-emptying so that he might be mediator and priest. Many others have been, and are, like Archbishop Romero, and this is why there has been, and is, priestly reality in Latin America. What remains needful is a church not less, but more priestly.

—*Translated by Robert R. Barr*

8

Bearing with One Another in Faith

A Theological Analysis of Christian Solidarity

The New Phenomenon of Christian Solidarity

The early 1980s witnessed a growing movement of solidarity toward Christians and churches in Latin America. Because it is something new and yet quite sizable, this solidarity deserves study. Such a study ought to involve an analysis of what has actually happened, to be able to define in Christian terms what solidarity means. It also ought to uncover the deepest roots of solidarity and clarify what the rediscovery of solidarity means for the church and for faith.

The reflections I offer here are based on the solidarity shown toward the people and the church of El Salvador, so they bear the limitations inherent in any particular case study. On the other hand, I believe the solidarity shown toward El Salvador is an eloquent case history in the contemporary life of the church and quite sufficient for working out some theoretical guidelines for what might be called a "theology of solidarity." In any case, these reflections are based on solidarity as it has actually appeared, not on an a priori and merely conceptual formulation.

On a descriptive level, what I wish to stress is first the immense movement of solidarity toward the people and the church of El Salvador. Many individuals and institutions have made the church of El Salvador their "neighbor," in the gospel meaning of the term: They have not taken a detour in order to avoid seeing the wounded victim on the road, but instead have come closer to examine the situation and help. Cardinals, archbishops, bishops, priests, and religious men and women of the Catholic Church, delegations from Protestant churches, and theologians both Catholic and Protestant have come to this country. Many professional politicians, journalists, jurists, members of human rights organizations and aid agencies have also come, and many of them, in addition to their professional capacity, have shown their specific concern as Christians. They have carried out their visit in a Christian way, engaging in dialogue with church personnel, taking part in meetings and liturgical celebrations with other Christians, and, most of all, coming close to suffering Salvadorans in the countryside, in jails, and in refugee camps.

Many others who could not come here have nevertheless from afar made the Salvadoran church really their neighbor. There have been countless letters from grass-roots Christian communities from all over the world, especially from Latin American rural and urban workers and Amerindians belonging to such communities, as well as from priests, religious, academics, and professional persons. Bishops from various countries and sometimes whole episcopal conferences have made official statements denouncing the repression, the violation of human rights, and the persecution of the church, and they have supported the guidelines given by Archbishops Romero and Rivera, encouraging the poor to keep up their hope and remain steadfast in their just struggles. Groups of theologians have signed and sent letters of solidarity, circulated theological and pastoral writings emerging from Central America, and offered their own thinking to shed light on Central American problems. Many institutions have sent material aid for the poor and persecuted, for refugees and exiles, for social and humanitarian works of the church, and for its communications media. Persons in many countries of Europe and the Americas have organized solidarity committees in order to receive and share reliable information, raise funds, pressure their governments, and organize liturgies and solidarity demonstrations.

Finally there are those who have come from outside and have stayed close to their neighbor, working in isolated parishes and aiding the suffering population in pastoral, humanitarian, and theological ways. As a symbol of this kind of solidarity, we may recall those who have remained forever at the side of the people as martyrs. The martyrdom of the four women missionaries from the United States and of priests who have come from other countries is the supreme expression of their really coming close and giving all.

What first strikes the eye in this vast movement of solidarity is the aid that other Christians and other churches have offered the Salvadoran church. Nevertheless, in order to describe correctly what has happened and adequately work out a theological concept of solidarity, we must analyze more deeply what is behind this phenomenon and delineate how it differs from other phenomena that seem to be similar to solidarity but, strictly speaking, are not expressions of solidarity.

Solidarity of this sort is not mere humanitarian aid, of the kind that often is prompted by natural disasters, for example. That kind of aid is obviously good and necessary and is a correct response to an ethical imperative. But if solidarity were no more than material aid, it would not be anything more than a magnified kind of almsgiving, where givers offer something they own without thereby feeling a deep-down personal commitment or without feeling any need to continue this aid. In authentic solidarity, the first effort to give aid commits a person at a deeper level than that of mere giving and becomes an ongoing process, not a contribution.

Moreover, when the initial aid is given, the giving and receiving churches set up relationships. It is not a matter of a one-way flow of aid but of mutual giving and receiving. This point enables us to get closer to what solidarity actually means, but again we must clarify what is specific to the kinds of relationships that solidarity creates between churches.

One could think of solidarity along the lines of an alliance between different churches to better defend their own interests, along the lines of solidarity as conceived in politics. But this idea would not explain the true origin of ecclesial solidarity; it has been generated by the self-interest of a particular church but rather in order to help the "other" church, which itself has turned to "others," the poor, the oppressed, the suffering. Hence solidarity is not an alliance formed to defend one's own interests, even though through solidarity many churches are discovering what their true interests ought to be. If the alliance model were the real basis for under-standing solidarity, the ultimate judgment on it would have to be that it was simply a matter of ecclesiastical self-centeredness, whether because the interests of the churches as a whole were given priority over the interests of the poor, or because one church sought its own advantage in helping another church. But neither of these approaches is what has actually given rise to solidarity.

If it is not simply aid from one church to another or an alliance between different churches in order to promote their interests, what is the specific element in solidarity? Further on we shall analyze this point in a more detailed way. At this stage it would be useful to single out the elements that have set solidarity in motion in recent history, to bring out what is specific in solidarity when seen from a Christian viewpoint. (1) Solidarity has been set in motion when some churches help another church that is in need because it has taken on solidarity with the poor and oppressed among its own people. (2) These helping churches find out that they not only give but also receive from the church they aid. What they receive is of a different and higher order: They usually describe it as new inspiration in faith and help in discovering their identities in human, ecclesial, and Christian terms and in relationship to God. (3) Through mutual giving and receiving, the churches establish relationships and make the discovery that in principle it is essential that a local church be united to another church and that in principle this mutual relationship embraces all levels of life, from material aid to faith in God.

This new way for Christians and the churches to be related (a matter of both fact and principle), which starts with the basic solidarity of the church with its poor and oppressed, is maintained as a process of mutual giving and receiving and is raised to the level of faith (although it takes its origins from ethical practices carried out in ongoing history). This is what is meant by solidarity. This is the way for Christians and churches to relate to one another in accordance with the well-known Pauline admonition, "Bear with one another." This is a conception of Christian life and a way of practicing it in which reference to "the other" is essential, both in giving and in receiving, both on the human level and on ecclesial and Christian levels, and the level of relationship with God, both in seeing in the other the ethical demand of responsibility and in finding graciousness in that other. Solidarity is therefore the Christian way to overcome, in principle, individualism, whether personal or collective, both at the level of our involvement in history and on the level of faith.

The Origin of Solidarity: The Fact of the Poor

The root of solidarity as I have thus far described it is something both real in history and effective. By "real in history" I mean that the present form of solidarity has not been set in motion by an effort of the will or by imposition from above, as if solidarity were something good in itself and therefore to be practiced. By *effective,* I mean that what has happened in El Salvador and elsewhere is of such a magnitude that it has been able to emancipate many churches from their centuries-old isolation.

The objective fact we are speaking of, which is both real in history and effective, is the fact of misery, oppression, and injustice in which millions of human beings live. The unveiling of this truth has amounted to a revelation for many persons elsewhere, including Christians, and they have felt questioned and challenged by this objective reality. The truth of the poor has therefore made its appearance, and many have grasped this truth and reacted appropriately.

There are two aspects to this discovery that, although they are related, should be distinguished if we are to understand solidarity: What has occasioned the discovery of the truth of the poor (the genetic focus, a question of fact); what has actually been uncovered (the systematic focus, a question of principle).

The Disclosure

From a purely genetic viewpoint, what began to attract worldwide attention and set in motion initial solidarity was the fact that some churches took up a stance vis-à-vis the world of the poor and accepted the consequences of that stance. What is involved is the kind of solidarity that is constitutive of a church and is prior to solidarity between churches, although it is basic to it: service in solidarity offered to the world of the poor. What has happened is that the desire of Medellín that "the church in Latin America be one that evangelizes the poor and stands in solidarity with them" (Poverty of the Church) has become a reality.

The Disclosed

It is clear that it was the murder of priests in 1977 that first drew attention to what was going on in El Salvador, because it provided the news media with something different. This spectacular fact served to uncover the persecution (unfortunately less spectacular and newsworthy) of the rural and urban poor, pastoral ministers, grass-roots Christian communities, and church institutions. In a word, the persecution of the church became known. (See, e.g., Martin Lange and Reinhold Iblacker, eds., *Witnesses of Hope: The Persecution of Christians in Latin America*, Maryknoll, N.Y., Orbis Books, 1981.)

This cruel and public persecution led to questions about the causes behind it or, in other words, to the mission of the church that brought persecution to it. Even though the answer had been known on a theoretical level, the reality of this mission finally broke through to many thoughtful observers: it was the overall liberation of human beings who live in inhuman conditions, whose most elemental human rights are utterly violated, and who are repressed in all their just strivings for liberation.

Persecution of the church therefore had two important effects. The first, which was more immediate and evident, was incipient solidarity with a persecuted church. The second, less apparent at first but deeper and more important in the long run, was the unveiling of the fact of the poor, of their situation and their future.

In the order of logic, coming to know the truth of the poor is independent of knowing what happens to the church. But for many Christians (and in general for persons of good will everywhere), the persecution of the church has been decisive in their discovery of the truth of the poor. If even the church is repressed and its priests are murdered, then it becomes quite credible that such is also the lot of the poor. What is worse and more tragic, the anonymous poor will be repressed with even fewer scruples and misgivings than those shown toward the church as a public institution. Moreover, because it was newsworthy, the persecution of the church brought to the attention of the world images, testimonies, and commentaries on the horror of repression. In this way the truth of the poor was communicated in a way that went beyond dispassionate narration; it managed to reach levels of feeling. The truth of the poor was not only made known; it unleashed indignation and protest. Finally, because it is the church that is persecuted and communicates the oppression and repression of the people through its own persecution, this truth is automatically presented as an ethical demand on others. The truth of the poor, thus unveiled, requires a response not only with a theoretical judgment but with a practical judgment that sets in motion some form of concrete action.

In sum, the truth of the poor, already known theoretically and often affirmed by the church, became a truth that was "more real," "more the truth," when it was proclaimed credibly by a persecuted church. Furthermore, it was proclaimed as a truth that must not only be registered in conscience but as a truth demanding a reaction.

This genesis of solidarity in ongoing history is thus an example of a common phenomenon: What comes first on the level of reality comes last on the level of knowledge, and vice versa. On the level of knowledge, what has set solidarity in motion has been the harassment and even murder of priests and of at least one bishop, Archbishop Romero of San Salvador. Nevertheless, on the level of (antecedent) reality, the sequence is the reverse. Awareness of these two levels or sequences is instructive both for individuals and for churches seeking to follow the dictates of their faith.

When persons have correctly grasped the two sequences for what they are in reality, then they are ready to sink deep roots in the movement of solidarity, including the dimensions of that movement relating to the church and God.

In principle, the discovery of the reality of the poor is the origin of solidarity, because this truth is a primal call to the human dimension within any person and a challenge based on the fact that each of us is socially a part of all humankind. It brings with it a demand for change and conversion, for persons to recover their true identity underlying a falsified identity. And it provides the opportunity to recover this identity through co-responsibility for the poor.

In theological terms, the basic issue is ultimately that in many places it has become clear that God's order of creation is threatened, debased, and repudiated. This elemental truth is often soft-pedaled or passed over in silence or, in any case, presented in such an undynamic way that it does not really register in personal or collective awareness. But concerned individuals and groups made it their business to dissipate deceptive smoke screens and "call a spade a spade."

The true condition of the poor has been discovered, documented, and disseminated. Their cry has not only gone up to heaven, but has made itself heard around the earth. Many men and women in Central America and elsewhere in the world are dying the slow death of oppression or the quick death of repression. This is the most basic fact in the world today, and it is a fact utterly in defiance of God's will.

This basic fact is a challenge to the very idea of humankind and its intrinsic unity. This fact unmasks the understanding of humanness imposed on others by analogy to its assumed "superior" Western prime analogue—the modern human being living in an affluent society, *the* human being.

The facts belie this facile assumption. The bulk of humankind is made up of poor persons whose lives are seriously threatened at basic levels. In comparison to them, the so-called modern human being of affluent societies is an exception. Taking the exception as the *analogatum princeps* of the human being is at least questionable. Those who want to maintain this position ought to recognize that Western humanity is the exception in the order of logic and ask themselves whether it is not also the exception in the order of causality: Is the exceptional life of some perhaps due to the large-scale exploitation or death of others?

Seen in this light, the unity of humankind cannot be conceived in an idealistic fashion as participation in the monolithic essence of what it means to be human, nor can the differences among human beings be explained simply in terms of different degrees of participation in the being of Western humanness. Much less may the differences be put forward (at least initially) as differences that are enriching and hence to be taken into account for planning a unified humankind. At present, humankind is not simply differentiated but deeply divided. The basic difference is between being close to life or close to death, between affluent societies where life and the most basic rights of the human person are safeguarded and societies where misery, blatant violation of human rights, and death prevail. What makes this division especially critical is that these differences do not simply coexist; they stand in a mutual cause-and-effect relationship.

Co-responsibility

Our reflection up to this point unavoidably simplifies matters, but it was important in order to understand the roots of solidarity. The unveiling of the de facto condition of the poor has served to force individuals and groups to reformulate the question of what constitutes the most basic problem in human history and the most basic division between human beings. It has served to relativize and unmask the Western world, which with its penchant for autonomy, development, and abundance has been taken to be the model of what is human and civilized.

Most of all, this unveiling has served to lead many to feel questioned and challenged in the social dimension of their personality, beyond the social aspect touching on family, civic, church, and national groupings. To put it most concisely, they have come to seriously question what it means to be a human being in this divided humankind where some live and others die, where the life of some partly depends on the death of others, and vice versa. The co-responsibility that must be shouldered if human beings are to be fully human has thereby been accentuated. The unveiling of the situation of the poor has prompted believers to reformulate and rethink the question of their faith in God, again at the most basic levels of life, beyond a faith simply imbibed from their ambient culture or one that merely tries to survive the threat posed by unbelief. It has served to make these basic realities a mediation of the question of God and the response to the mystery of God. Put simply, it has served to integrate into the nucleus of faith God's question to Cain, "What has become of your brother?" And it makes a positive answer to this question a fundamental mediation of the practice of faith.

This response to the suffering of the poor is an ethical demand, but it is also a practice that is salvific for those who enter into solidarity with the poor. Those who do so often recover in their own life the deep meaning they thought they had lost; they recover their human dignity by becoming integrated into the pain and suffering of the poor. From the poor they receive, in a way they hardly expected, new eyes for seeing the ultimate truth of things and new energies for exploring unknown and dangerous paths. For them, the poor are "others," and when they take on solidarity with them, they undergo the experience of being sent to others only to find their own truth. At the very moment of giving, they find themselves expressing gratitude for something new and better that they have been given. It is not difficult to recognize that what the poor provide insofar as they are others is a mediation of God's gratuitousness. But whether this gratuitousness is explicitly referred back to God or remains unidentified, it is clear that in aiding the poor one receives from them meaning for one's own life. In this manner the initial aid becomes solidarity—giving and receiving, bearing with one another.

The root of solidarity is accordingly to be found in what generates human co-responsibility, makes co-responsibility an imperious ethical demand, and makes the exercises of co-responsibility something good, fulfilling, and salvific.

The role of the church in setting this solidarity in motion has been twofold. First, in a more instrumental way, the church has played a positive role in helping others come to know the truth of the poor majority, so that those who are not poor will not, in Paul's phrase, "imprison the truth with injustice," but rather come to recognize the tragic situation of the majority of humankind as the bottommost fact of our present history. The church has been an instrument for giving voice to the cry of the poor majority, who by their very existence are trumpeting the proclamation that today one cannot be a human being *and* disregard the sufferings of millions of other human beings.

Secondly, to the extent that the church has itself become a church of the poor, it has become a real symbol of the poor, not only pointing to their truth from outside, but expressing that truth within itself. A church incarnate in the world of the poor, that defends their destiny and shares in their lot of persecution and death, visibly manifests the reality of the poor of the world.

In this way, the church shows how it can and must be church today and what its identity is. But it also shows how one can and must be human today and which road leads toward the utopia of a united humankind: It begins by turning to the poor and bearing their poverty. Such a church dissolves isolation between churches and helps dissolve isolation between the world of the poor and the world of those who live in affluence. But the root of this desegregation and positive solidarity is to be found in the first and basic solidarity with the poor of this world.

Solidarity as the Basic Way for Churches to Relate to One Another

The church's turn toward the world of the poor, whether in the universal church or in a particular local church, is the basic solidarity of the church, that with which it carries out and maintains its identity. Moreover, it is this basic solidarity that begins to dissolve the isolation of local churches and establish new, positive relationships between local churches. On the basis of this fact—always keeping in mind its roots in de facto history—it is possible to reformulate and better solve a series of theoretical problems regarding the essence and history of the church—problems with important practical consequences. These problems touch on the relationship of the churches with one another and the relationships between the different confessions. I am going to focus here concretely on the catholicity of the church, missionary aid from one church to another, and the ecumenical movement. I believe these three issues can be formulated better from the angle of solidarity.

The catholicity of the church, which has always been held to be one of the essential notes of the true church, means that there is one universal church realized in the multiplicity of local churches. There is only one church because there is only one God, only one Christ, and only one Spirit. This is what demands and guarantees the unity of the church. Inasmuch as this, rather than something created, is the ultimate root of unity, the church should in principle have the capacity to extend to different places and take on the peculiar features of those places. If such were not the case—if only certain places, certain situations, or certain cultures were suitable embodiments of the church—it would amount to a forceful denial of the transcendent origin of the church and would set quantitative and qualitative limits to what God can do. The true church is inherently both universal and local.

We have here in this theoretical formulation the problem of the one and the many, and how to combine them. It is very important to know which theoretical model is used to resolve the problem. Very serious practical consequences are at stake. Three theoretical models, none of which may be perfectly verified in the concrete, have been used to explain the nature and functioning of the church: uniformity, pluralism, and solidarity.

The Uniformity Model

The theoretical model of uniformity presupposes that the essence of the church exists prior to its concrete embodiments. Catholicity means that different local churches share in this essence. The model recognizes a minimum of diversity of participation—diversity resulting from historical and cultural differences in local churches. In the best interpretation of this model, such differences are regarded as possible enrichments of the overall composition of the universal church. But in practice the tendency was always to minimize differences, and the ideal proposed was that of the greatest possible similarity between local churches.

This model was the one in effect in the Catholic Church in the years prior to Vatican II. In the name of the universality of the church, the tendency was to encourage (sometimes through imposition by administrative means) not only the same doctrine and the same morality, but also the same liturgy, the same administrative policies, the same theology, and even the same philosophy. The tension inherent in catholicity was broken in favor of universality and the greatest possible resemblance between churches. This, of course, led to absurdities. To give just one example, seminarians all over the world studied philosophy from manuals written with a nine-teenth-century mentality and published in Spain. The element of ecclesial localness disappeared. In this model there was no allowance for positive and mutually enriching relationships between local churches. They were merely set alongside one another, and there was little to differentiate one from another as churches. This was seen as the ideal to be pursued for the sake of church unity.

The Pluriformity Model

The uniformity model fell apart in both theory and practice at the time of Vatican II. It ceded place to pluralism. The emphasis was now, in principle, on the necessity and importance of the local element in the church; diversity in liturgical, pastoral, and theological expressions were encouraged. This diversity was understood as being an enrichment for the universal church. There was no reason why diversity should threaten church unity; in fact it could only enhance that unity.

Nevertheless, two important factors are missing from the pluralist model, and even more from the uniformity model.

The first is that the localness of a church—that is, its character as formed by historical, economic, social, and political factors—is given virtually no ecclesial importance. In other words, no importance is given to the concrete world in which the church is incarnate. Nor is adequate consideration given to the need for a church to be incarnate in misery and poverty as basic elements of its localness, or for a church to specify and concretize its mission in accordance with these down-to-earth realities. These realities do not figure in either the uniformity or pluriformity models as mediations for faith, for the following of Jesus, for building the church. It is not clear in them how the fundamental differences resulting from milieus of misery and affluence, and the new responses of churches to these situations, can be seen as enriching the new liturgy, new pastoral practices, and the theology flowing from them.

The second thing missing is that, although pluralism is legitimized in order to do justice to the local church and enrich the universal church, there is no provision for relating local churches directly—and urgently—to one another. In other words, in this model there is no way for decisively introducing co-responsibility between churches, mutual giving and receiving, bearing with one another, as a form of catholicity. Therefore, the pluralist model, although legitimate and necessary in itself, and although it marks an advance over the uniformity model, does not get much beyond being a legitimate demand (in the liberal mold) that the right of local churches to autonomy be recognized.

The Solidarity Model

The third possibility is to understand catholicity in terms of solidarity between different local churches. In the tension between universality and localness, the latter is given preference for the sake of authentic Christian universality.

To begin with, catholicity means co-responsibility between local churches. Mutual love is seen as the essential and primary element for relating local churches with one another and unifying them. This loving co-responsibility is achieved through the mutual giving and receiving of churches to and from one another. This giving and receiving should be extended to diverse areas of the life of the church—liturgical, pastoral, and theological—but based on something yet more fundamental: giving and receiving in the practice of faith. Catholicity thus means bearing with one another in faith.

This bearing with one another in faith should not be understood in a formal and abstract sense but as practiced in the concrete. That is why it is all-important to determine what practice of faith it is that actually sets in motion this bearing with one another in faith. Such practice should include responding to God's will regarding the life and death of human beings. Solidarity between churches therefore presupposes that somewhere in the universal church there is ecclesial solidarity with the poor. That is how bearing with one another is practiced today.

Catholicity understood as co-responsibility is not an obstacle to the universality of the church, but rather helps to build it up. If this co-responsibility penetrates to the level of faith, the catholicity of the church is simply the building up of the faith of the universal church in history, a faith made up of pluriform and different faiths. Bearing with one another in faith is how the faith of the one church is embodied in ways that are related to ongoing history, differentiated and complementary. In no way does this deny that in the church there are universal levels and procedures for judging different expressions of faith. But these levels and procedures do not create the reality of the universal faith, which is built up when there is a genuine readiness for giving and receiving the faith to and from one another. Unity in the content of the faith is guaranteed by the magisterium of the church, but unity in embodying faith in that content is made effective when faith interacts with faith.

Within the universal church at particular moments there are some local churches that are privileged. It would be a mistake to think of the universal church simply as an agglomeration of all the local churches, with no one of them more important for the universal church at a particular moment. However it is to be explained, at certain periods one local church better incarnates the suffering of humankind, better announces the good news to the poor, denounces sin more clearly, suffers persecution more than other churches do, and gives the witness of supreme love in martyrdom. In a word, it better carries out the mission and embodies the essence of the church, is more clearly seen to be the sacrament of salvation, and gives greater witness of faith in God, in Christ, and in the Spirit.

As a result, some local churches are a leaven for the whole church, as the church should be leaven for the world, and these local churches should be seen as occasions of grace for the universal church. Naturally, this in no way gives such churches any reason to be arrogant, but it does demand that the universal church not overlook these occasions of grace and certainly that it should not reject them, but rather that it should turn its eyes to these churches. That is where it will more easily find God's will through the signs of the times, and also learn how to respond to them.

I hope that these reflections will aid in understanding a little better what the catholicity of the church is, and how important it is. Catholicity means direct co-responsibility between local churches, giving and receiving the best they have, teaching and learning their most valid insights, bearing with one another. At particular moments there emerge privileged churches that set this process in motion. It is their right to do so, because they embody better the essence and mission of the church. When this process takes place, the universal church is built up and the unity of the church is made real in history. The foundation and ultimate guarantee of this unity is transcendent: God, Christ, and the Spirit. But unity in history is based on incarnating this faith—that is why it is all-important to examine where this faith is best being incarnated—and on doing so together, "bearing with one another in faith."

Mission

A concrete and important form of catholicity is missionary activity. Traditionally, "to engage in mission" means going to other places to announce the faith to non-Christians and founding local churches. Here, however, I understand by missionary activity the sending of missionaries (even if they do not refer to themselves that way) from local churches in the First World to local churches in Latin America in order to help extend and strengthen the faith in our churches, which suffer from a shortage of priests, sisters, and lay pastoral ministers. I understand this activity as solidarity— that is, as the way that local churches of the First World and those of Latin America bear with one another on the basic level of faith.

In a number of First World churches, and certainly in the most perceptive, the meaning and purpose of sending missionaries to Latin America has become a problem. One indication of it is that different orders and congregations in the United States that send religious to the Third World have had to hold conferences on the issue.

Part of the problem comes from the danger (and often the fact) of neocolonialism and domination. Although this problem is serious, there is in theory an answer on how to overcome it: acculturation and an attitude of service. Nevertheless, I believe that at a deeper level the difficulty demands answers to two questions arising out of missionary activity itself and not simply *how* it is carried out: What does it mean to engage in mission in Latin America today? What does it mean to be sent unilaterally to provide a service? Although they are expressed here in an abstract manner, these questions arise out of the experience of missionaries and the churches that have sent them. Let us examine them in some detail to see how the solidarity model may aid in answering them.

The problem involved in the first question may be expressed as follows. Missionaries come in order to communicate the faith they already have, the faith already embodied in their local church, and indeed it could not be otherwise. They come in order to communicate generously what they have—their faith. The question that arises is whether this faith, inevitably in the concrete form of the faith of a local church, is adequate for doing missionary work in Latin America. Furthermore, the aim one has in announcing the faith to others depends on how one understands the faith. To put it very simply, the missionary (or any Christian) faces this question: Does the faith that I possess at this point give me any reason to communicate it to others?

Two basic answers, different but complementary, can be given to this question. The first, more traditional, reply is that faith is communicated so that others, as individuals, may come to possess faith or have it strengthened. This is the understanding of mission as the gaining of converts, in a positive, not pejorative, meaning of the term. The second answer is that faith is communicated so the kingdom of God may become a reality. In this view, mission is understood as evangelization, in the sense the term has for Isaiah and Jesus—that is, liberation. Logically, the first line of missionary activity would emphasize the truth of what is announced; the second would rather emphasize putting love into practice. The question then put to the missionary, particularly to one coming from a distant environment, is how to fit together these two notions of doing mission.

We now turn to the problem involved in the second question. When First World churches send missionaries, they are providing a service, they are giving of what they have, sometimes the best they have, and along with missionaries they provide other resources of all kinds. Missionary activity thus formally consists in giving. But by their own experience they know that besides giving they also receive from the churches that are the object of mission. They know that they, as First World churches, give out of their manifold abundance, but that they also receive from the poverty of the churches to which they are sent in mission.

Hence the question: Is it correct to see mission as a one-way service of one church to another? Is it enough to understand missionary activity as the unidirectional sending of missionaries? Putting it more sharply, can we correctly understand missionary activity today without a prior willingness to be the object of mission from those to whom mission is directed? It is a Christian truth that one who gives receives, and throughout history many missionaries have expressed their gratitude for how much they received when they engaged in mission. The question here, however, is structural rather than personal: Are local sending churches willing to receive from mission-receiving churches?

These questions are not abstract but concrete. They are questions posed by mission-sending churches of the First World, which are in fact member churches of the same universal church that subsists in Latin American churches—churches in the world of the poor. In this concrete situation, answers to the questions posed above can be framed in terms of missionary activity conceived as solidarity, as mission sending and mission receiving churches bearing with one another.

The framework of solidarity broadens the focus on missionary activity as moving only in one direction. In the concrete, sending missionaries means the service of one local church to another, but also the possibility that the mission-sending church may be evangelized by the mission-receiving church. In this formulation, mission is a positive concept for both mission-receiving churches of the Third World and mission-sending churches of the First World.

When missionaries are sent not only to respond formally to the mandate that there be missionary activity and not only as an expression of the generosity of a local church (although this is very important), but also with the awareness of their own need to be evangelized, overseas missions become very important for the local sending church. When persons go to an overseas mission and bring its reality back to the First World in their writings or other forms of communication, or when they return temporarily or permanently, then their First World church acquires a new principle for its own growth. This principle is simply the admission of the presence of the poor into the First World church so that it may find a broadened Christian way to its own conversion, its own faith, its own ecclesial mission. To set out to engage in missionary activity "with all the consequences" will shatter the one-way image of mission and view it instead as solidarity.

This conception of mission modifies and completes the theological notion of sending. Missionaries are sent by their own church to other churches, and this sending ultimately derives from God. It is God who sends, and hence all missionary activity has an essential component "from above." However, if mission is conceived as solidarity, then missionaries are re-sent to their original local churches by the poor of Latin America. This sending has no canonical status, but it is no less real on that account. It is a sending from the poor, "from below."

Solidarity thus introduces a circularity into the theological category of sending. In de facto experience, that is the way it has often happened. Many missionaries who come to preach the faith of their sending churches later return to them with the faith of the poor with whom they have worked in mission. But the circularity is also theological, given the twofold presence of God, both in the institutional aspects of the church and in the poor. In the former, God is present with the mandate to "go to all nations"; in the latter, God is present evangelizing from the side of the poor. Therefore sending cannot be adequately understood in a one-way sense. Christian willingness of local churches to send missionaries entails an openness to having them sent back by the poor churches of Latin America.

A circular understanding of sending is an aid in carrying out missionary activity as solidarity—that is, as not only giving but also receiving. With this point we have clarified the second question posed above. We now have to answer the first: What does it mean to engage in mission in Latin America? In my view, answering this question means taking seriously the one who is to be evangelized. The one at whom evangelization is aimed is not simply the "person," nor is it the "pagan." It is ultimately the "poor person." According to Christian faith, the poor are the privileged object of God's love and Jesus' ministry. If we take this correlation with utter seriousness, if we accept with utter seriousness that God loves the poor just because they are poor and that Jesus announced the good news directly to the poor, then it is from the vantage point of the poor that the missionary will best understand the content of evangelization and the best way to evangelize. This is valid for the missionary's own faith as well as for his or her missionary activity.

Simply by being poor and having the theological significance we have noted, the poor person is, for the missionary, first of all a question and a challenge. That person is not just someone ignorant who must be taught, but someone from whom (or at least through whom) the missionary must learn what is most basic in the Christian faith. The poor person relativizes the missionary's knowledge, despite whatever prior knowledge he or she may have possessed. The poor person's abundance of not-knowing, which may make the missionary uncomfortable, is nevertheless the precondition for concretely putting into practice what the missionary knows. In a word, and stating it in a radical form, the otherness of the poor person provides the not-knowing that is essential for knowing God. This otherness, however, because it is the otherness of the poor person and not simply of someone else like the missionary, drives one back to God's otherness in a manner that is specifically Christian. We shall not arrive at God's otherness simply by extrapolating what we already know of God, but rather in discontinuity from what we already know of God. The poor person is the one who in de facto history relativizes and even contradicts what missionaries coming from affluent countries believe they already know of God. Accepting this relativization and contradiction brings missionaries to a better knowledge of God. The same could be said of other basic contents of the Christian faith such as Christ, the church, love, truth, and so forth.

When missionaries have been taught the faith, they then understand what it means to communicate it to the poor and how to maintain the tension between announcing the faith so it may be believed (making converts) and practicing the faith (building up the kingdom of God). To be a missionary to the Latin American poor means proclaiming to them the truth of God and Christ and making real what they want in a manner that is both dialectical and unified, in such a way that announcing the faith moves toward the practice of the kingdom and that the practice from within itself clarifies the content of the proclamation.

This complementarity could conceivably be discovered in an unhistorical manner by analyzing the texts of revelation, but it is in fact discovered when persons go to engage in mission with the poor. The discovery in ongoing history is what has made it possible to discover such complementarity in revelation. The proclamation of God's truth so that it may be believed is important because it is the truth, but also because this truth not only speaks of salvation but, once it is pronounced, it also becomes an integral, salvific element in history. The practice of the kingdom of God is important because it is a Christian exigency—and in Latin America an exigency that is urgent and indispensable; but that practice is also important because it sheds light on God's truth as believed.

It is the poor who make possible in history the synthesis between announcing God's truth and incarnating God's kingdom, between announcing Christ and following Jesus, between truth and charity, between proselytism to increase the number of believers and deepen their faith, and work for liberation. When missionaries from abroad take with utter seriousness the fact that the object of their mission is the poor person, then they begin to understand the reason for coming to Latin America and what it means to engage in mission.

Missionary activity is therefore solidarity between local churches. We have already hinted at what the poor give to mission-sending churches. Obviously they have "neither gold nor silver" to offer. But when they send missionaries back to their local churches, the poor offer their own poverty as a questioning of the way that being human is understood and as another possible way to be human. When the poor live their poverty with spirit, with gospel values, with courage in persecution, with hope in their struggles, with the kind of love that can sustain martyrdom, what they are offering is simply their faith.

They also offer, not for rote imitation but to serve as inspiration, the Christian creativity that poverty with spirit generates: new pastoral and liturgical experimentation, grass-roots community enterprises, new forms of lay ministry, new modes of theological reflection. All this they offer gratefully to those who help them from outside.

What mission-sending churches offer has also been suggested. They provide all kinds of necessary resources. They send missionaries, many of whom work resolutely, some to the point of offering their lives in martyrdom. They offer the humility of respecting the values of others and learning from the faith of others. When they do all this, what they are offering is simply their faith.

Moreover, under present circumstances, solidarity with Latin America and the sending of missionaries constitute a kind of reparation by First World countries for what was done in the past. Mission as here portrayed is not only a Christian obligation, it is also an obligation derived from history: reparation for other kinds of church involvement and political intervention of an enslaving nature. Solidarity cemented by mission becomes a small and indeed utopian sign of how relationships between the First World and Latin America should be. For the "vital interests of an empire" they substitute the interests inherent in the life of the poor. The service that missionary solidarity renders here is not slight—although, admittedly, it is utopian—when it shows how international relationships can be mutually beneficial and denounces types of "aid" that are nothing but intervention. At least some churches will stand out as a sign of true international solidarity.

Ecumenical Movement

It is in the ecumenical movement that the different Christian confessions relate to one another today. The issue it deals with is how the different "universal" churches (composed of local churches) should be related.

As is well known, there has been a change, in both theory and practice, in the understanding of what these relationships should be and what purpose they serve. There is an awareness among the different confessions (except for some extremist Protestant sects and similar Catholic movements) that disunity is not willed by God, that it is an evil whose origin is to be found in sin, although it is not a sin to belong to one confession or another, and that it is a scandal. The evil of disunity is no longer attributed to a particular confession separated from the rest, but to disunity in itself. It is this disunity as such and the scandal it produces that must be overcome.

On the other hand, there is also recognition today that the diversity among the confessions, with their different emphases regarding the understanding and practice of faith, bears an aspect of mutual enrichment, inasmuch as historically and in practice some confessions have emphasized certain elements that are basic to faith and other confessions have emphasized others. It is a diversity that is enriching both in principle and in what it has yielded in practice.

This new ecumenical attitude therefore presupposes that a confessionally based sort of Manichaeism and mutual condemnation between confessions has been overcome. It assumes mutual respect and acceptance, and it especially assumes the urgent need for unity between the different confessions.

The point I want to develop is that the ecumenical movement will function better if the relationship between the different confessions is understood in terms of solidarity, "bearing with one another." This is simply an extension of the formal framework I have been using for this entire analysis. But what I wish to underline is that for such interconfessional solidarity to exist there must be an antecedent and underlying solidarity of each and every confession toward the poor. This is so for the general reasons already set forth and specifically because ecumenism is based on overcoming disunity and scandal. The diverse confessions will not overcome them in a Christian manner if they do not overcome the basic disunity and scandal afflicting humankind itself. I therefore intend to reformulate the premises of ecumenism, with a view to understanding it as solidarity between confessions.

Interconfessional solidarity without a preliminary solidarity with the poor of this world is out of touch with reality, anti-Christian, and difficult to achieve in real history. I therefore want to analyze how the primary solidarity with the poor relativizes and unmasks certain assumptions of the ecumenical movement and at the same time provides premises for building ecumenism upon a firmer foundation.

Division

The ecumenical movement assumes that in itself, division is something evil and not willed by God. But we must examine the seriousness of this evil and its varying degrees. If division means simply the existence of differences between confessions, that would not be an evil at all, and might even be enriching.

If division means the lack of unity in some formulations of the faith, in the liturgy, and in the way the church is organized, that might be an evil for a church that understands itself as "one," but it would not in general be regarded as a grave defect. However, if division means noteworthy and opposed differences in the substance of the faith and practice of the gospel regarding God's will for the world of the poor, that division would be an evil, inasmuch as it would simply reproduce among the diverse Christian confessions the basic division existing in humankind.

The division that is the most striking and scandalous is the division between the poor and the opulent, between oppressed and oppressors. That division is not simply a lack of unity, and it is not simply the expression of the fact that the hoped-for unity of the human race awaited in the eschatological eon has not yet arrived. Rather, in itself it is sin, and fundamental sin. The fundamental division in humankind is that between life and death, between those who die because of oppression and those who live because of it.

It is on the basis of this fundamental division that the evil involved in other divisions must be judged, and it is on the basis of the urgency of overcoming this fundamental division that the urgency of attaining any other kind of unity must be judged, including the unity of Christian confessions. Confessional division would be fundamental if some were to stand on the side of oppression and others on the side of salvation. Fortunately, there is no such division that actually occurs. What I have in mind in making such a drastic description of what a fundamental division would be is to propose what the fundamental unity should be: conceiving and practicing a faith that stands in favor of life and not of death for human beings. This kind of unification around such a central point would unify the churches in an interconfessional way.

Scandal

The ecumenical movement assumes that division, in addition to being evil, is a scandal—that is, it seriously impedes the acceptance of the faith and entails loss of credibility for the churches vis-à-vis the world. But again we must recall the fundamental scandal the churches may give, so that we may better understand how much scandal there actually is in their division. In the New Testament, the greatest scandal a Christian and believer can give the world is inconsistency between what is expressed as faith and the practice of that faith. Addressing Jewish believers, Paul says:

> Now then, teacher of others, are you failing to teach yourself? You who preach against stealing, do you steal? You who forbid adultery, do you commit adultery? You who abhor idols, do you rob temples? You who pride yourself on the law, do you dishonor God by breaking the law? (Rom. 2:21-23).

And Peter says to Christians:

> Among you also there will be false teachers who will smuggle in pernicious heresies. They will go so far as to deny the Master who acquired them for his own, thereby bringing on themselves swift disaster. Their lustful ways will lure many away (2 Pet. 2:1-2).

The effect of this inconsistency is described with words that could scarcely be more harsh: "Because of you God's name is blasphemed among the nations" (Rom. 2:24, *Bibl. Lat.*). "The way of truth will be defamed" (2 Pet. 2:2, *Bibl. Lat.*).

For believers, blaspheming God's name is undoubtedly the greatest scandal. And it takes place on the level of ethical conduct, of the practice of the faith at primary levels. Today the name of God is blasphemed—and unfortunately it does happen—when churches of any confession whatsoever ignore the problems of humankind, relativize them in God's name, or worse yet actually stand on the side of those who oppress the poor.

That is the point from which we must judge how great a scandal there is in disunity, and not the other way around. That is why a formulation of the ecumenical movement that, in the legitimate search for unity, would not seek at the same time to overcome the primary scandal and indeed give its overcoming a logical primacy would in itself be scandalous. It would also be scandalous to formulate the ecumenical movement in such a way that the topics it took up, the expectations it evoked, and the accomplishments it celebrated would ignore overcoming the fundamental scandal or treat it as something secondary. Such a course would not lead to a Christian way of achieving church unity. It is in the effort to overcome the fundamental scandal, in basic consistency with faith in God and a practice in accordance with that faith, that the churches will gradually unite—even though there remain differences in the way things are formulated.

These reflections point to a suspicion and an exigency. The *suspicion* is that down at the bottom of the ecumenical movement there lies a fundamental division that is not between confessions as such but between different ways of living the faith in a Christian and ecclesial manner, and that this division runs through the diverse confessions. It would follow that the unity sought and achieved on the level of the way the faith is formulated covers over a division that is real and profound, and that, on the other side, running through different formulations of faith there may be a fundamental unity in what is primary in faith.

The *exigency* is that the ecumenical movement must be relativized, for both theological and ecclesial reasons. Theological relativization means that the ultimate aim of the ecumenical movement ought to be the overcoming of the fundamental division in humankind, and that it is around this task that the work to overcome interconfessional differences ought to be carried out. Relativization in an ecclesial sense means that the boundary line today is not between different confessions, but that in fact it passes through them all. Before seeking unity of the churches, we must therefore seek that truth of the church wherein the different confessions can be united.

Such a relativization would be quite fruitful for the ecumenical movement. Without it, the movement toward church unity would be absolutized as something ultimate and definitive, and that would simply be proof of ecclesiastical concupiscence. However, when it seemingly forgets itself as it strives to provide the world with a way to solve *its* division, the church becomes truer to itself and lays down the true foundations for interconfessional unity, as indeed the experience of recent years has shown.

The ecumenical movement should not assume that the basic elements of faith are sufficiently assured in the different confessions and that the point now is to draw closer on relatively minor points of faith. Rather it should aim at tempering the foundations of faith in an interconfessional way: faith in a God of life, liberating and crucified; faith in Jesus as the one who announces the good news to the poor, denounces and unmasks the sin of the powerful, as the definitive servant of Yahweh, who shoulders the sin of the world and is executed by this sin, and is therefore raised up by the Father; a faith that is translated into the following of Jesus in the changing situations of history as it unfolds.

Seeking ecumenical unity through mechanisms that are purely ecumenical is not the answer. The answer must be sought in what can really make possible and set in motion a true unity. And that is nothing else but what I have called the foundations of faith.

Such a common basis for ecumenism has in fact led to a deep solidarity of different Christian confessions with the poor, at least in Latin America. Most of the poor in Latin America are Catholics. It would be a mistake to understand the ecumenical movement in Latin America as aid from Protestant confessions to Catholics. The wider and better view is that aid has come from different confessions to Christians who are poor.

This approach to the poor has unveiled the fundamental division in humankind and automatically relativized divisions between the churches. It has posed the problem of unity in faith more from the side of faith than from the side of unity. It has emphasized as an essential ingredient in this faith the defense of the poor and the struggle for their liberation. It has clarified the essential elements of the faith that really come to be shared in common, even though differences in formulation do not disappear. The result has been an important movement toward unification between the different confessions within Latin America, and also in the First World as its churches relate to Latin America. At the same time, other divisions have deepened, not between the confessions as such, but within any church of any confession to the extent that its members have or have not entered into solidarity with the poor.

The different confessions have their own doctrines of faith and their own particular formulations. The poor question and challenge the reality of both. The poor present the different churches with an otherness that is greater than their mutual differences, and that is why they can be so challenging. But they also are the ones who make unification possible. The poor are a mediation of God in ongoing history, a mediation of the Lord who is present in those who are crucified, the ultimate criterion of the faith around which all the confessions must be united. The poor actually bring to pass what is called—because it is so difficult to achieve—the "miracle" of union. They are also mediators of God's captivating power. The unending prayer of the churches to God that the grace of unity be granted is to a great extent being answered through the paradoxical power of the poor, through the mysterious creativity that solidarity with them produces.

Unity in faith between different confessions may be described as a movement toward unity in faith that is set in motion and kept in motion by solidarity. The greater the solidarity of the confessions with the poor, the purer will be their faith and the truer it will be in practice. By the same token, it will be a faith that is increasingly shared in common.

Within this movement of basic solidarity, the ecumenical movement among the diverse confessions can itself be viewed as another instance of solidarity, as different confessions bearing with one another, each giving the best of its unique tradition and also receiving from the other confessions. Although the following summation is in no way an exhaustive or exact description, it is undeniable that the Catholic Church has emphasized the necessity of works for salvation, the importance of the sacraments as focal points where grace is conferred in history, the importance of tradition as a historical and ongoing mediation of God's revelation, a certain autonomy and substantivity to be found in nature. Protestant churches have emphasized the importance of personal faith, the gratuitous nature of salvation, the efficacy of the word. The Eastern churches have emphasized the importance of contemplation, the liturgy as celebration, and a view of salvation as affecting not only human history but the very cosmos.

This diversity of emphases that some years ago was often presented as reflecting basic opposition is now seen as mutually enriching. The ecumenical movement as conventionally understood has no doubt been a help. But I believe that the real synthesis of these varied emphases is being accomplished within grass-roots solidarity with the poor. At least in Latin America, this synthesis is taking place, even though it is not being done formally in order to achieve ecumenical unity. Word and sacrament, revelation in Scripture and in the signs of the times, faith and works, prayer and justice, understanding of the present and reevaluation of church history, basic autonomy and trust in God—all these are different aspects being brought together in synthesis because that is what basic solidarity with the poor demands when that solidarity is worked out without any limits imposed a priori. In this way, we find a model for understanding the ecumenical movement. It is a model at once formal and yet historical: solidarity among the different confessions, with each one contributing the best it has and each advancing in faith, starting from the true foundations of that faith, and hence converging toward unity in faith, "bearing with one another in faith." All this is set in motion by basic solidarity with the poor.

Solidarity as Bearing with One Another in Faith

Our aim in the previous considerations has been to show how solidarity furnishes a model that enables the different churches or confessions to maintain, recover, and enhance their identity in relation to other churches and confessions. What we now want to show is that solidarity may also be applied to the faith of believers—that is, that the personal act of faith, what is ultimate in each person, should be made with an openness to the personal faith of others. Thus "bearing with one another" reaches the realm of personal faith.

It is quite clear in Christian revelation that faith is the act of an individual person. It is an act by which the person stands before God to hear and receive God's self-manifestation, to respond to that manifestation with a total commitment, and in so doing to correspond fittingly to the reality of God. This act is deeply personal; there is no way to delegate to anyone else the responsibility for making it. That is why the scriptures often dramatize the "solitude" of the act of faith, as is shown prototypically in the faith of Abraham, who must leave his land and what he knows and enter the unknown; in the scene of the annunciation to Mary, whose only response is her fiat; in Jesus' prayer in the garden, where he is alone with God—the way the scene is set emphasizes this solitude—and accepts the will of the

Father. There is something personal and nontransferable in the act of faith, and in this sense the "personalist" conception of faith is correct and continues to be valid.

Nevertheless, in the scriptures the act of faith in its personal and nontransferable dimension is often directed to the faith of others. Personal faith has a relationship to the faith of others. One expression of it is that of confirming others in the faith. Thus we read that those who are strong in faith "confirm" (Luke 22:32, *Bibl. Lat.*), "strengthen" (1 Thess. 3:2, *Bibl. Lat.*), and "complete" (1 Thess. 3:10, *Bibl. Lat.*) the faith of others, and those who are weak in the faith can find help in the great witnesses of faith (Heb. 11), especially in Jesus, who lived faith in its originating and full sense (Heb. 12:2).

Another way of seeing the relatedness of faith, and one that is applicable on a wider scale, appears in Paul's words to the Romans, "For I long to see you . . . that we may be mutually encouraged by our common faith" (Rom. 1:11-12). What he is speaking of here is not one-way help from the believer Paul, a teacher and moreover an apostle, to the faith of others who are presumed to need help. It is two-way aid, a mutual giving and receiving of faith itself—in other words, bearing with one another in faith.

Being related to the faith of others is therefore inherent in personal faith. That is in fact what these New Testament passages show. What I should like to clarify is that this mutual, horizontal relatedness to the faith of others is something essential and inherent, just because the content of faith is nothing else but the mystery of God. Precisely because God is mystery, faith in the mystery of God must be related to the concrete faith of others in this mystery.

The mystery of God has been formulated in an authoritative way in revelation and in the magisterium of the church. For that purpose, delimiting formulations have been employed. Thus it is stated that God is love, truth, omnipotence, absolute origin and future, grace and salvation, tenderness and mercy, precept and admonition, and so forth. Nevertheless, these formulations are not of such a nature that all believers will grasp them in an equal manner or degree. They are circumscribed formulations, and no one individual can grasp any of them exhaustively. They are different, though complementary, aspects, and no one person can grasp equally their different emphases. When these delimited truths are grasped in the concrete—and that is where faith takes place, and not simply in the cataloging of its contents—different elements in the concrete history of believers are at work: their personal situation, age, sex, culture, their own life story, their social and economic position, and so forth. These circumstances of their own history are both what make possible and what condition the way that the mystery of God is grasped differently and in differing degrees. They are what "concentrate" the comprehension of God's mystery in real circumstances, in real events, with the result that certain persons come to accent one or another aspect of this mystery. Although the mystery of God has been expressed formally in revelation, its being grasped in history nevertheless depends on the concrete way that the believer's own life unfolds.

The diversity of ways of "concentrating" the mystery of God is what actually makes it possible for us to keep God as mystery, beyond simply repeating in orthodox fashion that such is in fact the case. As there appear new ways in which the mystery is embodied, the mystery proves that it is indeed unmanipulable mystery. These new aspects are what break with our natural tendency to think that in a particular embodiment we possess God. Moreover, the different embodiments sometimes emphasize aspects of God's mystery that seem irreconcilable in ongoing history justice and mercy, liberation and peace, tenderness and imperation, and so forth. The mystery of God is "reduplicative" mystery.

The conclusion here is that, inasmuch as the content of the mystery of God is precisely "mystery," the faith of one person must be related to the faith of others. This is a way to preclude absolutizing one's own grasp of the mystery of God or trivializing the utopian aspect of its content. It is the practical way to retain the degree of not-knowing that must be part of any authentic knowledge of God. The others, with their different embodiments of the mystery of God, are those who enable one to avoid falling into the temptation of absolutizing one's own grasp and thus really trivializing the dimension of mystery in God. Those who would in principle refuse to open their own faith to the faith of others would be rejecting the mystery of God.

In a positive sense, we must be actively open to the faith of others if we are to continually grasp the mystery of God and allow it to be revealed in all its richness. In this way, with everyone taking part, we may ever more fully grasp the mystery of God. In a back-and-forth fashion, our conception of God comes ever closer to the reality.

The same thing must be said of faith as the real commitment of the human being to God. This commitment, as faith made real, cannot be delegated to anyone else. Theologically, what makes it possible is simply God's grace. That, however, does not mean that a person should not be oriented to the actual faith of other persons in the very process of making the commitment of faith. The real faith of other persons is, as it were, the way that the grace leading to one's own commitment is mediated within ongoing history.

The commitment of faith is described in formal terms as *total* commitment of the human person to God But again this commitment has specific nuances that arise from the actual circumstances of the particular believer. Depending on these circumstances, the commitment of faith will be manifested as humbling oneself and kenosis, as the practice of love in its different forms (humanitarian aid, justice, pardon, marriage, friendship, and so forth), as the sacrifice of one's life—martyrdom.

It is through all these things that the commitment of faith is made but, as a result of differing situations, sometimes one aspect will be emphasized over another. By way of example, believers who live in affluence will not emphasize prayer of petition so much, because one petitions when one does not have, whereas the poor will indeed petition in their prayer (and it does not necessarily indicate superstition or alienation). Poor believers, who have been kept down, will show their commitment precisely in their efforts for liberation, whereas believers who enjoy abundance will have to make a conscious effort to give up the trappings of their "superiority." Poor believers will be more ready to express gratitude and will demonstrate what it means to give out of poverty, whereas others will encounter radical demands on their generosity. Believers who find themselves in a conflict will go all the way to the point of martyrdom, whereas others will lend their support from outside to try to stop it. Believers who live in the Third World will manifest the simplicity and security of their faith, whereas what others offer will be their fidelity to the faith in a secularized world that is full of doubts and challenging questions.

Much more could be said about the concrete shape of each act of personal praxis that the act of faith implies. The point to emphasize is that the concrete reality of every believer's life at once conditions and yet makes possible the external act of personal response. The fact of being male or female, married or single, white-collar worker or blue-collar, for example, and the specific impact that they have on one's life, are major components of what shapes one's concrete reality. But what we most want to stress is that each believer's concrete personal commitment is something that challenges, stimulates, and opens possibilities for the commitment of others.

In this fashion, the very act of faith, which is personal and nontransferable, is made in solidarity with others; it lives from the faith of others. For example, a readiness to accept a lowering of one's own status or to be involved in the struggle for justice is certainly spurred by the real faith of poor Christians. On the other hand, the poor are remotivated in their own faith when they are supported by others. The prayer of petition by the poor no doubt will help well-off Christians discover areas of impoverishment in their own personalities and lives, and so they will turn to God through the prayer of petition. And active faith, the readiness to work and struggle, can enrich the faith of those who have tended to concentrate on petitionary prayer.

We could go on to list and analyze many other examples. But what is most important is the conclusion: The faith of others is important for one's own faith. In the de facto course of events, it is essential, as has clearly been shown in Latin America.

Insofar as it is the faith *of the other,* it always challenges one's own faith and questions whether one's commitment is enough or whether important aspects of commitment to God have been left out. Insofar as it is the *faith* of the other—that is, an embodiment of the miracle of faith—it is something enabling and encouraging for one's own faith.

When all, or a significant group, express and embody their own faith in connection with the faith of others, the process of mutual giving and receiving takes place, and through this mutual interchange there occurs what would be total commitment to God if it reached the ideal and utopian stage. In actual practice, it never reaches it fully. To conceive of personal commitment to God through faith within a process of giving and receiving the faith of others is the practical way to avoid placing limits on the commitment of faith. By not putting a priori limits, we are again affirming that the correlate of this commitment is the mystery of God.

All I have been saying may be summarized in the following statement: It is the person who believes—but not in isolation. The traditional way this idea has been expressed is that it is the person who believes, but within the church. In a more up-to-date form, we could say that it is the person who believes, but within the people of God. In both cases, the "within" is not just a spatial representation, nor is it meant to suggest two instances of faith positioned side by side, as it were, and logically independent of each other. Rather it signifies an essential openness to others in order to give to them, and receive from them, faith in its concrete form. In this sense, it could be said that we believe together, and together we approach the mystery of God.

This statement should have a priori plausibility: There will be a better grasp of God's mystery and a better response to it when it is the whole of God's people, the sum total of partial and complementary faiths, that approaches God.

Viewed a posteriori, this in fact seems to be what has happened. To the degree that the people of God has been better established, faith has been made real, both as comprehension of the mystery of God and as commitment to that mystery. But what is important to realize—and here we end where we began—is that is this people of God is being built up from the poor; and the "church" has become "people of God" in its solidarity with the poor. This solidarity is what has set in motion a process wherein the people of God and its faith is being built up.

Once we seriously understand that to be a human being is to be co-responsible with other human beings and especially with the poorest, that to be church is to be co-responsible with other churches, especially the most persecuted, we then understand that to be a believer is to be co-responsible in and with the faith of others, especially of the poorest. Solidarity in the faith is not a routine and empty formula; it brings out how faith is made real, a "bearing with one another" in the direction of the realm of faith.

Let us be mindful, however, that this solidarity in faith is not made simply because one decides so with an act of will and in an idealist manner. This kind of solidarity, one that reaches the depths of faith, becomes real when it starts out from the human solidarity of bearing with one another on the primary levels of life, where the death and life of human beings are at stake. This primary solidarity is not something optional for solidarity in faith, for in it is expressed what is new and scandalous in the Christian vision of history: a circular relationship between God and the poor. Puebla says the poor are "made in the image and likeness of God . . . to be his children [but] this image is dimmed and even defiled." Hence, independently of their moral or personal condition, "God takes on their defense and loves them" (§1142). Because of this primordial circularity between God and the poor, any ecclesial solidarity in the faith must of necessity pass through solidarity with the poor. And contrariwise, when this occurs, there emerges the miracle—not likely to be achieved through other means—of churches bearing with one another, and Christians bearing with one another, in faith.

A Closing Word in Memory of Archbishop Romero

In all I have said, I have made a presentation of solidarity that is idealized but not idealist. It is idealized because we have not mentioned or examined the other side of the coin: unconcern for the poor, divisions within the church, new efforts in the church to return to imposition from the top. Nor have we examined how insufficient is the solidarity shown toward the gravely serious situation of the people and the church in El Salvador, Guatemala, or Haiti.

But this presentation is not idealist: I have based it on historical facts that are more than enough for elaborating a Christian theory of solidarity. To give just one example from the hundreds that could be cited, let me quote the words of an English Catholic. "I am a Catholic," he said. "I teach a religion class. And yet I find atheistic humanism attractive. But when I hear what Christians in El Salvador are doing and I recall the witness of Archbishop Romero, without exactly knowing why, I really feel like a Christian. My darkened faith becomes real again." This English Catholic is one of so many who support El Salvador from afar.

If I had to provide examples to make what I have said understandable, nothing could shed more light than would reflection on Archbishop Romero. He launched a massive process of solidarity and, once it was in motion, he knew how to live the reality of the church and his own faith in solidarity with others. I shall therefore close with some brief quotations that may illustrate everything that has been said here.

Archbishop Romero understood quite well that at the root of this process is the solidarity of the church with the poor and oppressed, and he stated it in an utterly radical way: "The church suffers the lot of the poor: persecution. Our church is proud that the blood of its priests, catechists, and communities has been mixed in with the massacres of the people, and that it has continually borne the mark of persecution" (Feb. 17, 1980).

He was extremely happy to see how this solidarity with the poor led to solidarity with the people and the church of El Salvador: "There are countless letters offering solidarity and encouragement for us to continue living out this witness" (Second Pastoral Letter, 1977). And he responded to it at the end of his life, a month and a half before being murdered, when solidarity had reached great proportions:

I could find no better place and time than this opportunity so kindly offered by the University of Louvain, to say from the bottom of my heart: thank you! Many thanks, fellow bishops, priests, sisters, and lay persons, for so generously linking your lives, your strivings, your economic contribution to the concerns, works, weariness, and even persecutions we encounter in the fields of our pastoral work (Feb. 2, 1980).

He was also happy to see how ecumenical solidarity arose and grew: "We have received endorsements from many separated brothers and sisters, both inside and outside the country, and we wish to thank them publicly for their gesture of comradely and Christian concern" (Second Pastoral Letter, 1977). And he pointed to the root of true union:

[It is the] hope of union, which is present in prayer now being made in all Catholic and Protestant churches that do not allow the gospel to be manipulated, who know that the gospel is not a toy of either politics or of particular interests, but that it must remain on a higher level and be capable of rejecting anything that muffles the true gospel message. Along with our Protestant brothers and sisters we will continue to seek a gospel that will be really at the service of our peoples, who have suffered so much (Jan. 21, 1979).

It is harder to document with quotes the impact the faith of others had on Archbishop Romero's personal faith. Because of his natural modesty, he did not speak of what was deepest in him. But there is no doubt that contact with his people changed him also at the deepest levels and that from the poor of his people he gathered strength for his own faith and his own hope: "With this people, being a good pastor is not hard at all. It is a people that presses into service those of us who have been called to defend their rights and be their voice" (Nov. 18, 1979). "I believe the bishop always has a great deal to learn from the people. And it is in the charisms that the Spirit gives the people that the bishop finds the touchstone for his own authenticity" (Sept. 9, 1979).

Finally, Archbishop Romero saw that any solidarity relating to the church, ecumenical concerns, or even God must of necessity be rooted in the primary human solidarity—that with the poor. As he used to say, the suffering of the poor touches God's heart. "The church of my archdiocese has striven to incarnate itself in this world that lacks a human face, which is presently the sacrament of the suffering servant of Yahweh" (Feb. 2, 1980). "My position as pastor obliges me to stand in solidarity with everyone who suffers and to back every effort toward the dignity of human beings" (Jan. 7, 1979). Five days before he was murdered, a reporter asked him what could be done for El Salvador and he answered, "Anyone who believes in prayer should realize that it is a power we need very much here and now.

Anyone who believes in human fellowship should not forget that we are human beings and that persons are fleeing to the mountains, hiding there, and dying there" (March 19, 1980).

They "should not forget we are human beings." Perhaps there is no simpler or deeper way to describe the root of solidarity or to lay down firm foundations so that humanity may find full expression in the human race, Christianity be fulfilled in the churches, and the believer in God be fulfilled as a human being and a believer. When this "forgetfulness" is really overcome, the human being and the Christian believer are not alone; they are advancing along the road with others, and the miracle we have described occurs: They bear with one another.

The Salvadoran church and people have helped many individuals and Christians not forget about the human being, and so they have grown in their humanity and their faith. Many have shown their gratitude to this church and this people for that reason. May what I have written also serve to express gratitude, along with Archbishop Romero, for the aid given to this people and the encouragement given to the faith of the Salvadoran church.

9

The Legacy of the Martyrs of the Central American University

It is a Christian truth that wherever there is death like the death of Jesus on the cross for having defended the victims of this world, and with a great cry, there is also resurrection, a word continues to resound and the crucified endure through history.

The martyrs of the UCA, Ignacio Ellacuría, Segundo Montes, Ignacio Martín-Baró, Amando López, Juan Ramón Moreno, Joaquin López y López, Julia Elba, and Celina Ramos, together with Monsignor Romero and so many thousands and thousands of Salvadorans, died like Jesus on the cross, and that is why they must stay alive like Jesus. If this were not so, our faith in the resurrection of the crucified would be in vain, but if it is so, we must ask ourselves what those crucified persons have left to us.

One year ago, just a few days after their murder-martyrdom, I tried to say what that was, with pain and passion at the time, but it is important to take it up again, although I may do so today more calmly and with the perspective that time affords.

As with all human beings, with their death they have left us what they were in life. Their legacy as academics has already been explored in depth,* and so I will not delve into this aspect. Rather I will focus on the human and Christian legacy they left us, reflected in their university work, and which also made that work possible. Seeing them as a whole, I would like to say that these martyrs were human, merciful, truthful, just, lovers of mankind, blessed and believing, and that is what they leave to us: humanity, mercy, truth, justice, love, blessing, and faith. Let us say a few brief words on each of these.

The Incarnation Which Humanizes: Coming to Be in the Real World

We are born men and women, but becoming humans is not a simple matter. Above all, it means existing and being in the real world, and not in

---

* See Sobrino, Jon, and I Ellacuría, *Companions of Jesus,* Maryknoll, N Y : Orbis Books, 1990

the exception or the anecdote of reality. It is easy to determine what the real world is in El Salvador, but it is essential to remember that, in order to understand the human side of our martyrs.

In contrast with other societies of plenty in the countries of the First World and in the First World enclaves in El Salvador, what characterizes our Salvadoran reality is the unjust poverty of the majority, which produces a slow daily death, to which can be added the speedy and violent death which occurs in the form of repression and war. The world which is more real and more Salvadoran is thus the world of poverty and injustice. This is in a quantitative sense, since the majority are poor, and it is in a qualitative sense, because that poverty is not only one dimension of reality among many, but the one which cries out the most.

Things being the way they are, for these Jesuits—as for all—to ask oneself the question of one's own humanity was to ask oneself a question about incarnation, the question of where to stand: on these islands of plenty and well-being, which have nothing Salvadoran about them—in fact, almost without exception, they are anti-Salvadoran—or in the midst of the reality of the poor and impoverished majority.

Faced with this reality, our martyrs exercised the option, above all, to live in the midst of the true Salvadoran reality. This was their fundamental option for the poor, demanded of Christians by the gospel and ethically required by history. But above all it was a primarily human option—we could say even metaphysical—in order to become simply real and human themselves.

Their principal work, and the greatest part of their time, were spent in the UCA, although the cries of the poor also physically reached the UCA, and several of the martyrs assiduously stayed near the reality of the poor. But although they worked in the UCA, they did not live life from the UCA standpoint or for the sake of the UCA, but rather from and for the reality of the poor. This reality is what guided their actions and options. They worked at their desks, but not from the standpoint of a desk and not in order to pile up writings on a desk. The "from" and "for" of all their work was the impoverished and hopeful Salvadoran reality.

Their death shows perfectly clearly that in life they became incarnated in that reality. Monsignor Romero used to say in thunderous tones: "In a land in which so many horrendous murders are taking place, it would be sad if priests were not among the victims," a prophecy which was fulfilled in the case of the six Jesuits. But the reason Monsignor Romero was even gratified by these martyrdoms was also translated into reality: "They are the testimony of a Church which is incarnated in the problems of the people." If our martyrs suffered the most real form of death in El Salvador, it is because they lived the most real reality of El Salvador.

Thus, death made them participants in Salvadoran reality, but that same Salvadoran reality is what humanized them in life. In El Salvador there is not only poverty and death, but the poor also possess and transmit realities and values which are very difficult to find outside their world: hope instead of senselessness, commitment instead of selfishness, community instead of individualism, celebration instead of simple amusement, creativity instead of culturally imposed mimicry, a sense of transcendence instead of the blunt pragmatism and positivism of other worlds. With these values, the poor shaped them as Salvadorans and made them human. "Their pain converted and purified them, they lived on their hopes and their love seduced them forever," I wrote shortly after their martyrdom.

This is the primary and fundamental legacy left us by the martyrs: They were real human beings in El Salvador. And it must be added that they became so in the face of the temptation *not* to become so, since to be an intellectual in a university and a religious person in an order which frequently moves in another world tends to generate a bit of superiority and human artificiality, a tendency to live above and beyond true reality. But this did not happen with these martyrs. In Christian terminology, they were incarnated in truth, like Jesus, in the reality of our world. In the words of Luis da Sebastian, "they were where they had to be." In the simplest terms, they became human beings.

The Heart Which Is Moved to Mercy

To live truly and humanly in El Salvador inescapably means, as Jesus said in the parable of the good Samaritan, meeting up with a wounded person on the way, and they met one. But they did not meet up with an individual, but rather an entire people, and not just with a wounded people, but rather with a crucified people. And this meeting is where the human part is decided: Either you make a detour around him, as the priest and the Levite of the parable did, or you heal his wounds.

Our martyrs made no detour. Even amidst grave danger, they did not leave the country. Within the country, they did not even settle in those artificial islands in which one does not want to see the crucified people. Nor did they make that subtle detour—frequent in these cases—of taking refuge in science, in the university, in the religious life—there are always good reasons to do so—to avoid doing what had to be done with the wounded person. They stayed within the country, amid countless attacks and threats, when they could perfectly well have found comfort and gratification in other places. They turned the university and religious life not into a pretext to avoid dedicating themselves firmly to healing the wounded, but into an effective instrument for truly healing them.

But the most decisive part is knowing why they dedicated their lives to healing the wounded. The answer is extremely simple, but extremely fundamental in understanding how human these martyrs were. Just as with the Samaritan in the parable, in the presence of a crucified people, their hearts were moved and they were moved to mercy. They internalized the suffering of an entire people and responded to it. And they did all that without ulterior motives, without any more motive than the enormous suffering of the crucified people.

I like to think of these martyrs above all as human beings with compassion and mercy, for whom responding with effective love for the crucified people was the beginning and the end of existence. It is true that they worked and served in the university, in the Society of Jesus, in the church, but in the final analysis they were not serving and working for the good of the university, the Society of Jesus, or the church. They were working to bring the crucified people down from the cross, in the language of Jesus, to eliminate the anti-kingdom and build the kingdom of God. Thus, they did not use the poor as a means to further their academic or religious interests— an everpresent temptation, since we human beings manipulate for our benefit even that which is most sacred—but on the contrary, they used the latter as a means for practicing mercy.

This is what we mean when we say that mercy was the beginning and the end for them. These words should not surprise or shock us, as if in this way we were undervaluing the reality of the university, the Society, and the church. According to the gospel, the final goal is the kingdom of God, and for that reason, in the presence of the anti-kingdom, nothing can go beyond or before mercy. The Samaritan, who is presented as the perfect human being, acted only through mercy, and not to defend institutional religious interests or as a way to achieve his own perfection. The same thing is said in the Scriptures of Jesus and the Heavenly Father. If Jesus healed the sick and wounded, if God liberated an oppressed people, they did not do so with ulterior motives, but rather simply—as is said in both cases—because the cries of the poor moved their hearts.

Mercy was, therefore, much more for our martyrs than a feeling, or the willingness to alleviate some suffering or other, something which can exist in many people. It was a principle which guided their entire lives and work. Mercy was there in the beginning, but it stayed there throughout the entire process, shaping *them* as well. It is true that mercy is not everything for human beings, nor was it for our martyrs, since—as human beings—they were also necessarily confronted with knowledge, hope and praxis, as Kant said, and also with celebration. But the principle of mercy is what guided and shaped all that.

The Truth Which Defends the Victims

Mercy is what moved them to look at Salvadoran reality in order to understand it as it really is, and what guided their thought and knowledge. Moved by mercy, they sought the truth, analyzed it, and proclaimed it. They did all this in an academic way, as we will see tomorrow in detail, but here we would only like to emphasize one point.

We all know that truth does not abound in El Salvador, not only because ignorance exists, but because falsehoods prevail. Not only is the truth about reality unknown, but it is also covered up so that it may not see the light of day. In this way the realities of death and terrible massacres are unknown and relegated to oblivion, and very frequently fundamental truths are distorted to the point where the victims are portrayed as the executioners. This is not said as clearly today as before, but we should recall how Monsignor Romero and our martyrs were slandered, as if they had caused the violence instead of being its victims. In El Salvador, therefore, the same lie that provoked the terrible lament of the prophet Isaias, "Woe to you that put darkness for light, and light for darkness!" is repeated.

In this world of lies, finding the truth means not only overcoming ignorance. Our martyrs certainly dedicated their work to overcoming it, to obtaining the scientific and technological knowledge which is, of course, necessary to build a viable country. And they did so in research and teaching. But the first step they took, also in an academic manner, was to unmask the lie, because no just society can be built on that foundation, and with lies the necessary scientific and technological knowledge does not become liberating knowledge, but frequently becomes a new instrument of oppression.

Academically, they unmasked the original sinfulness of human beings which, as Paul said, consists in "oppressing truth with injustice," or in the words of John, in that "the devil is a liar." And they denounced that sinfulness as something real not only in the individual but also in society itself. A society which generates unjust poverty furthermore tends to cover up the fact, to justify it, even to try to portray it as something quite different, inventing euphemisms which cover over the fundamental sin. In this way, the Third World is often spoken about in terms of developing nations, of incipient democracies, without analyzing whether the Third World is really on its way to development or, on the contrary, if it is moving toward greater underdevelopment, or whether the democracies reach the "demos," the people, or not. And thus in El Salvador, although no one can any longer deny the tragedy of this country, they talk about democratic progress, progress in human rights, progress in the administration of justice, in the professionalization of the Armed Forces . . . Pretty words to cover up the lie of reality.

To speak this truth in a country like El Salvador, above and beyond anything else, means to unmask the lie. But whoever does so not only speaks the truth, but automatically becomes a defender of the poor. The poor are those who contain and express the most fundamental truth in their own flesh, although they cannot make it prevail. From this standpoint, we can understand the epithets repeatedly applied to Monsignor Romero in his time—for clearly speaking the truth—and which today I would like to apply to our martyrs. They were the voice of the voiceless, the intellectual words of those who have no words, even though they possess the truth.

With this, we wish to say that their passion to seek, analyze, and speak the truth did not, in the final analysis, come from a pure wish to further their own knowledge, although they were well aware of the need to increase their rigorous knowledge. Above all, it came from the wish to defend the poor, who have the truth on their side, and at times, that is the only thing they have on their side. The ability to seek and analyze the truth certainly came from their own intelligence, of course; but their passion for the truth was rooted in mercy. "Suffering precedes thought," said Feuerbach. These martyrs undoubtedly thought and tried to think in the best possible way, but they thought in order to defend the poor. A rare convergence of intelligence and mercy took place inside them.

Structural Mercy: The Paths of Justice

The wounded found along the way were actually an entire crucified people, not just an individual. For this reason, mercy took a certain shape in history and was not reduced to mere benevolent feelings or occasional help. It took the shape of justice, which is the expression necessarily taken by love for the poor majority, and took the shape of liberation, which is the expression of love for a majority who are unjustly and structurally oppressed. Returning to the parable of the good Samaritan, not only did they look at the wounded, but also at the highway robbers, those structures which necessarily inflict wounds. Not only did they wish to heal the wounded, but also to eliminate the causes of the wounds and propose the best solutions. In the final analysis, that is how they understood their university work, and they saw the university as an effective instrument for achieving their goals. All this is well known. What I would like to add is that their structural view of reality, the investigation into its causes and solutions, was guided by mercy, and that is why they always kept the concrete reality of the poor before their eyes.

This is also why, from a fundamental perspective of justice and liberation, which always guided their steps, they continually modified and changed their concrete views on how to implement those principles. And here they were very demanding in two aspects: in the rigor of their analysis, to avoid playing or experimenting with things which were such serious matters for the people; and in the creativity of their analysis to avoid falling into a dogmatism which always ends up prevailing over one's own preconceived ideas—as scientific as they may be—about the reality of the poor.

How they analyzed Salvadoran reality is well known. At this time I would only like to emphasize their willingness to change, to adapt their theoretical analyses to Salvadoran reality, and not vice versa. In simple terms, I wish to say that they were not dogmatic, although they were indeed firm in their positions. Nor were they purely pragmatic, much less opportunists, but they were flexible in order to be creative, and they were creative in order to respond to the demands of reality. It is sufficient to read the last twenty years of the magazine *ECA* in order to verify both assertions.

This is how they analyzed, as principles or at least as factors in a solution for the country, the elections of the 1970s, the coup of October 15, the revolutionary political-military solution, dialogue, negotiations . . . They analyzed the fundamental agents of social change, popular movements, the so-called and misunderstood "third force . . . " Whether or not all their analyses were correct is open to discussion—and in fact some of their positions were at times criticized—but what is beyond discussion is the objective of that flexibility and creativity: to find a solution for the popular majority. They greatly valued, and used, a variety of philosophical, socio-logical, political, and theological theories, but they never turned any of their principles into dogma, but rather used them insofar as they "opened" paths to solutions. The reason for that is the primacy they assigned to the reality of the poor over and above any theory about the poor. Just as Monsignor Romero said, "the Church will support one political process or another, depending upon how well it serves the people," so were the martyrs eager to find knowledge, theories, analyses which would benefit the people. If they held any immutable dogma, it was that of the suffering of the crucified people and the urgency of bringing them down from the cross.

The creativity of their thought undoubtedly stemmed from their own intelligence, but it was the people's pain that put it into motion, directed its fundamental course, and continually drove it to seek out new paths. Their thinking minds instilled the necessary intellectual rigor into their feeling hearts, but these feeling hearts were those which put vigor into their minds and moved them to produce knowledge for the benefit of the people. In the language of Saint Ignatius of Loyola, consecrated by Ignacio Ellacuría, their great question was always: "what are we going to do to bring the crucified people down from the cross?" But that question—as Ignatius of Loyola requested—was posed before a people who were actually crucified.

Enduring Mercy: The Greatest Love

When mercy takes the shape of justice and liberation in history, no matter how rational and reasonable it may seem, it must confront those who do not allow themselves to be governed by the principle of mercy. There are those in history who overlook mercy: the priest and the Levite, which is already a tragedy; but there are others who are governed by the principle of active anti-mercy: the highway robbers of the parable, which is a greater tragedy. This is why active and effective mercy for a crucified people must be maintained as mercy in the presence of active anti-mercy, in order to be enduring mercy. This means necessarily stepping into society's conflicts, running personal and institutional risks. And when, out of mercy for the victims, one touches the idols which produce the victims, it means risking one's life. Enduring mercy is that which leads to the greatest love, that of giving one's life, and when one gives one's life it means that mercy has truly been present and active in one's lifetime.

This is how the martyrs were: endearingly merciful, until the end. Mercy for them was the beginning and the end, and they put nothing before it, not even their personal safety, not even—and this was perhaps the most diffi-cult part—the safety of the institution. As we all know, during fifteen years they were the target of countless attacks, threats, and personal risks, and they also risked—but prudently—the institution, which was many times attacked and physically damaged, and always was threatened by the paralysis which is a product of the fear that some wished to instill into its members. Their deaths were thus the culmination of a process, and not the product of macabre and momentary madness.

But if this is so, our martyrs gave their lives freely—as did Jesus, as did Monsignor Romero—and they gave them in order to keep mercy enduring. Their deaths demonstrated, therefore, that what moved them in life was definitely their great love for the poor, and not any personal interest or hatred of anyone. Here is where, in the final analysis, their credibility lies. Their deaths, which they met consciously, are what convince the poor, more than any possible words, that they were with them, that in this cruel world there are human beings who have defended them and loved them.

The Joy of the Beatitudes

Joy and suffering also belong to the human world. These martyrs had some of each. The joy and suffering of daily life, when things turned out well or turned out badly, when—as persons—they felt gladness in their hearts or suffered tension, when they saw progress or setbacks in the processes they worked for. This joy and suffering were very real, and each one had his; but here we continue to move in a world of particular joy and suffering, not in that fundamental sphere which makes a life blessed or damned. Underlying, and going beyond, concrete and particular joy and suffering is the enjoyment of life or the pain of sadness.

Now at this level, in which the meaning of life is at stake, I would like to say that these martyrs were human beings who felt joy. This should be seen as a given, since if they were truly merciful, they were already blessed with one of the beatitudes of Jesus: "Blessed are the merciful." From this standpoint of the beatitudes—which we could call Jesus of Nazareth's theory of happiness—I would like to recall the joy they shared and offered to all.

"Blessed are the poor," says Jesus, and these martyrs shared—each in his own way—that joy. By carrying out their work from the standpoint and for the sake of the poor, they participated in their reality, which gave them a fundamental human dignity and filled them with joy. And their direct contacts in the refugee camps, poor parishes, and base communities filled them with a shocking happiness.

"Blessed are the clean of heart," says Jesus. By letting themselves be enlightened by the poor and see the world through purified eyes, they experienced the joy of holding the truth and serving the truth.

"Blessed are they who hunger and thirst for justice," says Jesus. By living and dying for justice for the poor, they found a superior food, one which satisfies the hunger of humanity and fraternity.

"Blessed are the peacemakers," says Jesus. By working to achieve peace amidst repression and war, even if they themselves were repressed, defaced, and slandered, they achieved true peace, not the kind afforded by the world but rather one upon which they could rest their hearts.

"Blessed are they who suffer persecution for justice's sake, for theirs is the kingdom of heaven," says Jesus. By stepping into conflicts and remaining with them until the end, until giving their own lives, they achieved the maximum joy, which is the maximum paradox. By giving their lives, they showed the greatest love, and that made them live.

Saint Ignatius asks the Jesuit to do everything "freely, without expecting any human payment or salary for your work," in somewhat ascetic language. Jesus says it to us in the language of the beatitudes: "It is more blessed to give than to receive." This is what was personified in our martyrs. They did not keep their lives for themselves, but rather gave their lives so others might live and live in plenty, as Jesus says. In this they lost their own lives, but by giving life to others they themselves came to life.

This is what their joy consisted of, and in this joy they were similar to the poor whom they served. Gustavo Gutiérrez often repeats these words he heard from a peasant: "The opposite of happiness is not suffering, but rather sadness. We have much suffering, but we are not sad." My brothers—I know it well—had much suffering, but I never saw them sad. And that joy of being human, that deep sense of life, is what they leave to all of us.

The Faith Which Walks Humbly with God through History

These martyrs were, finally, believers, and in a very concrete way. Their faith certainly did not separate them from being human, much less did it remove them from Salvadoran reality, as sometimes happens with people who, "because they are not of this world, believe that they are of God, and because they do not love men, believe they love God." The martyrs rather saw in Christian faith a requirement and the best opportunity for themselves to become human and humanize others, and they saw in it the great Christian principles which guide humanization: the kingdom of God as an ideal for society, and following Jesus as an ideal for human beings.

Thus, they verified and insisted upon the historical effectiveness of the gospel, but also believed in the gospel. In Jesus they saw the perfect human being, and believed that by following him one set into motion the essence of the truly human being, and all that we have said about them up to this point is nothing but concretizing in our time what it means to follow Jesus. But that following is also faith, since nothing—no philosophy, no ideology—can guarantee historically that following the path of Jesus leads to the right place. If, however, they followed that path until the end, it was because they believed in Jesus, because they were convinced that there is nothing more true than Jesus.

They felt attracted by the Jesus who says: "The spirit of the Lord is upon me, because he has anointed me; to bring good news to the poor he has sent me, to proclaim to the captives release, and sight to the blind; to set at liberty the oppressed . . . " (Luke 4:18). And to that Jesus they were true. That is why I wish to place on their lips these words taken from Paul:

> Who shall separate us from the love of Christ? Shall tribulation, or distress, or persecution, or hunger, or nakedness, or danger, or the sword? Even as it is written, "for thy sake we are put to death all the day long. We are regarded as sheep for the slaughter." But in all these things we overcome because of him who has loved us. For I am sure that neither death, nor life, nor angels, nor principalities, nor things present, nor things to come, nor powers, nor height, nor depth, nor any other creature will be able to separate us from the love of God, which is Christ Jesus our Lord (Romans 8: 35-39).

Our martyrs, perhaps because of their sober temperament which was Salvadoran, Basque, and Castilian, never used such lyric expressions to speak of Jesus, but they said as much in their daily stubborn efforts to follow his steps until the end.

Finally, by following Jesus, and like Jesus, they found themselves before the final mystery of personal existence and history: the mystery of God. God was, for them, a reality which must be reproduced in history, in a historical fashion, and limited to human beings, of course; but a reality which, in the final analysis, must be "practiced," as Gustavo Gutiérrez says. They saw that "practicing" of God as something very good for them and for history, but if they perceived it as good, it was because they believed in a just and good God, in a God the Father. Believing in God was for them an attempt to be in affinity with God.

Furthermore, God was for them a reality which was always impossible to embrace and manipulate, a reality whose word—whatever it was—had to be listened to and answered. God was the height of mystery, the greatest possible otherness, and to believe in God meant letting him be God. This presupposed standing before God, sometimes without hearing a word, asking God and crying out "My God, my God, why have you abandoned me?" in one's personal life and, above all, faced with the tragedy of El Salvador, without hearing an answer. But it also meant standing before God in terms of the utopia of this mystery, the God who draws everything to him so that all would be more, so that there be life and plentiful life.

They too lived their faith in this *chiaroscuro* of all that is human, I think with more light than darkness, definitely so. Like all human beings, and like Jesus, they struggled with God, and he vanquished them. In the midst of such darkness in history, they let themselves be seduced by God, like the prophet Jeremias, and the burning flame they carried in their hearts was not extinguished. They sought rest in God the Father, but he never left them in peace. But true to the mystery of this God, they walked humbly with God in their own lives, as Micheas says, and thus they walked toward God.

I think this is the faith shared by our martyrs, this is the faith they proclaimed, and this is the faith they left to us. In their lives, in their work, and in their martyrs' fate they united the human and the divine. In the words used by the Jesuits to define our mission in the world of today—words inscribed on their tombs—they united faith and justice, God and the victims of this world. In their words used by the Letter to the Hebrews to describe Jesus, they united faithfulness to God and mercy for the weak.

In this way, along with "many other Salvadorans," they united what is Salvadoran with what is Christian, and strengthened both. To some they offered the God of the Salvadorans, God of the victims as opposed to the idols, so that their faith would not be alienating or obfuscating. To others they offered the mystery of God, so that their liberating practice would not reduce or make smaller that which is human, but rather open it up more.

Ignacio Ellacuría said of Monsignor Romero something that neither he nor his fellow martyrs would have said of themselves. But the truth is that, with Monsignor Romero, with many thousands of others, with Julia Elba and Celina and the six Jesuits of the UCA, God passed through El Salvador. They leave us their faith, therefore, but above all, they leave us the mysterious passing of God.

Martyrdom: A Cry Which Continues to Resound

All this has been left to us by the martyrs of the UCA. In its concrete execution they undoubtedly did it with limitations, and for this reason what I have said is not intended as a eulogy. But I do hope it contributes inspiration and courage so all of us can reproduce the fundamental structure of what is human and Christian. What martyrdom adds to their lives is, on the one hand, credibility, and on the other, a great cry to the world saying that *that*—and not so many other deceiving offers—is what humanizes and christianizes, that *that* is what is human and Christian.

"Death is more eloquent than words," said Monsignor Romero. And Don Pedro Casaldáliga said of Monsignor's martyrdom that "nothing will silence your last homily." On November 16, my eight brothers and sisters spoke their last homily. Let us finally take a look at what they said with that last cry of theirs, although briefly and somewhat schematically.

Above all, their martyrdom has shaken the world in such a way that this time it cannot be silenced. In many places, and in many institutions which usually overlook our reality (governments, universities, churches, political parties), people have finally had to look Salvadoran reality in the eye. "Something is very wrong in El Salvador," our martyrs cried. And many of those who have heard that cry—although not as many and not as profoundly as we might wish—have felt called upon.

Politically, for the first time, the United States—which bears such great responsibility for our tragedy—has been forced to take a hard look at these martyrs, and through them, at El Salvador. For the first time, the Salvadoran Armed Forces has felt strong pressures to renounce its aberrant practices. The cut in military aid and the way in which this contributes to a negotiated solution is a great contribution made by our martyrs. The same can be said of the Salvadoran negotiations now underway, whose pace has been accelerated by the murders.

Solidarity with El Salvador, so necessary and so difficult to maintain for the duration of the tragedy, and which suffers understandable discouragement on the part of some, has increased. The celebrations being held these days in El Salvador and in many places around the world—in the United States alone there were activities in over 200 cities—is strong evidence of this.

But beyond this shakeup and the important fruits the moment has produced, they leave us something more fundamental and lasting, since that cry—like the cry of Jesus on the cross—is also good news.

From their crosses, the martyrs are, paradoxically, feeding hope, and this was seen by the recent celebrations. There is weeping, but more from emotion than from hopelessness. There are songs of thanks, of commitment, and of hope.

From their crosses, the martyrs unite us as a Salvadoran people and as a Christian people. Around their crosses have gathered Salvadorans and people from many other countries, Christians of different churches, and even nonbelievers, intellectuals and peasants, religious workers and trade unionists. This true ecumenism is a great benefit for all of us, in human and Christian terms.

From their crosses, the martyrs tell us, finally, that in this world it is possible to be human, to be academics, to be Jesuits, and to be Christians. Although this may not appear to be exceedingly good news, it is. And they proclaim it decisively, because they tell us that it is possible to live with a great love in this world and to place all our human abilities at the service of love. My personal impression of the recent celebrations is that all of us who participated in them came out with greater firmness, inspiration, and courage to be a little better, a little more human, and a little more Christian.

At the beginning I said that all who die crucified like Jesus will rise again, and that is what is also happening with the martyrs of the UCA. One year after their deaths, they continue among us, and they are becoming—as Monsignor Romero said—a "tradition," a permanent source, already objectified in history, of inspiration and courage. Their names are already on schools and libraries, on streets and plazas of important cities, and in little villages and repatriate communities. But let us also remember how the resurrection of the crucified is described in the gospel: he appeared before "witnesses," not before mere "seers." That is what is now our task: To bear witness for our martyrs, pursue their cause, and in that way keep them alive in a world which so deeply needs what they were and did.

I would like to close by using, one year later, the same words I wrote just a few days after their martyrdom:

My six Jesuit brothers now rest in the chapel of Monsignor Romero beneath a large portrait of him. All of them, and many others, would have given each other a firm embrace and would have been filled with joy. Our fervent desire is that the heavenly Father transmit that peace and that joy very soon to all the Salvadoran people. Rest in peace, Ignacio Ellacuría, Segundo Montés, Ignacio Martín-Baró, Amando López, Juan Ramón Moreno, Joaquin López y López, companions of Jesus. Rest in peace Elba and Celina, very beloved daughters of God. May their peace give us hope, and may their memory never let us rest in peace.

EPILOGUE

A Letter to Ignacio Ellacuría

Dear Ellacu:

For years, I've thought about what I'd be saying at the Mass of your martyrdom. I've had the same feeling as I had about Archbishop Romero. His martyrdom was inevitable, too, and yet I never wanted to admit to myself that it would finally come. But your death was so likely that it was simply impossible for me to get the idea out of my head. And here are the two things that have most impressed me about you.

The first is that, while I was struck by your intelligence and creativity, it always seemed to me that these weren't your most specific traits. Even to you they were quite important, of course, but you didn't steer your life in the direction of becoming a renowned intellectual or prestigious college president. Here's an example. I remember how, in one of your exiles in Spain, you wrote a manuscript that would have made you famous in the world of philosophers. But you didn't ascribe all that much importance to it. You didn't even finish it when you came back to El Salvador. You had other things to do—more important things—from helping solve some national problem, to attending to the personal troubles of someone who'd asked you for help. For me the conclusion is really clear: Service was more important to you than the cultivation of your intelligence and the recognition it could have meant for you.

But service to what, and why? You served *at* the University of Central America, but ultimately not the University of Central America. You served *in* the church, but not ultimately the church. You served *in* the Society of Jesus, but not ultimately the Society of Jesus. The more I came to know you, the more I arrived at the conviction that you served the poor of this country and of the whole Third World, and that it was this service that gave your life its ultimacy. You were a faithful disciple of Xavier Zubiri, that philosopher and theologian of liberation, that theoretician of popular movements. But you didn't fight for his theories as if they were some kind of dogma.

Read at Mass, November 10, 1990. Originally published in *Carta a las Iglesias*, no 223 (1990), pp. 12-13.

Instead, you changed your viewpoints. Inflexible you! And when you changed them, it was always for the same reason: the tragedy of the poor. So I think, if you were bound by any unshakable "dogma," there's only one thing it could have been: the pain of the crucified peoples.

This led me to the conclusion that, over and above everything else, you were a person of compassion and mercy, and that the inmost depths of you, your guts and your heart, wrenched at the immense pain of this people. That's what never left you in peace. That's what put your special intelligence to work and channeled your creativity and service. Your life was not just service, then: It was the specific service of "taking the crucified peoples down from the cross"—words very much your own, the kind of words that take not only intelligence to invent, but intelligence moved by mercy.

That's the first thing I'd like to mention. The second thing about you I recall—and this one is more personal—is your faith in God. Let me explain. Your contact with the modern philosophers—unbelievers, most of them, except for your beloved Zubiri; the atmosphere of secularization—in fact, of the death of God that prevailed at the time you were coming to your intellectual maturity; your own critical, honest intelligence, so disinclined to credulity; and the great God-question, which *in se* is the unjust poverty of Latin America—none of that made your faith in God easy. I remember one day in 1969, when you told me something I've never forgotten. Here's how you put it. You were talking about your great mentor, Karl Rahner. Suddenly you remarked, "He managed his own doubts very elegantly." I asked you what you meant. And you explained. You meant that neither was *your* faith anything obvious. It was a victory.

And yet I'm convinced you were a great believer. You certainly communicated faith to me. You did it one day in 1983. You had just come back from your second exile in Spain. You were saying Mass, and when the time came for you to speak to us, you talked about the "Heavenly Father." And I said to myself that if Ellacu the brain, the critic, the honest intellectual, used those words, then it wasn't just sentimentality. If you talked about the Heavenly Father, it was because you believed in the Heavenly Father. You communicated faith to me a great many other times, too, in what you said and wrote about Archbishop Romero and his God, or when you spoke so simply about the piety of the poor. And you communicated it to me in your way of talking and writing about Jesus of Nazareth. In your writings, you expressed your faith that, in Jesus, we've had revealed to us what we human beings truly are. But you also expressed in those writings, gratefully, your faith that, in Jesus, an "ever more" surrounds us all—the ultimate mystery and utopia that draws all things to itself. I don't know how much you wrestled with God, like Jacob or Job or Jesus. But I believe that God won the match, and that Jesus' Father gave your life its deepest direction.

Ellacu, this is what you've left us, or at least left me. Your exceptional capacities could dazzle, and your limitations could confuse. I think, Ellacu, that neither the one has bedazzled me nor the other obscured what, to me, is the rock-bottom thing you've left me: that there's nothing more essential than the exercise of mercy in behalf of a crucified people, and nothing more humane and humanizing than faith. These are the things I've had in my head for years now. Today, on the first anniversary of your martyrdom, I say them. With pain and with joy—but especially, with gratitude. Thanks, Ellacu. For your mercy, and for your faith.

Jon

—Translated by Robert R. Barr

NOTES

1. "The Samaritan Church and the Principle of Mercy"

1. In his *Teología de la liberación: Respuesta al cardenal Ratzinger* (Madrid, 1985), pp. 61ff., Juan Luis Segundo shows in detail that the finality of the Exodus is simply the liberation of a suffering people, contrary to the position of the first Vatican Instruction on the theology of liberation to the effect that the finality of the Exodus was the establishment of the people of God and the worship of the Sinai Covenant.

2. Mercy ought to be directed toward "natural" sufferings, as well. But its ultimate essence, we hold, is expressed in persons' attention to those whose suffering is precisely that of "victims." The latter, in their turn, may be the victims of either natural or historical evils, but Scripture generally ascribes far more importance to the victims of human history than to those of "natural disasters."

3. Without acrimony, and in all sibling simplicity: It is surprising that, in the last ten years of ebullient, eventful historical (and ecclesial) life in El Salvador, practically no Spanish bishop has ever paid a visit to our country and its church, with the exception of the bishop in charge of missionary work and Msgr. Alberto Iniesta, who came to Archbishop Romero's funeral at the behest and expense of his faithful of Vallecas.

4. To me, it is altogether clear that Ignacio Ellacuría allowed himself to be guided by the "mercy principle" in all his activity and specifically in his intellectual work in theology, philosophy, and political analysis. We mention this in order to emphasize that mercy is much more than either a sheer sentiment or mere merciful activism: It is also the principle of the exercise of the intelligence.

2. "Theology in a Suffering World"

1. I emphasize this here, in this volume, since the United States, in what it does and what it should do, is related in a special way to the suffering of the Third World. Certainly the U.S. is related to the other two themes of this volume—cultural and religious diversity—but its responsibility for Third World suffering is direct and immediate.

2. To carry out the usual task and teachings of theology properly, it is extremely important to determine whether and how the sufferings of the world are present in the conventional places of theological activity (universities, departments, seminaries, etc.) Inversely, it is essential to determine whether and how these places make it easy or difficult for theologians/students to stand within the actual reality of a suffering world. In general, the physical locales where theology is carried on and taught veil much more than make present the suffering taking place in our world. To overcome these impediments, the theologian must make a personal option to do theology "from within" the suffering of the poor—no matter what her/his actual place of theological study. Such an option naturally requires a certain material proximity to the suffering of the poor.

3. The theology of liberation is becoming more aware of these other forms of structural oppression which do not always coincide with socio-economic oppression. Thus there is more talk today of the indigenous peoples of Latin America and of poor women who suffer under a twofold form of impoverishment. Liberation for such groups, though it will have to be

multiple, can still be simultaneous—at the same time, liberation from both socio-economic poverty and from cultural, religious, or sexual poverty.

3. *"The Crucified Peoples"*

1. I dedicate this article to Ignacio Ellacuría because he dedicated his life to the crucified people and in his death assumed their fate. He also made them the object of his theological reflection. See his article written in 1978: "El Pueblo crucificado. Ensayo de soterologia historica," *Revista Latinoamericana de Teología* 18 (1989), pp. 305-33, and "Discernir 'el signo' de los tiempos," *Diakonia* 17 (1981), pp. 57-9. On 1492, he wrote *Quinto Centenario. America Latina. ?Descubrimiento o encubrimento?* (Barcelona, 1990).

2. "The 'Crucified' Indians—A Case of Anonymous Collective Martyrdom," *Concilium* 163 (1983), p. 51.

3. Ellacuría, "Discernir" (n. 1), p. 58.

4. *La Voz de los sin Voz* (San Salvador, 1980), p. 208.

5. Ibid., p. 366.

6. Ellacuría, "Discernir" (n. 1), p. 58.

7. Here I repeat much of what was said in "Meditacion ante el pueblo crucificado," *Sal Terrae* 2 (1986), pp. 93-104; "Brief an Ludwig Kaufmann aus El Salvador," in *Bioteppe der Hoffnung* (Olten & Freiburg im Breisgau, 1988), pp. 392-8. See also *The Crucified Peoples* (CIIR pamphlet), London, 1989.

8. *Quinto Centenario* (n. 1), p. 11.

9. Ibid.

10. "The Kingdom of God and Unemployment in the Third World," *Concilium* 180 (1982), pp. 91-6.

11. *Quinto Centenario* (n. 1), p. 16.

5. *"Five Hundred Years"*

1. Ignacio Ellacuría, "Fifth Centenary of Latin America: Discovery or Cover-up?" *Latin American Theological Review, RevistaLatino-americana de Teología* 21 (1990), p. 272s.

2. Luis de Sebastián, "The Situation of the World: Data and Interpretations," *ECA* 513-514 (1991), p. 725.

3. Ibid.

4. X. Gorostiaga, "The XXI Century Already Began: North Against South," *Envio* 116 (1991), p. 35.

5. Franz J. Hinkelammert, "The Crisis of Socialism and the Third World," (San José 1991), p. 8.

6. Ibid.

7. The information is taken from an IPS cable of February 5, 1992. According to the cable, the proposal was made by the World Bank economist, Lawrence Sumner. "The economic logic of depositing toxic waste in low-income countries is indisputible." To demonstrate this he pointed out that the demand for a clean atmosphere is concentrated principally in countries where life expectancy is relatively high, which he illustrated with the following example: "The concern that pollution can increase the risk of prostate cancer is greater in countries where the population lives long enough to be affected . . . [the concern] is naturally less strongly felt in countries where mortality of children under five is as many as 200 per thousand."

8. Franz J. Hinkelammert, op. cit., p. 6.

9. This is illustrated by these words of Monseñor Rivera, which appear extremely simple but are of a profound truth. "With the fall of real socialism, the Church—enlightened by her solid social doctrine—will be the only one left to continue fighting for justice and for the integral welfare of the poorest of the poor." Letter of Archbishop Rivera Damas, Archbishop of San Salvador, taken from "Letter to the Churches" 236 (1991), p. 8.

10. Franz J. Hinkelammert, op. cit., pp. 4, 6.

11. X. Gorostiaga, op. cit., pp. 34, 36.

12. Luis de Sebastián, op. cit., p. 729.

13. Investment in the Seville International Exposition could reach figures twenty times

greater than the annual budget of El Salvador. In the Barcelona Olympics, time and distance records will be beaten, while in the Third World, records of hunger will continue to be beaten.

14. Ignacio Ellacuría, op. cit., p. 278.

15. *Selected Works II* (Madrid, 1957-1958), p. 51 1b.

16. Collection in Josiene Chinese, *History and Culture* (Lima, 1970), pp. 97-152.

17. Ibid., p. 142.

18. "The cause of this deception . . . was a monk of St. Dominic called Bartolomé de las Casas . . . His qualities were that he was a very good religious, but very passionate in questions of Indians, and in most of what concerned them, very mistaken," op. cit., p. 106.

19. "Through the Eyes of a European Theologian," *Concilium* 232 (1990), p. 491.

20. "In comparison to the pillage of Holland, France, England, Germany, Belgium, and the United States (to speak of some illustrious western nations), if there is anything which distinguishes the Spanish conquest it is not the proportion of crimes (a point on which none of these nations have any cause for which to envy the others), but the proportion of scruples. The conquests carried out by these other countries had no lack of murder or destruction, but they lacked men such as Las Casas, or internal polemic such as that raised by the Spanish Dominicans about the legitimacy of the conquest which shook the Hispanic empire." R. Fernández Retamar, in the prologue of the French edition of *Las Casas*, taken from J. González Faus, "Letter to Juan Carlos I about 1992," *Letter from the Churches* 253 (1992).

21. *Letter to the Churches* 252 (1992), pp. 11-12.

22. After his death, this was reproduced in the *Revista Latino-americana de Teología* 18 (1989), pp. 305-333.

23. Ignacio Ellacuría, op. cit., pp. 281-282.

6. "Personal Sin, Forgiveness, and Liberation"

1. See what we have written in Chapter 4 in this volume, "Latin America: Place of Sin and Place of Forgiveness."

2. This remarkable fact ought not to be overlooked in designing the pastoral activity of the church, where we hear so much insistence that the option for the poor must be only preferential, and not exclusive. The gospels do not hesitate to show that it was very difficult for Jesus to change the mighty, except in the case of Zacchaeus and, more modestly, Joseph of Arimathea.

3. Matters grow worse with Anselm and the Anselmians, who reappear in theology time and again. To cite but two examples: Theologians will dictate what "the poor" must mean in order for God's attitude toward them to be logical—and even the suitability that a priest be a male. The problem lies not in conceptualizing revelation, or even in the use of certain inevitable anthropomorphisms, but in the attitude that God ought to be dictated to as to how things ought to be done—even if it is after the event—instead of letting God be God.

4. Joachim Jeremias, *Teología del Nuevo Testamento*, vol. 1 (Salamanca, 1973), p. 187.

5. Hubris (Gr., *hybris*) is the radical arrogance that, once it has infected its human subject, enslaves that person and therefore formally requires a liberation. Furthermore, hubris has a genesis: It is something that comes by way of a process, although it will have been present somehow from the outset. In the words of González Faus, Saint Paul views it, synthetically, as a "process of subtle self-deceit, . . . of the divinization of the 'I' through the divinization of desire" (José Ignacio González Faus, *Proyecto de hermano*, as cited at the end of this note), to the point that it becomes idolatry, with its enslaving counterpart expressed anthropomorphically in the Pauline "God delivered them up in their lusts" (Rom. 1:24). In Ignatius Loyola, the process is quite precise: first wealth, then honors, then pride (radical arrogance), and thence to all the vices. Paul Ricoeur describes *hybris*, in its meaning for the Greeks, as follows: "Success engenders self-complacency, in the same way that the latter engenders arrogance" (cited by González Faus, *Proyecto de hermano*; see end of this note). To fall into *hybris* is to reach a state of radical slavery. It means arriving at the state of sin, and of that sin that, for the Greeks, "was the only sin the gods punished." Christian faith shares this conviction of the radical negativity of *hybris* and of its formally enslaving reality, which stands in need not only of absolution, but of genuine liberation, and this precisely is one of the ultimate formalities of liberation: By grace, God has the power of delivering us from ourselves. For this note, see José Ignacio González

Faus, *Proyecto de hermano: Visión creyente del hombre* (Santander, Spain, 1987), pp. 202-11; quotations in this note, pp. 207ff.

6. Gustavo Gutiérrez, *We Drink From Our Own Wells* (Maryknoll, N. Y.: Orbis Books, 1984).

7. Ignacio Ellacuría, "Las Iglesias latinoamericanas interpelan a la Iglesia de España," *Sal Terrae* 826 (1980, no. 3), pp. 219-30.

8. See our *Spirituality of Liberation: Political Holiness* (Maryknoll, N. Y.: Orbis Books, 1988), pp. 13-45.

9. As González Faus insists in his *Proyecto de hermano*, pp. 194, 200, 509-10.

10. Karl Rahner, *Escritos de teología*, vol. 6 (Madrid, 1969), pp. 295-337.

11. In its "Message to the Peoples of Latin America," Puebla says: "For all our faults and limitations we pastors, too, ask pardon of God, our brothers and sisters in the faith, and humanity" (John Eagleson and Philip Scharper, eds., *Puebla and Beyond: Documentation and Commentary* [Maryknoll, N. Y.: Orbis Books, 1979], p. 117). The more usual "acknowledgment" runs something like, "We recognize that we have not always been consistent." The important thing, of course, is not the words, but what words seem to conceal: a fear of coming right out and naming the persons the church has offended, a fear of accepting forgiveness by them, or indeed the failure to so much as notice this possibility and need. Puebla's words are clear, and—at least logically—are to be explained by an attitude of standing before the poor and accepting the fact that they evangelize (as well as, we add, forgive).

12. A thesis cannot be argued from one case, but an enlightening example can clarify a thesis, and we have just such an example in Archbishop Romero. His "conversion" sprang from various roots, but the most decisive of these, in our opinion—in that it enabled him to persevere in the radical change that had taken place in him, amid such grave difficulties—was his interior knowledge that he was welcomed and accepted by the communities of the poor. The communities with which he had had serious conflicts before his conversion welcomed him and accepted him, in all sincerity, and with great joy. One of them, at least, he explicitly asked for forgiveness for his earlier conduct. Archbishop Romero's later work was obviously performed in behalf of these communities and the people of the poor in general, but at the root of this fact is that he had been accepted by them, that he had been *forgiven* for what he had done before. Therewith, and on this basis, he perceived the inadequacy of his earlier pastoral practice. It gave him acceptance and consolation and unlimited courage in the maintenance of his mission. And this process, so plain in Archbishop Romero's personal life, came to form part of the structure of his entire ecclesial mission. A dialectic sprang up: an endless oscillation between allowing himself to be accepted by the people and throwing himself into his mission to that people. So far as we know, Archbishop Romero did not formulate it in our words; but two well-known formulations make the same point with utter clarity. "It is so easy to be a good shepherd with these people. Here is a people that drives you to its service" (November 18, 1979). "The Church is with the people, and the people are with the Church. Thanks be to God!" (January 21, 1979).

7. *"Toward a Determination of the Nature of Priesthood"*

1. As for the New Testament, the novelty of salvation was such that, at the very beginning, there were no priests in the communities. But the important thing is to understand why. "If it is true that the first Christians had no priests, then their manner of understanding God and practicing their faith and their relation to God must have been profoundly revolutionary for that time and that society" (J. M. Castillo, "Sacerdocio," in C. Floristán and J. J. Tamayo, eds., *Conceptos fundamentales de pastoral* [Madrid, 1983], p. 888). As for Luther, his rejection of priestly Order as a sacrament and his restoration of the common or universal priesthood to its ancient place are due not only to the fact that, according to his methodology, there is no foundation in Scripture for Order as a sacrament but, on a deeper level, to the fact that priests were mediating not salvation, but oppression: They promoted not Christian freedom and siblingship, but slavery. Our point here is that a profound change in the priestly occurs when there is a profound change in the understanding of salvation.

2. As for Archbishop Romero, there can be no doubt of his esteem of the ministerial priesthood or of his efforts to restore to it a more authentic dignity and value (see *Voice of the Voiceless* [Maryknoll, N. Y.: Orbis Books, 1985]). And we are familiar with his even more novel

restoration *in actu* of the universal priesthood, which so powerfully enhanced lay participation at the various pastoral, liturgical, and administrative levels, and at the decisive level of the practice of salvation. But the root of it all lay in his acceptance of the fact that the very faith, the seizing of God's manifestation in the present, was being made real by the church in its totality (see *Lumen Gentium*, no. 12). Hence Archbishop Romero now had everyone sharing in the church—in the interpretation of the signs of the times and in decisions on how to respond to them. Before writing his fourth pastoral letter, and before presenting his report to Puebla, he consulted the people of God, and did so very seriously. Thus, he did not reserve to the hierarchy that which ultimately, and customarily, differentiates its priesthood from that of the faithful: the faculty of seizing the manifestation and will of God.

3. The theology that inspired and flowed from Vatican II strove to overcome a theology of the priesthood shaped in terms of worship and separation from the world in favor of a theology fashioned in terms of word and incarnation, especially in its christological methodology for determining the reality of priesthood. See the classic articles by Karl Rahner in his *Escritos de Teología* (Madrid), vols. 3 (1961), 4 (1964); Josef Ratzinger, "Zur Grage nach dem Sinn des priesterlichen Dienstes," *Geist und Leben* 41 (1968): 347-56; Walter Kasper, "Die Funktion des Priesters in der Kirche," *Geist und Leben* 42 (1969): 102-106; Hans Urs von Balthasar, "Der Priester im Neuen Testament: Eine Ergänzung," *Geist und Leben* 43 (1970): 39-45; and the classic exegetical work of H. Schlier, "Grundelemente des priesterlichen Amtes im Neuen Testament," *Theologie und Philosophie* 44 (1969): 167-80.

4. F. Wulf, in his commentary on the Conciliar Decree on the Ministry and Life of Priests in "Das Zweite Vatikanische Konzil," in *Lexikon für Theologie und Kirche*, vol. 3 (Freiburg, 1968), pp. 142-69, recognizes the positive reforms we have mentioned, but emphasizes that the Council did not consistently found the ministerial priesthood on the more comprehensive priesthood of the entire people of God (pp. 147, 148, 152).

5. It cannot be denied that, generally speaking, the church shows far greater reserve and lack of courage when dealing with concrete theological problems having to do with itself, especially with its institutional aspects (ministerial priesthood, ministry of the sacraments, women's ordination, and the like), than it does in addressing the grand theological themes such as Christ, God, evangelization, and so on. At work here, consciously or unconsciously, is a defense mechanism of the institution and hierarchy as such.

6. Priestly renewal in Latin America has been implemented more on the basis of a practice committed to the world of misery and hope than on the basis of doctrinal texts. The spirit of Medellín has been present in this new practice, but not so much its document on priests, which substantially reproduces what Vatican II says, with some mild concretions bearing on the importance of participating in "the process of the continent's development" (no. 18) and on the call to evangelical poverty (no. 27). The same must be said of Puebla, although Puebla recognizes more explicitly the urgency that the priest work for an integral liberation (no. 696), praises a greater nearness to the people and greater priestly poverty (no. 666), and incorporates into priestly existence a readiness for suffering and martyrdom (no. 668). At the theological level, we do not think that the priesthood has been directly and systematically approached, but there can be no doubt that the theology of liberation has posed the question anew, if only implicitly, and has indicated avenues to a response to the series of problems involved.

7. Castillo, "Sacerdocio," p. 888.

8. G. Baena, "El sacerdocio de Cristo," *Diakonia* 26 (1983), pp. 123-24.

9. Albert Nolan, *Jesus Before Christianity* (Maryknoll, N. Y.: Orbis Books, 1978), sees Jesus' mercy as one of the keys to an understanding of his mission, and its specific element.

10. Baena, "El sacerdocio de Cristo," p. 130.

11. Ibid.

12. Ibid.

13. Ibid., p. 133.

14. A Vanhoye, *Le Christ est notre prêtre* (Rome, 1969), p. 19.

15. See Leonardo Boff, *Passion of Christ, Passion of the World* (Maryknoll, N. Y.: Orbis Books, 1987); Ellacuría, "Por qué muere Jesús y por qué le matan," *Diakonia* 8 (1978), pp. 65-75; Jon Sobrino, "Jesús de Nazaret," in C. Floristán and J. J. Tamayo, eds., *Conceptos fundamentales de pastoral* (Madrid, 1983), pp. 496-501.

INDEX

Alexander VI, 75
Alfaro, J., 40
Anthropology, the Reign of God and, 86
Anti-mercy, 19, 24
Assmann, Hugo, 32

Beatitudes, the, 25
Bloch, Ernst, 16
Boff, Leonardo, 37-38

Casaldáliga, Don Pedro, 183
Casas, Bartolomé de las, 75, 76, 87
Catholicity, 152
CELAM, 76
Central American University, 173-85
Central Intelligence Agency, the, 76
Church, the: catholicity of, 152; "de-centered," 21-22; joy and, 25; mercy and, 15-26; persecution of, 148; pluriformity model of, 153; poverty and, 22-23; the Reign of God and, 23; solidarity and, 151-55; the uniformity model and, 152-53
Compassion, Jesus and, 37
"Contempt as Destiny" (Galeano), 78
Conversion, 79-80, 92
Co-responsibility, 150-51, 154
Covenant, 131
The Crucified God (Moltmann), 49
The Crucified People (Ellacuría), 54, 78-79
Crucified peoples, the, 49-57
Curia, Roman, 76

"Dogmatic slumber," 1-3

Ecumenical movement, the, 160-65
Elba, Julia, 173, 185
Ellacuría, Ignacio, 3-5, 11, 80, 81, 179, 187-89: The Crucified People, 54, 78-79; on crucified people, 36, 49, 51; on the "discovery" of the new world, 70; on hope, 56-57, 81; on Latin America, 74; martyrdom of, 173, 185; on poverty, 22; on praxis, 38
El Salvador, solidarity and, 144-72
Eurocentrism, 2, 77
Europe, Latin America and, 69-82
Evangelii Nuntiandi (Paul VI), 109-10

Faith, 56, 165-70
Faus, J I Gonzales, 66, 97
Forgiveness, 83-101: communal, 67; Latin America and, 58-68; as liberation, 92-93; the poor and, 97-100; of the sinner, 62-64; spirituality of, 64-68
Freedom, Jesus and, 11

Galeano, Eduardo, "Contempt as Destiny," 78
Gaudium et Spes, 109
God: human access to, 111, 115; mercy and, 16-19; the mystery of, 8-9, 36, 40-41, 43, 166-67; partiality to the poor, 113-14, 117, 121; suffering and, 34
Grace, 69-82
Gratuitousness, God's, 86, 87, 93, 151
Gutiérrez, Gustavo: on happiness, 181, 182; on liberation theology, 94; on the poor, 32

History, God and, 114
Hope, 80-81: the crucified peoples and, 55-56; love and, 43-44; the poor and, 6
Human being, the ideal, 17

Humanity, Western understanding of, 6-8

Idols, 9
Ignatius of Loyola, 96, 179, 181
Incarnation, the, 113
Indigenous peoples, South American, 72, 77
Injustice, Latin American, 71-78
Intellectus amoris, theology as, 27-46
Intellectus justitiae, 36-45
Intraecclesialism, 117, 124

Jeremias, Joachim, 92
Jesus Christ: compassion and, 37; mercy and, 17-19; the priesthood of, 111-13, 115, 117, 127-37; the Reign of God and, 20; the sinner and, 89-92
John Paul II, 97, 98: *Solicitudo Rei Socialis*, 33
Joy, the church and, 25
Justice, love as, 36-45

Latin America, 58-68: Europe and, 69-82; poverty in, 49-50; priestly service and, 137-43
Letter to the Hebrews, 129-38
Liberation, 83-101
Liberation theology, 27-46: attacks on, 76; as *intellectus amoris*, 28; Leonardo Boff on, 37-38
Liturgy, 123
López, Amando, 173, 185
López y López, Joaquin, 173, 185
Love, 80: the crucified peoples and, 56; forgiveness and, 63-64
de Lubac, Henri, 40
Lumen Gentium, 109

Martyrdom, 80, 173-85
Martín-Baró, Ignacio, 173, 185
Medellín 1968, 33
Mediation, 112, 131, 132
Mercy: the church and, 15-26; costliness of, 23-25; the exercize of, 10-11; God's, 16-17; Jesus and, 17-19, 132-33; the principle of, 16-20
Metz, J. B., 77
Mission, solidarity and, 155-60
Moltmann, Jürgen, *The Crucified God*, 49

Montes, Segundo, 173, 185
Montesinos, Antonio, 71-72, 77
Moreno, Juan Ramón, 173, 185
Mystagogia, 42-45, 88-90, 127

"The Opinion from Yucay" (Toledo), 75-76
Option for the poor, the, 25, 33
"Otherness," 69

Paul VI: *Evangelii Nuntiandi*, 109-10; *Populorum Progressio*, 33
Paul the apostle, 96
Peguy, Charles, 118
Plunder, justification of, 74-78
Poor, the: forgiveness and, 97-100; irruption of, 32-33
Populorum Progressio (Paul VI), 33
Poverty: the church and, 22-23; Latin American, 49-50; solidarity and, 147-51; Third World, 72-74; unjust, 59-62, 174
Praxis, 37-39
Presbyterorum Ordinis, 109
Priest, the, 133-34
Priesthood: the nature of, 105-43; problems of, 105-11; sacrifice and, 136-37; the theo-logical dimension of, 111-27
Priestliness, the apostolic character of, 118
Priestly service: Christological dimensions of, 127-37; fields of, 120; historical verification of, 125-26; Latin America and, 137-43; liturgy and, 123; locus of, 122; mediation and, 131; salvation and, 131-32; the traditional priesthood and, 135-36
Puebla 1979, 33

Rahner, Karl, 188
Ramos, Celina, 173, 185
Reagan, Ronald, 76
Reality, forgiveness of, 58-62
Reason, liberation of, 1
Reign of God, the, 19: building, 86; the church and, 23; Jesus' proclamation of, 20, 128; liberation theology and, 39, 42, 43; priestly service and, 119; proclaiming, 15

Revelation, divine, 33-34, 40-41, 84, 89, 93, 94

Rockefeller, Nelson, 76

Romero, Oscar, 3, 5, 10-11, 24, 81, 183, 185: on the crucified peoples, 51; on forgiveness, 65, 67; on idols, 9; martyrdom of, 173; on priestly service, 142-43; solidarity and, 170-72

Sacrifice, the priesthood and, 136-37

Salvation: the crucified peoples and, 55-57; forgiveness of sins and, 133; mediation and, 112, 115, 116; priestly service and, 108-109, 131; sin and, 89, 91; sociopolitical groups and, 117-18

Science, personal sin and, 85

Sin: acknowledging, 83-88; communal, 66-67; the crucified peoples and, 53; death and, 60; forgiveness of, 62-64, 133; historical, 43, 83, 93-97; Latin America and, 58-68; the priest and, 112; recognition of, 88-91; personal, 83-101; structural, 69-82

Society of Jesus, the, 1, 187

Solicitudo Rei Socialis (John Paul II), 33

Solidarity, Christian, 144-72

Spirituality, priestly, 123-25

Subsistency, the principle of, 24

Suffering: fundamental form of, 29; God and, 34; historical, 29-30; theology and, 27-46

Theology: end purpose of, 39; as *intellectus amoris*, 36-45; the place of, 30-36; praxis and, 37-39; revelation and, 33-34; suffering and, 27-46

Toledo, Garcia de, "The Opinion from Yucay," 75-76

Trinity, the, 113

Truth, 35-36, 79

United Nations, "Declaration of Human Rights," 7

University of Central America, the, 187

Values, humanizing, 80

Vatican II, the priesthood and, 117, 118, 142

Vitoria, Francisco de, 78

"Works of mercy," 16, 18, 19, 23

World Bank, the, 73

Zubiri, Xavier, 187